Ernie,
Thanks for
your leadership.
Let's launch a
renaissance!
God Bless,
Pastor Carl

A Development Plan for Black America

BY
Carl L. Livingston, Jr.

INCLUDES CRITIQUES OF *THE COVENANT* AND *POWERNOMICS*

CLASSIC DAY
PUBLISHING

Seattle, Washington
Portland, Oregon
Denver, Colorado
Vancouver, B.C.
Scottsdale, Arizona
Minneapolis, Minnesota

P.O. Box 12249
Seattle, Washington 98122
www.carllivingston.com

ISBN: 978-1-59849-049-7

Second Printing March 2010

Printed in the United States of America

Editor: Cherie Tucker
Design: Soundview Design Studio

Classic Day Publishing
2925 Fairview Avenue East
Seattle, Washington 98102
877-728-8837
info@peanutbutterpublishing.com

I thank Elliott Wolf of Classic Day Publishing, Cherie Tucker of GrammarWorks, Soundview Design Studio, and Fiona Henderson for their unique and necessary contributions to this publication.

I offer my highest thanks to my wife Evie, my confidant; my parents, Carl Sr. and Geri, stepfather and stepmother, Charles and Queen; my siblings, Brian, Monte, Gary, April, Tony, Lysander, Senora, Tray and Tony; my parents-in-law, Early and Ethel, and their children; my kids Ashante and Walter; the rest of my and my wife's great extended families, as well as to Providence for all of the stalwart support and empowerment. You all made the difference.

~CL

INTRODUCTION

On 17 January 2004, Rev. Dr. Robert Jeffrey, Sr. invited me to give the keynote address for the joining of "Local Initiatives" to "Black Dollar Days Task Force." The event was held at the Esquire Club, an African-American establishment. I spoke about the need to ensure that this joint effort did not leave Seattle African Americans behind, as past initiatives too often have done. I explained that in order to guarantee success, we need a comprehensive plan that is centered in economics. I endeavored to dissuade this business-savvy crowd from seeing the answer to Black development as government-based programming, for we have done this much too long. I said this:

> *In a country primarily capitalist in structure the answers have to be primarily capitalist in nature. This means that most programs, and most people acting like they are trying to help us, need to help Blacks and the poor create wealth. For you cannot help a people as a people who will not as a people help themselves.*

I went on to outline what the plan should cover. Then I challenged both Blacks and non-Blacks present to develop and institute such a plan. Before sitting down, I took the risk of stating that certain groups in attendance were from healthy American ethnic communities, communities that were developing businesses and doing great self-investment. Yet their main contribution in African American communities were not-for- profit measures to do things like "Just Say 'No' to Drugs"; "you major in for-profit endeavors in your non-Black community, and non-profit measures in the Black community; instead, do for us what you do for yourself—help us build wealth." For wealthier communities are healthier communities.

Afterward I sat down, satisfied that I had stirred thought, interrogated motives, and touched hearts. Within about fifteen minutes, Pastor Jeffrey came to me and told me something I was not ready to hear: "I have spoken to my board and they have authorized me to ask you to propose a plan about which you have just spoken." For a few moments I was frozen.

My angst had to do with my feeling that I did not know enough to do it, coupled with my sense that I had not the time to devote to such a large-scale project. Medical professionals should propose health plans; educational professionals, education plans; and so on. I am an attorney and Political Science professor; this would be a stretch.

I was rallying myself to tell him "No" when other thoughts led me to think otherwise: Why can't you just propose what you know? Why wait for more credentialed and experienced people to do what they could have but had not—and may never do? And, what if this is your opportunity to uniquely contribute to your city, an opportunity that may not come to you again? Besides, having spoken so boldly about doing this work, I would have felt hypocritical were I to run away from the very work about which I had just made an appeal. I figured that this must be the hand of God.

I gingerly said I would do it, but that I would need time to do this work right. Little did I know that between now and then I would become a local pastor of an established predominantly African American United Methodist church with all that entails both with the clergy and laity. How my life has complicated and busied! This has much to do with the delay in making timely good on my promise to submit this work to Black Dollar Days Task Force.

Nonetheless, here it is: a development proposal, not just for Seattle's Black community development, but for any Black American community. I hope that this work leads to an effort that not only achieves a new birth, but that spurs a renaissance in Black communities across this country.

TABLE OF CONTENTS

EXECUTIVE SUMMARY

Give us a plan of action... a 10 Black Commandments; simple, strong, that we can carry in our hearts, and in our memories no matter where we are and reach out and touch and feel the reassurance that there is behind everything we do a simple, moral, intelligent plan that must be fulfilled in the course of time even if all of our leaders, one by one fall in battle, somebody will rise and say 'Brother!! Our leader died while we were on page three of the Plan. Now that the funeral is over, let us proceed to page four.

(Ossie Davis, First Annual CBC Dinner 18 June 1971)

This is a plan for the development of African American communities through an economically-led, comprehensive plan. This plan presents a program geared at Black associations—their leaders and especially their members—connecting and mobilizing Blacks for their own development. While society owes African Americans for its mistreatment, this plan is not dependent on that help for its success. As actor and activist Ossie Davis proposes above, this is a "plan of action" but one that is longer than "10 Black Commandments, simple and strong." Still, it is a plan clear enough that, were our leaders taken from us one at time, the community would have the written guidance to say, "Our leader died while we were on page three of the Plan. Now that the funeral is over, let us proceed to page four."

Common sense tells us that without a plan the people perish; they do not flourish. In point of fact, the Bible says these very words (Proverbs 29:18). This plan is for the kind of development that causes Black communities to flourish. Picture after 15 years Black income growing by 400% because of this plan instead of merely slightly above 40% without it. Imagine children reared in two-parent homes going from 45% to 75% of Black households. Ponder three times more Blacks in college or vocational school than in prison, as it is today. Consider Black health dramatically increasing, increasing physically, socio-psychologically, and spiritually. These are the goals of this plan. I write here of a renaissance so impressive that it can only be compared to the rise of Jewish Americans in the 20th century. How does that sound?

This plan speaks to what is needed to accomplish this renaissance on a community-wide level, and includes measures at the associational and household levels. So, I do call for the convening of leaders to supervise this plan; however, the real base of the plan is our associations—particularly the churches—and our households, even though we are spread out all over the county. In other words, this is a macro and micro, economically led, comprehensive plan.

The title mainly concerns what Blacks should do to pick themselves up. Part of this, though, has to do with social and political action to move the larger society to help us, as we have historically done. What society does for Blacks is the shoestrings; what we do for ourselves is the bootstraps. After 300 years of slavery, 100 years of segregation, and 50 years of tokenism society is duty-bound to finally give Blacks who have been in the U.S. for a century the modern equivalent of their 40 acres and a mule. Alas, a society good at pushing certain groups down but bad at picking them up is unlikely to give Blacks any reparations or long give to them affirmative action. For far too long Black leadership has majored on what society should do for us, as opposed to leading the Black community to effectively help itself. So, this plan reverses this tired approach. In the main, Blacks have to pick themselves up by themselves, as all other groups have had to do. For instance, Native Americans have not been compensated for the trail of broken treaties, when a treaty is the highest legal promise a people can make. So, if they have not, then we are not likely to be. This is not to discourage Black groups from trying. Do try to get it—just do not give it your best. Save your best for self-help.

Shoestrings and Bootstraps is a comprehensive, mainly self-help plan that clearly and without apology makes economics the driver in the short term. In the midterm, educational and social development has to be paramount to sustain what the economic development launches into place. In the long term, spiritual development has to be renewed or else we will loose all of the gains we have made. Still, economics drives the plan from the beginning.

Economics has to be the immediate basis for any comprehensive plan to work well with mass support. For, he who provides the jobs is the one the people will follow. It is as simple as that. Moreover, we are in a mainly capitalist country. Hence, the problems are in a mainly capitalist context and the answers have to be mainly capitalist in character. Additionally, we have gained our civil rights, and thus economic development is the natural progression. Furthermore, the case studies of groups like Jewish, Vietnamese, and Ethiopian Americans reveal that economics led them up after they secured citizenship rights. Finally, our own leaders pointed Blacks to economic development, including Marcus, Malcolm, and Martin. There you have it: five reasons why we must launch extensive economic initiatives first. The fact that the present cast of Black leaders does not quite get it, or will not do it (will not forge community-wide capitalistic solutions), is a grand failure of leadership. Happily, a new surge of wiser leadership is upcoming.

As stated above, this plan covers non-economic areas as well. Certainly, Blacks need help across the board: educationally, socially, medically, politically, artistically, and spiritually. After the economic initiatives are launched, then the emphasis will turn to education and strengthening Black families. With respect to education, Blacks have to learn from more successful ethnic groups how to better stress and finance academic excellence. Similarly, we are obliged to improve relations between Black men and women in order to promote and strengthen successful marriages. This has many benefits: increasing household income, providing more custodial childcare, and promoting companionship. After achieving the midterm educational and social development, Blacks need to revitalize their spiritual development: rededicating their lives to God, increasing their participation in a religious institution, and advancing in good works to the point that the golden rule becomes the general rule. Now you have it: spiritual renewal built on socio-educational revitalization, built on economic resurgence.

In a perfect world, no one of these would be more important than the other—except maybe the spiritual area. Albeit, in this world, in this country, at this time, economics must lead the way. No one should know this more than Black leaders of the 21st century, and no one should be doing it more than they.

The plan has been influenced by other developed plans, especially Claud Anderson's *Powernomics* and the Black Dollar Days Movements in Seattle and around the country. On the other hand, the plan springs from my understanding of the lessons of Black leadership history, having run a small business, and teaching International Political Economy. I believe that leaders like Marcus Garvey and Martin Luther King told Blacks very clearly that the front of the battle is economic. Having practiced law in a firm and then run a small legal business, I learned about capitalism first hand. Then I discovered development insights teaching Political Economy.

My Political Economy course apprised me of the two main development approaches Southern countries adopted. These ideas, adjusted a bit, are the concepts behind this plan. I call them import substitution commercialization and export led commercialization. The former has to do with spending more on businesses in one's community. The latter involves investing in businesses within one's community to enable them to compete outside the community. I do not parse these scholarly ideas until the end of this work. I want the main part of this plan to be approachable and understandable.

Around the economic strategies we will add the social, political, educational, medical, artistic and spiritual measures that we will need. Because I know more about these areas, this plan details the economic, political, and spiritual measures. For the social, educational, and medical aspects I have very little to add; others will have to develop these areas into well devised sub-parts of a comprehensive plan.

This plan has a healthy role for Black associations, especially the church, as the base for implementation of economic strategies. The leaders of the Black church could lead this renaissance alone; conversely, without Black church leaders there will be no Black renaissance.

This plan requires that a group of leaders come together in order to learn about and adopt the plan. They must make sure that every area is covered: politics, health, relationships, and education will be folded into the economic plan. They are tasked with proposing the economically centered, comprehensive plan to the people, and facilitating the people adopting the plan.

This committed core must sacrifice making money from the endeavors this plan employs so that the people will not feel exploited and end up opting out before the great community gains occur. The leadership has to shepherd both the execution and the quality control of the plan. The agreed target that all must be dogged about exceeding is **growing the Black community 10% annually**. Folks must be reconciled to advancing this plan beyond the annual target for the long haul: if so, the results will be significant at first, impressive after a few years, and then stellar in just 7.5 years.

How do we know that the results will be stellar in just 7.5 years? The *Banking Rule of 72* tells us so. The Banking Rule says divide any rate by 72 and one will know how long it will take money to double at that rate. At 10% sustained growth, Black income would double in 7.2 years, a season short of 7.5 years. If we can stay on the plan for 15 years, the Black community will quadruple in economic output alone! Our money will quadruple! This is how we exponentially grow our resources so that we can employ the unemployed, house the homeless, educate the uneducated, and give hope to the hopeless. Said another way, this how we rebuild our own households, neighborhoods, and communities economically, socially, educationally, and in every other way.

To accomplish these great gains, the leadership must get the plan to the various associations so that they can initiate the portions of the plan that apply to them. Each church, each mosque, each sorority, each fraternity is to help its own members go from owing to owning, and from buying mostly outside of the community to buying mostly inside of it. In our patience possess our souls: in other words, *if the people will hang with the plan then they will experience a greater renaissance than we had in the 1970s.* Associations are the key to our unity. They are the under-utilized resource in the Black community for connecting groups of our dispersed people into a working whole. We may be disconnected bones now, but just as the ole spiritual reads: da foot bones [is about to] connects to the ankle bone, and so on.

Members of every household are to try to live below their means, invest the difference, and support Black businesses more. Middle and upper class households must lead the way, because they can better afford to support our businesses whose prices may be a bit higher. Every Black household is to improve its education, health, voting, relationships, and spirituality. As we are hurting in all of these ways, we have to help ourselves in all of these ways. Moreover, one solution builds upon another.

The unique parts of this plan are the incentives and sanctions critical to enforcement. I present controls we can put in place to encourage Black people to buy Black, and Black businesses to hire Black. How many know we have to watch out for those who will 'front' like they are working the plan, but be undermining the plan on the 'down low'?

There are five other important features of the plan. The first are the larger-scale **development projects** that the community will launch every five years or so. With Blacks doing the design, construction, bonding, and labor, these projects will pour millions of dollars of revenue into Black businesses. They will also provide hundreds of thousands of dollars in income into the households of Black workers. This is an independent way of making sure that the 10% growth goal is met.

The second special feature is the targeting of **businesses to expand** for one of two reasons: either to provide inside of the community what Blacks have been spending money on outside of the community (import substitution commercialization); or to export Black goods or services outside of the community similar to what other more successful ethnic groups are doing (export led commercialization). These will be smaller scale endeavors than the development projects discussed above. At least every five years the community should be assisting a business along one of these two lines so that a dollar will multiply in the Black community closer to the number of times it circulates in the White community. Examples of such projects are these: expanding a beauty supply business, assisting the establishment of a gas station, and promoting the franchise of a Black restaurant outside of the Black community. The businesses invested in should be those that have the best combination of track record, resources, and commitment to the community.

The third feature is that the plan fully utilizes its **captive audience**. The captive audience are both those who are the first to receive personal or business income from the plan, as well as the leaders espousing it. Those who benefit financially from this plan will have an incentive, and will in fact be urged, to make use of the education, health, and other non-economic parts of the plan. So, the leaders will make a demand on the business owners enjoying increased income to comply with all aspects of the plan, and those owners should be more than happy to do so. The leaders will ask these owners to promote in their company the education initiatives our educational leaders have outlined. The same holds true for the social and political parts of the plan. However, the leaders will not wait for business owners to do this out of inclination. Leaders will go by and make sure [with a smile] that the owners are working the entire plan.

This equally applies to the workers getting jobs as a direct result of this plan. As a condition of their employment they will need to agree to pay their child support, read about Black history, and work on their relationship issues—doing all parts of the comprehensive plan that apply to a person. This means that the leaders will not have to be the examples to the rest of the community alone. Those who benefit will be examples as well. In other words, we will have a growing captive audience of benefactors to assist with getting the entire community to live the complete plan.

The fourth measure is the model, called an **econometric model**, that will estimate graphically the money and jobs this plan will likely provide from year one to year twenty. The econometric model in this book is a basic one. Economic professionals can do a more masterful job. The community must demand of its professionals of all types the best of their expertise when the community is in pursuit of its renaissance.

The fifth effective components of this plan are the **case studies** we used as examples. Those examples are Jewish Americans, the most successful ethnic group in the United States in terms of wealth, post-graduate degrees, and SAT scores; Vietnamese Americans who have risen impressively in this country over the last 25 years, starting often in African American communities; and Ethiopian Americans who are ascending now in society in dramatic fashion, in or near a historically African American neighborhood. Jewish Americans showcase how high a group may catapult in the U.S. Vietnamese Americans demonstrate that non-White groups can advance in the post-Reagan era. Finally, Ethiopian Americans evidence that Blacks can economically accelerate in U.S.

society, as the typical Ethiopian American is a shade darker than the typical African American. These groups pulverize Black excuses about whether, and how high, ethnic groups can still rise in the U.S. Moreover, Jewish, Vietnamese, and Ethiopian Americans have each advanced largely because of ideas like those set forth in this plan.

Perhaps what is stated in this Executive Summary could stand some whittling to about a page. Maybe thousands will need to copy solely one page that pretty much says it all. Accordingly, on the next page are the answers in brief to the big questions concerning this plan: what, who, and how.

THE PLAN IN A NUTSHELL

WHAT: The development of a plan to achieve 10% a decade economic growth for Black America, and to use this economic productivity as a platform to develop politically, socially, medically, educationally, artistically, and spiritually.

Why emphasize economics first? With political and legal equality, the civil rights front has shifted to economic equality. Too many of our people are underemployed or unemployed. With good reason it is said that 'the best welfare program in the world is a good job'. When we come centrally with economic assistance we get our people's full attention in order to help them with the other things they need. This is where both Martin Luther King and Malcolm X were going shortly before they died, and where Marcus Garvey long was during his leadership in this country.

WHO: This plan is for African American communities. Because no such community can be practically served without effective leadership, the 'Who' has to be a core of African American leaders who care more about the development of the community than about their personal development, and who are prepared to show it by sacrificing in order to see this plan to fruition. As well, leaders in every profession must heed this call to prepare sub-plans in their areas.

HOW: The leadership must engage this plan on three different levels: the community (macro), associational, and household levels (micro). At each of these levels it advocates owning instead of owing, and investing more inside instead of outside the community.

At the household and associational levels, the leaders will provide this plan to every Black association and household. Moreover, leaders must facilitate every association and family doing much more to help their own members into family ownership and community investment. Associations are the under-utilized vital bridge between Black families and our community. They can connect us into a working whole.

The community strategy is a modified application of two "third world" development strategies: *import substitution industrialization* and *export led industrialization* explained in the appendix. Simply put, African Americans need to spend more on businesses owned by African Americans. Then we need to promote businesses within our community by investing in them so as to enable them to compete outside the community. We can do this by community measures to expand Black businesses selling inside or outside of the Black community. We can further promote these efforts by larger-scale real estate development projects that the community will launch every five years.

DO WHAT WITH THE PLAN? Call the community leaders together by next year, in order to approve one of 1 – 2 proposed plans for primarily economic development (i.e. *Powernomics* or *Shoestrings and Boostraps*). I need your help to mobilize a committed core of leaders, and an army of volunteers who will do the work of carrying out this plan. I especially need those who will continue the work for the necessary years so as not to do what we have done too often: leave unfinished the work that would lift us.

SHOESTRINGS & BOOTSTRAPS

A SHOESTRING ON THE HISTORY OF BLACK AMERICA

❖ ❖ ❖

A shoestring is a skinny thing. A thin but long piece of woven fabric, a string does not have a lot of girth. If a shoestring were a person it would be Reggie Miller (formerly of the Indiana Pacers basketball team) not Shaquile O'Neal (of the Lakers)—someone lanky but who can get the job done.

As effective as they are, shoestrings probably did not arrive with the first shoe. No, they are a great adaptation on the strap that tied a piece of wood or leather to the foot and ankle. They have so revolutionized shoes, however, that a person can get strings with any type: tennis, dress, and formal shoes—even boots. But shoestrings have their negatives.

They can break more easily. They get dingy. They have to be replaced before the shoe wears out. Personally, I have had so many pairs of tennis shoes on which I have had to replace the strings. When I was younger and lacked the wherewithal at the time to get strings, I had to back the string out of one of the eye-holes of the shoe and tie the strings together at a lower point. As useful as they are, shoestrings just are not a bootstrap: they are neither as rugged nor as enduring.

As I stated at first, shoestrings are what others do for Blacks; bootstraps are what we do for ourselves. Government and corporate assistance are types of bootstraps. Getting governmental services that lasted a longer period of time was a great adaptation for Blacks and other poor folks just as shoestrings were an adaptation in shoe binding. It was a good thing to be able to count for a while on aid to families with dependent children, retirement security payments, and even affirmative action. All of these were better and more reliable than were the programs coming out of slavery that did not last long.

Like shoestrings though, the services have not been rugged and enduring enough. The pages to come manifest that the programs on which Blacks have relied have not broken the back of poverty nor catapulted them into the middle class. Now the programs like older strings have gotten dingy, worn thin, and in some cases broken. Thus, Blacks, while faring better than in slavery, languish still at the bottom of society in America. We will remain at the bottom until we learn the difference between shoestrings and bootstraps.

THE CHALLENGE FACING BLACK AMERICANS

With its Black owned taxi services, banks, stores, insurance companies and the like Tulsa's thriving Black community was the Black Wall Street of the West. . .The 1921 race riot so devastated Black Tulsa that it took ten years to rebuild to a semblance of its former glory . . .What devastated Tulsa more than the race riot was integration. With integration Black Tulsans stopped supporting their own businesses. This was a blow from which Black Tulsa has not recovered.
(Black Wall Street: 1921 Tulsa Riot, video)

The above quote crystallizes what most devastated formerly thriving Black Tulsa: it was not racism. What decimated it—and continues to decimate us—was, and is, our failure to sufficiently support ourselves economically. Every Black community in the U.S. is struggling with how to achieve sustained economic development. African America is facing the same thing. In addition, Blacks will continue to experience something less dramatic, but just as serious as Black Tulsa, unless it comes together and invests in itself to a great degree. Before it can fully discover how to do this, it has to understand in detail the dynamics.

CHALLENGES COMMON TO BLACK AMERICA

Since their first arrival, and continuing after they started receiving wages, black Americans have figured disproportionately among the nation's poor. (Hacker, Two Nations 99)

The African American community around the country has lost economic and social ground from where it was in 1975. One of the first things to disappear from the Black community were the federal funded programs like VISTA, Model Cities, and, later, City Crew summer jobs. Republican Gerald Ford was in office and he had less of a commitment to the programs, and President Carter did not have the power to stop the Southern Democrats from joining with the Republicans in Congress to cut funding.

The de-funding was fueled by mistakes Blacks in these programs made. Whenever Blacks misappropriated or absconded with the funds the White media gave this prominent attention. At times it competed with itself in programming and for financing. It played up each other's excesses and miscues. Blacks also could have done much more to support their own businesses, particularly as integration flourished. Thus, most of what happened to Blacks occurred from outside of our community, from forces seeking to shut helpful programs down. However, a great deal that undermined Black efforts came from within, as Blacks did things to sabotage our upward mobility. What is so sad about this is that this pincer action occurred during the time of the largest transfer of wealth into our community that we had seen heretofore. Yet, these were not all of the outside forces arrayed against us.

Another factor was that the *Bakke v. University of California, Davis* decision made conservatives feel they could do things their way, which meant going back to the old way of doing things. The *Bakke* case outlawed U.C. Davis' affirmative action program that set aside a number of seats in their school exclusively for minorities. (Washington actually had a case destined for the Supreme Court that would have made similar law before *Bakke* when a gentleman named DeFunis challenged the University of Washington's law school admissions program; he was accepted eventually which made the case moot.) With gusto, affirmative action measures countrywide were being proscribed and watered down. Despite Arthur Fletcher's connections to this area, affirmative action did not look as scary to the establishment in 1979 as it had looked in 1973. Fewer African Americans were hired in the private sector to positions that mattered.

Blacks were freer to move out of their community and freer to patronize businesses outside of their community. Surely, these they did with dispatch, at a terrible cost to ourselves, a cost of which we remain ignorant. From the outside, though, whites established "front" businesses to divert money from, or subvert, the affirmative action programs in place. While many White and Asian Americans regularly patronize Black businesses, most do not. The results were bitter. From forces inside and out, black businesses withered on the vine.

Even the non-profit sector has diminished.

You cannot help a people as a people who as a people do not help themselves.

This is not to say that the various Black business owners always did things correctly. To the contrary, they over-spent or were rude at times. But these things were rectifiable.

What could not be fixed was too little support. This is an example of a maxim I coined: you cannot help a people as a people who as a people do not help themselves. What we lost, we lost, because we did not help ourselves as a people. In the early 1990s, so many businesses went by the way side rather quietly, but the significance of their demise thundered against African American development.

So, we remain unemployed at twice or thrice the White rate, twice as likely to be poor, and experiencing half the marriage rates. Our household income is two-thirds of that of Whites, while our household assets are at one third. We have less insurance coverage, live with greater disease, and die almost ten years earlier than those in the larger society. So, we lag on almost every good measure; we excel on almost every bad one.

There is a place where our numbers and representation are increasing rapidly. There is one place where we are booming most, a place that is a growth industry: that place is in the jails or prisons. In fact, Washington's Black incarcerated population is among the worst in the country. This likewise is occurring across this country.

Fortunately, the news is not all bad. The major black churches are still around. Many respected African American clergyman remain to provide a type of protection, if not guidance. While most black businesses have failed, a number of black businesses remain. Black media are still around and are a wall of protection in our communities across the country.

There is a place where our numbers and representation are increasing rapidly. There is one place where we are booming most, a place that is a growth industry: that place is in jails or prisons.

There are a number of Black politicians countrywide. Where Black communities are at or near the majority, the numbers are impressive. Even where Blacks are a distinct minority, one will still find Black politicians of some standing. For instance, Seattle, a city with less than 10% Black population had a Black mayor Norm Rice; its county—renamed in 2007 Martin Luther King County—has had a Black executive for over six years. Black politicians can be quite helpful.

> *Evidence from case studies had already indicated that black mayors place a high priority on municipal contracting with minority-owned businesses. A comparative analysis of the 28 areas was conducted to see if black business performance, as a whole, has been aided somehow by the presence of black mayors. The examination found that it has in*

fact been so aided. Compared with black-owned firms elsewhere, those located in black-mayor areas are (1) more likely to be run by college graduates, (2) started up with much larger financial investments by their owners, (3) much larger in sales and employment levels, and (4) characterized by lower rates of business failure. (BATES, BANKING ON XX)

We should say that most of the mayors are in places with two to three times the black population, or more. Also, a conservative backlash since 1998 has made it difficult to get government funding that aides Black businesses.

Albeit, while the average Black may be better off, the Black community in the 21st century is languishing as most all of the programs and institutions of the 1970s have fallen by the way side.

While the black community has lost numbers and institutions, it might be individually more prosperous now than it was then. This is primarily because housing prices have spiked and more blacks own homes. Howbeit, while the average Black may be better off, the Black community in the 21st century is languishing as most all of the programs and institutions of the 1970s have fallen by the way side.

This presents a cold and throat-lumping challenge. Being at the bottom of societies with continued educational disparities and high incarceration rates, Blacks will be consigned in the future to under-performance, lack of actualization, and continued bottom status. They will be so consigned all across this country, unless we do something major and effective about it everywhere we are.

We should study the 1960 – 2000 era to see what it took to get what we had, to learn where we went wrong, and to determine what we did that was right. We are embarking on an era in which we shall have hundreds of millions of dollars for our community and we need all the learning we can get so as not to make the same old mistakes. Those who do not know the past, it is said, are doomed repeat its mistakes in the future.

For encouragement, all we have to do is look over our shoulders at all we have done in order to be inspired. We are the people who have survived enslavement in Africa … We are the people who survived the Middle Passage … We are the people who survived chattel slavery … We are the people who survived Jim Crow.

We face a future of serious need. Reports by the Urban League have shown that Blacks nationally gained in household income in two-wage earner homes, and that their home ownership improved. On the other hand, per capita incomes have been stagnant or have declined since 1970. These studies followed those of the National Research Council (*A Common Destiny* 1989) showing a decline in Black worker income since 1969, and Danzinger and Gottschalk (1986) demonstrating a decrease in benefits just as poverty increased. The National Research Council warned of a bleak future for Blacks. It should be noted that none of the studies of the 1980s took into account the effects of the welfare reform act of the middle 1990s. Black America has work to do.

Something has to be done, given what we face. I am confident that something will be done, given who we are. For encouragement, all we have to do is look over our shoulders at all we have done in order to be inspired. We are the people who have survived enslavement in Africa from ancient times. We are the people who survived the Middle Passage of the fourteenth through nineteenth centuries. We are the people who survived chattel slavery for 300 years. We are the people who survived Jim Crow from the 1870's to the 1960's. Yes, we are the people who survived the "Southern Strategy" from the 1960's to the early 21st century, a Republican strategy to clean up racists and move them into leadership in the Republican Party (many of them are leaders mainly in the Republican Party and some in the Democratic Party). We are survivors and we are over-comers.

Speaking in terms of strings, Blacks have been strung along, strung up, and strung out.

The geographic, psychological, social and political challenges raised above frustrate development. They make advancement harder here. These idiosyncrasies also force the tailoring of any generic plan or any plan being tried here that worked somewhere else. Yet, they are conditions that we have to do something about. They demand our attention.

As a result of these challenges, especially in light of the history we have gone through, Blacks have been uniquely tried, stressed, and oppressed. We suffer as a consequence. Speaking in terms of strings, Blacks have been strung along. Governments and social programs generally promise more than they can deliver to a people. We have been strung up. We have been consigned to poverty as a people and at times tied from trees as individuals. Then we have been strung out. Drugs and alcohol are the most prevalent commodities in our more impoverished neighborhoods. We make neither ourselves. Blacks have been strung along, strung up, and strung out. These are the tough details. Thank goodness, the news is not all bad.

To be sure, we are not where we should be, we are not what we used to be, and we are not what we are going to be. We have to be cognizant of our special resources as we act to go where we should be. We have benefits of which we can make maximum use. . . . and that is exactly what we should do.

A SHOESTRING IS TOUGH TO LIVE ON

If you are "living on a shoestring" or "hanging by a thread", then you are not doing well financially. Living by a shoestring means that you are barely making it; things are tight. The ends are scarcely being met.

Hanging by a string is not a good thing. It conveys being in a touchy, precarious situation. One pictures a person hanging on a rope that is shredding so that it can no longer be called a rope. The hundreds of twisted and woven strings that made it so redundantly strong have frayed to simply a few, and now the desperation is registered on the face of the person so hanging. No, this cannot be a good thing. However, this is a not too exaggerated a depiction of our plight.

In some ways Blacks are having it tight but making it all right. In other ways Blacks are in a precarious place. This is what life is like for the large group of Blacks in the lower class.

In a capitalist world, this should be understood if not expected. Capitalism serves those who own assets that others want to use or buy. One cannot even gain a foothold in a capitalist world living on government benefits, as opposed to living on one's own earnings. Such is the difference between living on another's shoestring instead of on your own bootstrap.

Common sense tells us that capitalistic problems in a capitalistic world require capitalistic answers. Whether hanging by a string, or simply living on a shoestring, life is a tough; tough, indeed.

THE NEED FOR CAPITALISTIC LEADERSHIP

The large majority of the Negroes who have put on the finishing touches of our best colleges are all but worthless in the development of their people.
(Carter G. Woodson)

The greater Seattle area has a waning African American population, one that saw its more populous and, sadly, its most institutionally-powerful days in the 1970s. During the heady days of the 70s and 80s, we did not support our institutions as we should have, particularly our businesses. These debilitating circumstances here are the very circumstances Blacks are experiencing elsewhere around this country.

Seattle sadly proved true the maxim: you cannot help a people as a people who as a people do not help themselves. We did not use our unique benefits to overcome our unique challenges. As a result, we remain in need of action on a precise plan. Specifically, we need to achieve 10% decade economic growth, and to use this economic productivity as a platform to develop politically, socially, medically, educationally, artistically, and spiritually. Notice that this is a decidedly economically based plan. To agree on and engage it, Black communities in cities like Seattle will need extraordinary leadership.

Now, leadership is skill and art. The skill of leadership is to take the people where they want to go often, but to take them where they need to go always. The art of leadership is the legitimacy and glory of the job. Our leaders are failing in the *work* of leadership: we are not leading the people where they need to go. We are reactive instead of proactive. We are governmental in an entrepreneurial world; in other words, we are socialists when the country is capitalist. Our thinking does not match, hence our programs do not fit.

In the next two chapters I endeavor to show that our leaders have missed the centrality of economics, with certain exceptions. What our leaders are missing is hurting us in this capitalist country, something our leaders should have figured out. This chapter looks at the general way in which we are downplaying economics. The next chapter treats the two most impactful books on the subject: *Powernomics* and *Covenant*. The subsequent chapter deals with where Marcus Garvey, Malcolm X, and Martin Luther King either saw the centrality of economics, or were headed in that direction.

We need a plan. However, we do not need just any kind of plan. Instead we need a certain plan, a plan that is unapologetically economic, and beyond this, has more to do with what we are going to do to pull ourselves up by our own bootstraps, than about getting society to give us shoestrings. We need our own bootstrap program notwithstanding how small they may seem to us.

There are five separate and independent common sense reasons why economics must lead the comprehensive effort for Black development: capitalism, civil rights, case studies, and counsel —

1. Capitalism: the U.S. is primarily capitalist.
2. Civil rights: Blacks have experienced political liberation.
3. Case studies: this is how other groups have risen in this country.
4. Counsel: this is what our leaders, especially our greatest leaders, have advised.
5. Common sense: a decent job is so important in the life of a person that a person will do almost anything to get it, and listen most to the one who provides it.

I cover these reasons in order.

NOT THINKING AND ACTING CAPITALISTICALLY

You cannot pull the wage-earner up by pulling the wage-payer down. (Abraham Lincoln)

There is a fiend in the Black community that is worse than anything a racist could do to Black America. This fiend zaps our community of capital so reliably that the community is as porous as a sieve. This fiend has our community in such a state that no matter how much money is put in, it will always run out to other communities. It is what took Black Tulsa down to its knees for good. Until this is fixed, the community's economic problems will remain unfixable. We want every Black who wants to work to earn at least a living wage. Well, Lincoln taught that investing in "wage-payers," business owners, is the key. We cannot allow circumstances to pull our business owners down, if we want our wage earners to rise.

Of all of the circumstances pulling us down, the greatest fiend since the end of segregation is Blacks failing to support our own businesses. We pale in comparison to how groups like Jewish Americans support their community. Our lesser relative support of our own businesses hurts us most. When will we wake up, lift up, and walk out of our stupor? We are robbing ourselves. If we do not learn the lesson of Black Tulsa, then we will remain in our tizzy; if we do not heed Lincoln, then we will hibernate through another season of our would-be liberation.

Segregation required that Blacks support our own businesses by default. Now we have to support our businesses by design.

Suffice it to say, neither the Black community in general, nor its leadership in particular, recognize this. Some do not see it at all (they are really in the dark). Most see it as a factor but do not realize that it is the main factor robbing us (they are partially darkened). Leaders and the people alike have to see that a community that does not self-invest is like a pocket with big holes in it. Such a pocket cannot hold coins. Money pours in the black community and flows right out of it. This is what happens to a people in a capitalist country who have not figured out how capitalism works. To be sure, the U.S. is more capitalist than it is anything else.

Clearly, our community is too ignorant of capitalism. We do not see that our only answer to our capitalistic problem is itself capitalistic. Our capitalistic setting demands capitalistic structures. For we are in a country that is more capitalist than democratic. Again, the U.S. is more capitalistic than it is anything else. For that matter, the West, and increasingly the world, is more capitalistic than democratic. We were more capitalistic when we had to fend for ourselves and could only buy from ourselves. This was the case 50 years ago, during segregation. Segregation required that Blacks support our own businesses by default. Now we have to support our businesses by design.

Let's talk some long-delayed sense. Ladies and gentlemen, we have got to figure this out, and to do so despite the fact that many of us see capitalism as strange or as boring. We have got to get comfortable talking about its terms, talking like economists.

Capitalism will not change for us; we have to change to it. This is what it means to be a "minority". It means that, for the most part, we have to deal with the majority; we have to deal with the establishment. So, we have to approach capitalism on its terms.

It is critical that we understand utterly that capitalism is the catalyst for the comprehensive development of people of darkest color.

I am not happy to tell you this. I am not in love with capitalism (to use Churchill's words on democracy: "[capitalism] is the worst of all systems, except for all the other ones"). Yet, I feel I have no choice. As the young kids say, "We have to be real." Being "real" means facing things as they are, not how we want them to be in some fantasy world. We have no choice but to master capitalism in this country if we are going to craft a Black solution out of our White problem; and in actuality, solution is not really going to be White or Black —it is green.

So, it is critical that we understand utterly that capitalism is the catalyst for the comprehensive development of people of darkest color. Do I have your attention?

AFTER POLITICAL LIBERATION COMES ECONOMIC DEVELOPMENT

Martin Luther King was right, and Booker Taliaferro Washington was wrong: Blacks free from slavery but bound by segregation needed to direct most of their efforts to continued political liberation, and not to economic development. Political liberation has to precede economic development. This is the second reason why economics must be the centerpiece of Black development: the acquisition of civil rights. Whereas citizenship was the challenge of political liberation for most groups that came to the U.S., segregation was the post-slavery challenge for Blacks.

Segregation was an all-encompassing bar to Blacks being able to help themselves. Blacks could have for a while a Harlem Renaissance or establish a Black Wall Street of the West in Tulsa, but they found in time an entire system against them. That system, at its best, kept Blacks over-crowded, under-educated, under-employed, uncompetitive, and under siege; while at its worst, boiled over into race riots or lynch mobs that either burned Blacks out or burned them up.

Martin Luther King, Jr. saw this and gave his life to free us. This gave Blacks enough equality to concentrate on economic development without government-sanctioned harassment or oppression confining them to third-class citizenship. Booker T. Washington did not see this, and thus everything his leadership helped Blacks do for themselves was always too small for a Black renaissance and too vulnerable to attack. For instance, Mr. Washington is known for establishing Tuskegee Institute, his Atlanta Compromise speech of 1896, and for his advocacy on behalf of the Black community. While the institute trained thousands who influenced tens of thousands, they could not make much headway against dusky segregation. The same holds true for Washington's advocacy. Mr. Washington's Compromise Speech debuted him nationally as the accommodationist who urged Blacks away from protest and the white-collar professions which would make such protest even more effective. While Washington's work did promote the development of Black people, it lacked the transformative, sacrificial girth of Martin King.

Now the thinking behind this work can be stated in three points:

DEVELOPMENT PLAN SYLLOGISM

1. **Politically liberated ethnic groups** in the U.S. need to help themselves in every way, but with economics leading the way, in order to rise in this country.
2. Since the civil rights movement, **African Americans are a politically liberated group** in the U.S. that has yet to adequately rise.
3. African Americans need to help themselves in every way, but **with economics leading the way,** in order to rise in this country.

Before leaving the subject of political liberation, I have to make a couple of points. First, liberation is not empowerment. Blacks have achieved political liberation, but I know that they have not gotten political empowerment. Liberation concerns the removal of major barriers to citizenship rights. Empowerment is political power commensurate to Whites. Blacks have quite a way yet to go before they have their proportionate share of the power of the dominant group in the U.S.

OTHER GROUPS DEVELOPED ECONOMICALLY AFTER POLITICAL LIBERATION

Across the board, ethnic groups that have come to the U.S. have experienced some degree of intolerance and even discrimination in their early period in this country. Uniformly, they have all had to struggle to get a foothold in this country (the only exception to this rule being the British and perhaps the Scots, although the Scots have experienced some intolerance from the British).

The first groups to come across the Atlantic had little to no problems with U.S. citizenship. By 1800, however, the country began to make more particularized the process of citizenship naturalization. Scottish, Welsh, French, Irish, Italians, Greeks, Germans, Scandinavians, Armenians, Chinese, Japanese, Filipinos came in waves in the 1800 and early 1900s and worked their way into citizenship and ownership. Of the ethnic groups, Latinos, Chinese, and Native Americans had special challenges relative to discrimination and citizenship.

Latinos, mainly Mexicans, have had a protracted struggle with citizenship rights, even though some in the Southwest were living on the land that became the U.S. longer than European Americans in the Southwest.

Chinese Americans have had their struggles with U.S. citizenship. State and U.S. law restricted their numbers and Chinese women from making a home here. New scholarship is revealing the wave of towns and cities that discriminated against the Chinese and Filipinos even to the point of forcibly driving them out of town. Other Asian Americans have had problems from this country too. Japanese Americans did not have their citizenship repealed, but they were interned, and those wanting to come over to this country around the war years had great difficulty.

Then there is the experience of Native Americans, the very Americans whose sharing of these shores put them in the ironic position of having later to become citizens in a process that had to have been as foreign to them, as it was bizarre. Many Native Americans never became citizens for over 100 years, not because they could not, but instead because they did not want to. There are still Native Americans who do not consider themselves citizens of the U.S. The discrimination and violence against Native Americans was very likely the worst any ethnic groups faced here.

Having recounted this information, no Black should ever again entertain the notion that only Blacks have struggled with discrimination and citizenship. All of these situations just described put the above ethnic groups in a compromised position with regard to acceptance in this country and building wealth. I am trying to say that Native Americans have suffered in a way equal to or greater than Blacks; I am not saying other groups have suffered equally; I am saying that almost all, if not all, ethnic groups suffered to some degree after arriving in this country. Where they suffered the delay or denial of civil rights, there they had problems thriving.

It is the problem of political disenfranchisement: it puts an obstacle course in the way of economic development. Winning political liberation (usually in the form of citizenship with full rights and responsibilities) removes the big barriers of the obstacle course. Irish, Italian, and German Americans had to remove such barriers before they gained their foothold in this society.

But once this was done, ethnic groups began to make their way up the ladder that is the American dream. Groups have had to make their own way with little to no help from the government. Each has their sojourn to tell, stories that would require more space than I have room for to portray. Space has to be made, though, for three groups that have risen in ways that are particularly noteworthy to African Americans. The three groups are **Jewish, Vietnamese**, and **Ethiopian Americans**. I deal with them briefly here, but at length in the appendix.

Jewish Americans have had the most spectacular ascent of any ethnic group to come to this land. No single group compares to them when it comes to where the first generation started and the heights to which multiple generations have climbed. From about 1890 and the arrival of very poor eastern European Jews, to 1990 and the preponderance of Jewish Americans in the professions, their economic excellence has become a subject in ethnic studies. Shortly after entering the country, Jews by a greater percentage than other ethnic groups started small businesses—sometimes from a cart. They did well in the areas that they had historically thrived at as a people in Europe: they launched into the clothing, jewelry, and finance arenas from wholesale to retail.

Three groups have risen in ways that are particularly noteworthy to African Americans. The three groups are Jewish, Vietnamese, and Ethiopian Americans.

On the west coast they experimented with showcasing their plays using the newest technology at the time. In the process they established in Los Angeles a media core known as "Hollywood." As they rose financially they kept their families intact and invested generously in the education of their children. First they stressed education in the home and synagogue; then they added their financial resources to what they stressed; and finally they added facilities, when necessary, to their resources, setting up their own remedial or advancement programs, and then their own schools. All of this was shaped and buttressed by the insightful and community-building instruction of the rabbis in the local synagogues. They made sure that Jews in the U.S. patronized Jewish businesses as a matter of survival and godliness. They encouraged the structuring of no-interest lending societies to provide their entrepreneurs indispensable seed capital.

To see how high Jewish Americans have risen, one need only determine their percentage as attorneys, doctors, investment bankers, accountants, and managers of the most prosperous and prestigious companies. It will likely be something like 5 to 10% of the total, or much more. Then relate this to the fact that they are about 3% of the country's population. Whereas African Americans rate disproportionately high on the indices that are bad (i.e., unemployment, debt, and incarceration), Jewish Americans are disproportionately high on the indices that are good (i.e., stock ownership, income, and academic achievement).

Their economic growth parlays into economic and political power. Of late, at least one, and sometimes two, of the seven governors on the financially supervising Federal Reserve Board will be Jewish. They now have what is the most influential lobbying group as of this writing: the American Israeli Public Affairs Committee (AIPAC). Privately, AIPAC boasts of having successfully campaigned against the reelection of a number of members of Congress. That is power. Jewish Americans are disproportionately at the very locus of power in three important cities: in Boston, the investment headquarters of the U.S.; in Los Angeles, the entertainment capital of the country; and in New York, the banking and cultural core of America.

I want African Americans to listen to and learn from Jewish Americans. I have opened up a dialogue with one prominent rabbi and hope to extend this to others. Many have spoken in the past of a special relationship between Blacks and Jews, cemented in the Black-Jewish collaboration in the formation of the NAACP and with the rise of jazz. Its most glorious days may have been the facilitating of *Brown v. Board of Education*, the Mississippi Freedom Rides, and the joint work of the slain civil rights workers Schwoerner, Goodman, and Cheney. Its most tawdry days, at least from a Jewish perspective, may have been the riots and killing in Crown Heights, New York; presidential candidate Jesse Jackson's "hymietown" remark; and the coming to prominence of Louis Farrakhan. (A number of Blacks believe relations were strained long, long ago from both racism and only lukewarm support from Jewish Americans.) In an effort to rehabilitate this relationship, Cornel West and Michael Lerner together wrote a book about the strength and the strains of Black-Jewish relations entitled *Jews & Blacks: a Dialogue on Race, Religion & Culture in America.*

I am in favor of mending these relations. As I am in search of a Black renaissance, I need help from the group most successful at it. I am this serious about what I am seeking.

Vietnamese Americans are the next ethnic group to discuss. They also have sought economic development upon receiving citizenship rights (even before receiving such).

When I bring up Jewish Americans, Blacks who see development as a pipedream can counter, 'Well, the Jews are White.' But they cannot say that about Vietnamese Americans. The Vietnamese also deflect the argument that ethnic groups cannot rise now in White controlled U.S.A. For Vietnamese have forged their business corps mainly since 1975. This is pretty recent.

Finally, Vietnamese Americans remove from Black scoffers the counter that no group can rise from the ghetto. In point of fact, the Vietnamese moved into the poorest areas in whatever cities they gravitated too, as they escaped here from the persecution of the North Vietnamese in their country of origin. Sometimes they lived two families to an apartment. Many if not most started for a time on welfare. Many, if not most, did not know English. The Vietnamese lived so close to Blacks that their children went to school together, each group has a sense of the other's story, and they at times shared the same tenement buildings.

Blacks have watched from a distance the economic rise of Vietnamese Americans. In fact, some of the businesses that the Vietnamese purchased were Black owned or at least operated. Ironically, Blacks are the major patrons of some of the hair supply, auto, or clothing stores that the Vietnamese own. Theirs has been a remarkable success story. How did they go from many on welfare to many owning businesses in one generation?

How have the Vietnamese Americans done this? It has come as a result of an extended family and associational drive for prosperity. The Vietnamese emphasize their own economic development. Individually, they work as many jobs as they can handle upon entry in the country in order to save money. They keep their marriages and their families largely together (although this is changing, as they are approaching the incidence of divorce of the larger society) which provides social and economic stability. The younger family members respect the elders in the family, who direct the savings into investments that benefit the extended family members (although the males do slightly better in this system than do the females).

Vietnamese Americans minimize their expenses, and resulting in more savings. They accumulate their savings in family or associational pools. Their elders determined who would be the first to receive the accumulated business seed money. They jointly establish businesses, and their families assist with the work. In so doing they enjoy labor savings while, at the same time, increasing the demand for their labor.

Then they put heavy pressure on their children to excel in school. Vietnamese parents are earnest about telling their children that the family's honor rests on their performance in school and in business. Perhaps it is too much stress, but I, for one, love the academic results they achieve. Vietnamese children score high in science and math, rivaling the results of Chinese and Japanese children. The oldest child has the job of tutoring the younger children and of being the interpreter for the parents, if necessary. Clearly, everyone in the family has a role to play for the uplifting of the entire family (although Vietnamese women may lament that the role is traditional, maybe even sexist).

Be that as it may, who can argue with the results? Their formidable one generation advances augur well for them in the future. Who knows how far along they will be when they have been in this country as long as Jewish Americans. Their example can teach African Americans a lot, and can remove a bevy of excuses.

Jewish, Vietnamese, and Ethiopian Americans model before African Americans the truth that African Americans can rise and guidance as to how to do so. These ethnic groups showcase the importance of focusing like a laser on economic development after gaining citizenship rights. Similarly, they remove excuses that have a way of self-limiting a people.

Ethiopian Americans are the last group demanding consideration. They are still largely in the middle, if not early in, their first generation in the U.S. Yet, their gains can already be appreciated. Ethiopians in the U.S. are faring as well, if not better, than first generation Jamaican Americans, a group known over the years for doing markedly better than African Americans in general—that is, who do better in their first generation.

Like Vietnamese Americans, Ethiopian Americans nix a number of excuses that Blacks simply just have to overcome. Some African Americans (who have been in the U.S. 50 or more years) say, "Well Vietnamese Americans may not be White, but they are not Black either." Well, the typical Ethiopian is as dark, or darker, than the typical African American.

Other African Americans feel that with the Gingrich Republican Revolution of 1994, the country has turned against Blacks in a way reminiscent of the 1950s. Even if this is so, how does one explain Ethiopian Americans opening stores, restaurants, and gas stations; taking over the local taxi-cab industry; and acquiring a healthy percentage of the parking lot business? This is legitimate, lucrative business development that the footings of a renaissance can rest on. Ethiopian Americans have done this in a quarter of a lifespan.

How do they do it? As I have been able to determine, their methods are a mixture of what both Jewish Americans and Vietnamese Americans have done. With intact families, their elders guide family protocol. Family members get whatever jobs they can and work hard. They save as much as they can in order to raise start-up capital. The elders direct where the capital goes: to whom, and to what ends.

The church or mosque aids what family elders do. Ethiopian Orthodox Christians priests and other Christian pastors teach the necessity and godliness of transcending native tribal differences. They instruct on the ways Ethiopians in this country can work together, at least as separate families. They offer the churches and mosques as centers for society, education, and business development.

Ethiopian parents and pastors emphasize education as Vietnamese parents do. They may not as of yet invest the resources of Jewish parents, but they employ Asian- like pressure on their children to succeed. Ethiopian American children do well in school. Their success is much higher than the African Americans on the whole; Ethiopian children's success in school is comparable to Vietnamese American children.

As a result, Ethiopians have been rising as a people right before the eyes of African Americans. Viewing the economic accomplishment of Africans who arrived within a generation has not been easy for Africans who have been in the U.S. over a century. There has been some ill-will, perhaps even enmity, between Blacks and Vietnamese Americans, and now between Blacks and Ethiopian Americans. In Seattle, there have been incidents of violence between the groups, mainly from African Americans towards Ethiopians here. It has led to shootings on the streets and in the cabs.

Efforts are underway to stem this tide and to foster harmonious relations. Blacks and Ethiopians have good reasons to resolve their differences. African Americans who have been here longer than 50 years need to learn from Ethiopians about their ancient history, about family and culture. For, it is becoming increasingly clear that the earliest humans came from near Ethiopia in Africa, and the West Africans, from whom Blacks have come, came from East Africa. Moreover, Blacks still do not know a lot generally about families from the Motherland. Ethiopians can teach Blacks the eastern story, which may be the generic story.

Ethiopians in the U.S. can use the political assistance and cover African Americans can provide. As the government comes too harshly and broadly against East Africans under the guise of terrorism, Ethiopians here have needed to appeal to the NAACP and to Black churches for assistance. As Ethiopians experience discrimination, they feel the need to resort for advice to the people who know best the civil rights laws and activism. One group can help the other. But what Blacks need most to know from Ethiopians is what they are doing in detail to gain a foothold locally in pockets all around this country.

The Ethiopian story is still very new. There is still a question about whether they will fall victims to the experience of second and third generation Jamaican Americans. Something happens to the children of Black immigrants, even Jamaicans, which makes it progressively more challenging for them to produce the academic and professional results of the earlier generation of children to come to the country. What does this mean? It means that there is something real and sinister going on in the U.S., a covert racism that grinds down even those who come here with the best of intentions, the hardest of workers, and who start off as small entrepreneurs.

Alternatively, every year more of this institutional racism is confronted; every year it fades; every year its pillars are rooted out. So, maybe the combination of elders in intact families and the guidance of strong religious institutions will steer Ethiopians in the U.S. around the experience of Jamaican Americans. Time will tell. In the meantime, I am making overtures to the Ethiopian American community in order to give what I can and to learn what I can. Where they come from, and their success thus far here are all I need to sit at their feet to learn something.

Jewish, Vietnamese, and Ethiopian Americans model before African Americans the truth that African Americans can rise, and guidance as to how to do so. These ethnic groups showcase the importance of focusing like a laser on economic development after gaining citizenship rights. It starts with economic development. This helps hold the family together. Elders and religious leaders guide hard working family members who have to find a way to save more than they consume, even if it means living more than one family to a house, or two jobs per person. Then the savings have to be invested well.

Similarly, these groups help remove the excuses that have a way of self-limiting a people. This is a snapshot of how these groups have done it. Blacks should expect no more than these groups have gotten, and no easier a road than the one these groups have trod. We can hope for more, but we should not expect more; we have a case for more, but we should not wait for more. These groups show the way to travel down that road. The question is, "Are we learning from them where we have to go?" If our ancestors can survive slavery without reparations, and beat segregation without government programs, then we can lift ourselves by our bootstraps even if the government withholds the programs and reparations that would serve as shoestrings. I am not waiting for help; I want us to help ourselves now—and we can.

A NUMBER OF LEADERS DIRECT BLACKS TO ECONOMIC DEVELOPMENT

We have more than civil rights and case studies. We have counsel, as there are a number of Black leaders and thinkers who get it. They understand that what Blacks face now is an economic development problem. This section, and the two that follow, bear this out in more detail.

Harvard Economics Professor William Julius Wilson has written and spoken forcefully to the effect that the challenge for Blacks now is economic development. He believes that Blacks need to promote business formation and viability. He also believes that Black communities need more resources than they can provide themselves. Therefore, he advocates coalescing with other ethnic groups into a multi-cultural coalition for mutual assistance from the state and federal governments. His is an analytical and a well-documented voice for the need to focus our limited time and resources on capitalism in this capitalistic country (using some lobbying tactics for good measure). Then there is a broad movement with one thousand local leaders.

Black Dollar Days is a national movement with no one leader behind it. It is more or less a grassroots movement with various degrees of success that aims to foster a discipline in Blacks to support their own businesses as a matter of modern day survival. Most U.S. cities have something like a Black Dollar Days program. For the month of February Blacks are encouraged to buy Black. It is broader than Black people though; anyone who wants to support Black businesses is encouraged to do so, the thinking being that when the problem is green, the color of the hands that provide it do not matter.

The Black Dollar Days movement in Seattle and around the country has known only minimal success. The credit for that success is owed the Rev. Dr. Robert Jeffrey, Sr. Black Dollar Days is helpful as a forerunner. It is the right approach, searching for a mass following and other initiatives such as remedial education and preventative care to sit on its strong platform. Black Dollar Days is a prototype of the kind of measures Blacks must employ. The local leaders who institute this program in city after city are the kind of leaders who understand the times, and who have first things first.

The most prominent Black leader of the last thirty years is Jesse Jackson. Since the fall of Dr. Martin Luther King, Jr. in 1968, Jackson's life has been dedicated to Blacks receiving the completion of their civil rights. He has been stalwart in the final frontier of political liberation, something we have for the most part received. He added to his quest for government programs (Operation Breadbasket) a major initiative to enhance Black educational achievement PUSH/EXCEL. All of this is beyond commendable. Interestingly, Jackson has shifted his focus somewhat.

In the 1990s he started a Wall Street Initiative to increase Black managerial employment and company investment in Black communities. This is a shift from almost exclusively political endeavors. It is a far cry from the kind of program that would bring the development that Blacks need economically, but it is on the right track. Remember, during the years of primarily Jesse Jackson's leadership, our community has languished. He, and those like him, have helped us survive, but not thrive.

Jackson needs to continue in this vein. The strong organizations he has founded, his international fame, and his great oratorical powers, if turned wholly to economic development herein, could by itself turn the tide in favor of a renaissance. He would have to utterly advance, however, that investment from our own associations, not the least of which is the church, such Black self-help is far greater than the assistance we desire from the government. Until then, his help will continue to feel like he is the most valiant of soldiers, fighting yesteryear's war.

Two leaders, however, who merit discrete attention hail from different centuries. One is the greatest civil rights leader of the 1800s, Frederick Douglass. The other is the founder of *Black Enterprise* magazine, the main African American periodical on economic development hands down: Earl Graves.

FREDERICK DOUGLASS

Frederick Douglass devoted his words and actions mainly to political liberation: freedom from slavery and the undoing of the early thrust of segregation. However, Douglass' example and other words signaled how Blacks can attain economic development after first acquiring political liberation.

Frederick Douglass was born in slavery in Virginia. He spoke of freezing in the winter shack and baking in the summer fields, all occurring under the eyes of the master of the plantation, the man who was very likely his father. When Douglass obtained his freedom, hatching a deft plan and carrying it out to perfection, he fled to New York. There he discovered the abolitionists and William Lloyd Garrison. Mesmerized by their clear indictment of slavery, Douglass signed up for the abolitionist cause. Articulate and courageous, he became their greatest symbol and speaker.

Douglass traveled widely, speaking incessantly against the barbaric institution that had held him bound, and that continued to subjugate his mother, wherever she was. To add to the cause, as well as negate the naysayers who concluded that eloquent Douglass could have never been a slave, Douglass wrote the first part of his autobiography.

After returning from a brief exile in Europe and the publication of his autobiography, Douglass later started his own association and in time a newspaper, *The Liberator*. Frederick Douglass was a powerful force in crystallizing Black opinion in support of the anti-slavery movement, and its political appeals that included presidents from Franklin Pierce to Abraham Lincoln. All of this was in order to destroy slavery so that Blacks could be free.

Douglass advocated for Black soldiers, later signing up his son and helping to outfit a regiment, all so that Blacks could enjoy the pleasure of having participated in their own liberation. And participate they did admirably and wonderfully. With the end of the Civil War and the passage of the Thirteenth Amendment, Douglass witnessed the end of political disenfranchisement (at least for Black men). As Douglass helped shape the Reconstruction, he could savor for a time the feeling that political liberation was won. Next came economic development.

Douglass was successful with his own money. The mansion he left, now part of the country's museum homes, attests to his wisdom with his own money and his support of his family. His finances extended further though.

Douglass put money into his political activities from his anti-slavery efforts to the underground railroad, from publishing his *Emancipator* to the raising of Black troops during the Civil War. Douglass helped raise Black troops so that Blacks could fight for their own freedom. Then he turned his efforts to the Freedman's Bureau Bank both as an investor and the executive officer. When Douglass could have withdrawn his money from the bank when it was clear that it could not be saved, Douglass chose instead to suffer loss with the other depositors.

Douglass communicated more about Black economic development. He did this mainly post-slavery, as Blacks were sampling their first taste of freedom as a people. Douglass's great, great grandson gives us a taste of what Douglass did in terms of economic development:

> *[Interviewer Jacquie]* Changing the topic: could you tell me a little bit more about the houses that your great, great grand father built and why he did it, and, can you trace that area through time at all for me?
>
> *[Fred Douglass the Fourth, great, great grandson of Frederick Douglass]* Well, he built the houses on Dallas Street. He lived and worked in that area in Fell's Point and there was a church there called Strawberry Methodist Church that he attended periodically, so he came back and, number one, he was very concerned about the status of the area because he saw it falling down. So he built the houses as an effort to upgrade an area that he regarded, you know, that he had very much in his heart and loved. Also because he was concerned about the need to provide adequate housing for former slaves and those who were originally freed blacks, so those were his reasons. And he built those around 1890, when he built them and so they were rented out. But that was his improvement, I would say he was a visionary for approaching the whole concept of fair housing and accessible housing at that point in time and also the idea of just building houses to upgrade a neighborhood. So that showed his interest in economic development.
> (Jacqueline Greff, Producer, Tonal Vision LLC, transcr. By Mike Pierce 14 February 2004)

Then with the infamous *Civil Rights Cases of 1883* in which the Supreme Court whittled to nearly nothing the Civil Rights Act of 1875, the civil rights community at the time called old man Douglass back into action. It was apparent to Black America that the country had reinstituted Black segregation, and so the effort to achieve political liberation had to start over again. Back against it came Douglass with whatever strength he had left to muster. Douglass died in 1895 without making as much as a dent in segregation, but he left us a giant mark as to how to proceed.

No matter the position, Frederick Douglass was always focused on the development of Blacks as a people. He was this way as an ambassador, as a solicitor, and as a journalist. He could not be bought. He would not chafe. He did until the end what he directed others to do from the beginning of his adult life: agitate, agitate, agitate.

EARL GRAVES

Earl Graves is the author of the most successful business magazines in Black America: *Black Enterprise*. Black Enterprise is also one of the oldest Black magazines in continuous existence. Early, early on Earl Graves got it; and he has not stepped away from the bar. Even when it could be argued that ending segregation was preeminent, Graves was advocating that Blacks needed economic empowerment through business profitability, and that we needed economic empowerment now. The name of the magazine says it all: we need Black enterprise.

Mr. Graves gives an impressive speech in this regard. Standing tall and with a bold demeanor, he plaintively outlines his case of the amount of Black wealth, the examples of limited business success, how money works in this country, and the money that is being made either around us or from us. He then drops the gauntlet: when will we learn to use our great wealth to make money by ourselves, for ourselves? He said it this way:

> *Our program—developed with the input of our editors, financial experts and the esteemed BE Board of Economists—seeks to empower you by changing your attitude toward money management and revealing comprehensive savings, investment and consumer strategies. We encourage you to embrace the BLACK ENTERPRISE Circle of Wealth, which details the stages of wealth accumulation. We urge you to commit to the BLACK ENTERPRISE Declaration of Financial Empowerment. This historic document lays out your commitment to specific financial objectives. Join other financially savvy African Americans who are making wealth building their own personal goal by committing to the Declaration of Financial Empowerment.* (BLACK ENTERPRISE, "THE 10 PRINCIPLES OF WEALTH")

Savings, investment, and consumer strategies are all along the lines of what is described herein. What he says is a lesson for us all. It is a long awaited lesson in supply and demand, profits and losses. I urge you to get the *Black Enterprise* Declaration of Financial Empowerment and to learn its "10 Principles of Wealth."

THE COMMON SENSE REASON

Sometimes practical reasons can be the most effective. Arguments on capitalism, history, and scholarship can be compelling, but can be so in an abstract way. One may wonder whether these are really what make the average person do what he or she does. At times, the real motivation may be more simple and basic to human nature.

Perhaps the best explanation for why economics must now lead has to do with the power of a good job in the life of a person. A job can give means to a healthy existence, can provide a sense of value, and can offer a path to professional development. Not having a decent job can cause dislocation, depression and deprivation. There is a lot to having or not having job.

As a result, providers of decent work can gain the ability to really shape the lives of those who are looking for such work. People will do a lot to get certain jobs. They may be willing to finally do the things that can improve or even save their lives if it is a condition of their employment. They may be willing to follow a program that they would not otherwise give second thought to. Thus many people do almost anything to get it, and listen most to the one who provides it. This is the power of a job.

CAPITAL IMPROVEMENT: QUANDARA, BOLE & ATLANTA

Capitalism is complicated. It is about supply and demand, as well as about markets with individuals and firms providing competition. It is about labor being on the expense side of the equation. Capitalism exists mainly for owners of businesses—employers. Employees are labor, and labor is an expense that employers work to control. Any people who are almost exclusively employees will almost surely be controlled in ways that they profit from least. Disproportionately Blacks are employees and not employers. We are on the wrong end of the equation when we do not have capital in a sea of capitalism.

Quandara was a town in Kansas that is no longer a vibrant township. At one time it constituted over 10,000 farming family members who had their own "main street" core. Quandara had its stores, bank, saloon, post office, barbershop, restaurant, blacksmith, and boarding rooms for putting people up for a night. What was so unique about Quandara is that Blacks built this town—it was one of the original Black towns of the Midwest.

Blacks built their own farms and homes. They cut their own lumber and planted their own crops. They were the architects and contractors. They laid the foundations and erected the artifices. They built their own stores and shops. Blacks did it all.

Unfortunately, Quandara did not have the advantages of some settlements that allowed them to grow through the ups and downs (vicissitudes) of business cycles and catastrophes. Purposefully, the state and federal planners did not put Quandara on the railroad line. The townspeople had no mining rights, no oil, not even a large forest to which to lay claim. It was not a town that the federal or state governments invested in. They neither placed governmental assets there, nor did they support it as any kind of destination site.

Still, Quandara survived the downturns of the 1880s and the panic of the 1890s; however, these recessions kept farmers from growing. With numbers of towns bursting at the seams, Quandara grew relatively smaller and smaller. Many in the younger generation elected to leave the family farm life for northern expanding towns in hopes of becoming part of the upwardly mobile middle class. They would get a job and maybe own a flat, but would never command the assets that their parents had—not even close. Quandara could not survive the Great Depression and the ensuing dust bowl. Forces beyond their control drove Blacks off the land and to northern or western cities.

As more people left, the town increasingly became unsustainable. Once the population drain hit the critical mark, the main street businesses could no longer turn a profit. With main street becoming a ghost town, the vital services that provided farming people the essentials of civilization—markets for good exchanges, seasoning to give food the taste people demand, and spare parts to keep equipment in repair—were lost.

Yet, the lesson of Quandara is not lost. Blacks fresh out of slavery built a once vibrant town from scratch on their own. If Black Kansans then could do it, then Black Washingtonians now can do it. They built it not from government handouts or from acting chaotically. They did it from capitalistic efforts working in unity. This is the lesson of Quandara.

Boley is still in existence today as a surviving Black town in Oklahoma, what was called "Indian Territory." Blacks in droves left southern places like Mississippi and Arkansas and ventured West to what was the frontier. Once well into Oklahoma, some of them settled down and staked out territory of their own they could negotiate. Discrimination, even a lynching, in Memphis accelerated the process.

Ida B. Wells, activist journalist and devoted teacher, wrote about and then guided Blacks to pull up stakes in Memphis and to go to Oklahoma. She journeyed out herself and scouted the land. Many went to Tulsa; some went to Boley.

Like Quandara, Boley become a Black town of some dimensions. Unlike Quandara, it is still a going concern. Blacks built out Boley as a farming town that now is on the Black historical register as a destination point. It still has its main street with all that it entails: stores, bank, taverns, post office, barbershop, restaurant, blacksmith, and boarding rooms. Blacks built it all with little to no help from outside. Blacks developed these projects as private owners. Blacks there are the face of capitalism. What they are doing is sustained by Boley residents buying from Boley residents, as each supports the other.

In the short run, Tulsa, Oklahoma from 1910 – 1921 is the top example of Blacks building a thriving municipality. Black Tulsa was the Black Wall Street of the West. Harlem in the 1920s rivaled it because of its population and the grand scale of its arts scene. In the aggregate, no Black community anywhere could compare with Harlem's income or the number of its businesses. Yet, Blacks did not own most of the places where they worked; however, Blacks owned most of where they worked in early Tulsa. When owning instead of owing is the name of the game, then any place that owns the assets of its community is the penultimate. This makes Tulsa the short run example. Nevertheless, the long run example of Black capital improvement is Boley, Oklahoma.

Let's learn more about capitalism. We cannot end this chapter without doing so. To do so, we have to go deep into it.

Capitalism is about supply and demand. The first part of capitalism is analyzing demand or finding out what people want. Suppliers move in to fill this demand at a profit. Those business owners will maintain businesses that continue to have demand for the kinds of things that their businesses provide. Too often, Blacks have not presented demand for what they can provide, and so their businesses do not move in to fill that demand. When the businesses take the risk to attract Black demand for their goods and services, we do not show demand, or else it tapers off. We do not sustain demand. Thus, we do not maintain businesses. No businesses, no jobs. For jobs do not fall from the sky; they flow mainly from the businesses that provide them, in a capitalist economy.

Let's look at what a market is. In economics, everything happens within markets. Supply and demand occur within markets. Even labor (a type of supply and demand) happens in a market. That is why we speak of the "job market." Thus, suppliers of demand provide the employment. At a minimum, a business owner employs him or herself. This is the provision of at least one job.

When businesses thrive, more employment is available. When businesses suffer, their owners cut expenses, particularly labor, and thus fewer jobs are available. Employees should do what they can to increase the demand for their labor, whether through schooling, character, or image. Otherwise, they risk demand falling for their labor. One thing feeds off of another.

Now we are ready to understand in economic terms why Blacks are hurting as badly as they are. Black unemployment is a result of the lower demand for their labor. The lack of demand for black workers can basically be explained as business owners not wanting to hire them. Employers say the reason is because Blacks are lower skilled or are less reliable. What Blacks have to do is to work with those most likely to hire them in ways that increase the demand for their labor.

> *Black men, women, and children were brought to this country for a singular purpose: to work. Indeed, the demand for their labor was so great that slaves continued to be smuggled in even after that traffic had been banned. In the years following emancipation, former slaves found that their services would not necessarily be needed. Their labor, like that of other Americans, would be subject to the vagaries of a market economy. The capitalist system has been frank in admitting that it cannot always create jobs for everyone who wanted to work. This economic reality has certainly been a pervasive fact of black life. For as long as records have been kept, in good times and bad, white America has ensured that the unemployment imposed on blacks will be approximately double that experienced by whites. Stated very simply, if you are black in America, you will find it at least twice as hard to find or keep a job.* (ANDREW HACKER, TWO NATIONS: BLACK AND WHITE, SEPARATE, HOSTILE, UNEQUAL, 107-108).

Hacker explains above why Blacks are twice as likely to be unemployed: after slavery, they were just another set of workers competing for too few jobs, jobs that are easier to obtain the whiter a person is. Phrased more politically correct, employers have a greater demand for employees who share their same race. It is not only Whites and Asians who do this; Latinos and Blacks do this as well. Were each ethnic group similarly situated economically, this would all work out fairly. But Whites disproportionately own the businesses, especially big businesses, in the country, and the world, and so the meting out of jobs based on likes and dislikes is quite unfair. Those employers who hire those most like them racially greatly contribute to the unemployment and underemployment of those who are least like them.

As a result, Blacks are the last hired and the first fired. Persistently they suffer twice the unemployment as Whites. They are in an economic jam that requires fixing. Yet, the jam is systemic, and so the fix demands leadership and unity in order to be effective. Individuals working individually cannot do it. Black leadership has to understand the capitalistic context, how it has worked against Blacks, and how Blacks have worked against themselves.

PROBLEM OF LEADERS WHO DO NOT LEAD ECONOMICALLY

Black leadership is not leading the people in this primarily capitalistic country to primarily capitalistic answers to their primarily capitalistic problems. The leadership still does not get it. It is a failure of majoring on minor things and minoring on the majors.

Why are Black leaders so missing the mark? Some do not lead because they cannot. They simply do not understand what capitalism is, how it works, and how capitalistic the country is. Such leaders cannot be faulted, at least at the beginning. It just is not right to fault ignorance. However, after these leaders have led for a number of years, it could be argued that they should start figuring out what is going on economically. If nothing else, consultation, thought, and trial or error should lead them to the revelation.

One could argue that Malcolm X and Martin Luther King were in this boat. They had no economic classes that were relevant to the problem. King was steeped in religion, philosophy, and sociology. Malcolm X was educated on the streets, in prison, and in the Nation of Islam informally along the same lines as King. Neither had operated a business.

Notwithstanding, King had figured out that economics was the new ground of the struggle, and I think that he would have come around to the importance of, and the way to, capture more of the Black dollar for Black businesses. Malcolm X, because he was a quick study, I believe would have come to the same place. This, I admit is speculation; yet, it is what I believe.

Others do not lead in a capitalistic way not as a result of ignorance—they know about capitalism well enough. They do not because they will not. They have the expertise; they have business experience. So, what do they do? They do a few economic projects that have limited capitalistic gain without providing a complete plan or matrix for the next steps to completely develop a Black community. Many of the leaders who come from the professions like law are of this category: Maynard Jackson, former mayor of

Atlanta; David Dinkins, former mayor of New York; and Douglass Wilder, former governor of Virginia are examples. The projects they pushed through, often overcoming serious and sustained political resistance, they deserve credit for. Surely, something is better than nothing. On the other hand, our history proves that it is not enough; not enough for us countrywide, and not even enough in the very communities that these limited projects were done. Something capitalistic, comprehensive, and calendarable is needed to raise Blacks in every community, in every way, over time. Where is this type of Black community plan?

Some do not lead because they cannot; others do not because they will not. Either way, leaders are not leading effectively, and the community suffers as a result. We are good at a certain type of leadership. It is not described as capitalism.

CAPITALISM, SOCIALISM, AND TONY BROWN

If the problems are mainly capitalist in nature then the answers have to be primarily capitalist in structure. It is what fits.

Black leadership is too caught up with resorting to and relying on the government to solve our problems. Going to and leaning on the government are the right things to do when the government is socialist. Socialism has to do with the government controlling and often owning the producers of goods and the providers of the services in the economy. When the government is running everything, one has to go to it to get the help needed. Blacks in the U.S. are great at seeking socialistic measures for our problems. We have become expert at appealing to (or some would say "begging") the city, county, or national officials to solve our problems. It makes some sense because, first, our system is somewhat socialist; second, governments receiving peoples' taxes owe duties to provide the basics for their residents; and third, governments are doing a lot to help others in the U.S. These are logical reasons for seeking socialist answers.

Then there are historical reasons for doing so. Governments backed slavery and segregation; it was appeals to governments that helped end these institutions; governments prosecuted many of the civil rights cases; and in fact governments promoted affirmative action programming that provided greater opportunity for people of darker color. Furthermore, Martin Luther King died preparing a major protest rally in demand of the U.S. government passing major legislation to alleviate poverty for the poor of every stripe. King was the trainer or role-model of the Black leaders who lead us today. Oh, it makes some sense that Blacks are captivated with searching for governmental solutions to their many problems. It makes *some* sense, but it does not make the *best* sense. Tony Brown calls it blaming and demanding:

> *American's Black leadership sees its primary function as blaming Whites for the dire problems of the Black community and demanding more government intervention as the sole solution to this predicament.* (Tony Brown, Black Lies, White Lies 26)

Who is Tony Brown? For those who do not know, Mr. Brown is the producer and broadcaster of the syndicated show *Tony Brown's Journal*. It is touted as the longest continually regularly aired Black show on television. Tony Brown is the author of two books *Black Lies, White Lies* and *Empower the People*, the latter apparently an attempt to prepare himself for a presidential bid in 2004 that never materialized. Brown leans to the right in his politics amongst a people who lean to the left. Yet, Brown makes telling points that both our leaders and people must face. He helps us see how government-oriented we have become in our approach to everything that would lift us.

Brown would have us see that the problem with such governmental initiatives is that they do not work here. This country is primarily capitalist, not socialist. Capitalism in the U.S. is system of private ownership. Socialism is the government ownership and control of goods and services to achieve equality, or the more equal distribution of jobs, shelter, and health care. The United States is not completely capitalist; it is mainly capitalist.

Socialist solutions in a capitalist economy are like trying to put a square completely in a circle. They do not match. We have already visited the rule that "problems that are capitalist in nature demand answers that are capitalist in structure." Capitalist answers are what fit capitalistic problems. It should stand to reason that solutions forged from what only part of the economy is about can, at best, only solve part of the problem. We need solutions from what most all of the economy is about.

The U.S. government and the local governments hire a lot of people. Still, they do not hire most people, and they do not pay anywhere close to the highest compensation. A people reliant on the government for jobs and benefits are relying in this country on the smaller part of the employer base and compensation pool. For government employees compete for the smaller piece of the job market and hold jobs that will ever be vulnerable to budget cuts. To be sure, they will never truly be paid what they are worth.

When will we learn that governmental solutions in a primarily capitalist economy do not promote private ownership? Such solutions address the basic needs of life, and this they do inadequately. Thus, socialist solutions in a capitalist economy do not provide most of the jobs; they do not build wealth; they do not promote private ownership; and they do not adequately address a people's basic needs. At best they supply a few well-paid jobs for the program directors and subsistence living for the rest. Some of the top jobs will go to Blacks just to make the program look effective; the subsistence living keeps most of the people barely making ends meet.

Blacks need economic development through supporting our own businesses that we make sure continue to hire our people.

This miss-serves our people. What is worst, it disserves the interests of Black masses, most of whom are unskilled employees. These employees do not quite understand why they are in their weakened position of little demand for their labor. As a result, they are incapable (or little capable) of defending themselves against the greedy using of their labor and resources against them. They are rife for economic exploitation.

Our leaders should be our defense from this exploitation. What I am saying is that the preachers and teachers, the lawyers and doctors, the chief executive officers and the executive directors should have long ago figured out that our people need massive private sector initiatives. They should have discovered that social programs were only taking us so far. Then they should have spoken and written about the answer until the people came together to make the difference. So many different thinkers, from so many different walks of life, should have said the same thing, so many times, to the same people, that the same message finally became crystal clear. To wit, Blacks need economic development through supporting our own businesses that we make sure continue to hire our people. This should have happened everywhere. Instead, it occurred only here and there—not nearly enough to get the community on the same page.

This is why we must renew our leadership in order to have resolution. Tony Brown said it best when he wrote:

> *Even when the government responds with more opportunity—education, welfare, preference programs for the middle class—these leaders are too shortsighted to mobilize the public largesse* ***into a private self-help initiative*** *to attack the collective problems of the Black community. No amount of government intervention can solve the problem of an*

> *inept, failed leadership.* ***Therefore, White racism has had a partner, a co-conspirator,*** *in the marginalization of Black Americans. Black economic development and social equality have, in part, been subverted by the very Black leaders who pointed their fingers at Whites.* (TONY BROWN, BLACK LIES, WHITE LIES 46-47)

What Tony Brown states here may not be what we want to hear, but hear it we must. We need much more "private self-help" or else we are a "partner", a "co-conspirator" with racism. This is tight, but it is right.

Generally speaking, customers patronize to a slightly greater degree the businesses of those who share their same ethnicity. The ethnic groups who do this help the businesses owned by members of their own community to survive. Such businesses provide greater employment in their community, which promotes jobs.

Everything else feeds off this dynamic. The social benefits are tied to economics, as are the political benefits. In other words, a people generally want to socialize with those who have money, and groups generally want to mix with other groups that are financially more successful. Blacks have to know what this means and how to deal with it.

So, suffice it to say, I am in wholehearted agreement with Timothy Bates, who laid the hammer down by saying that our development rests on the growth of Black businesses. Bates has the most detailed book on banking in the Black community. He wrote,

> *My emphasis throughout this book has been to identify the most viable black-owned businesses—those large-scale firms that are most likely to remain in operation and to create jobs. This emphasis is dictated by my choice of policy objectives—enabling black-owned businesses to fulfill their potential as catalysts of economic development in minority communities.* (BATES, BANKING ON BLACK ENTERPRISE 14)

Now I do not necessarily agree with emphasizing large-scale firms, but I wholeheartedly agree with businesses being the catalysts for economic development. Bates is also right about this generally: this works for any minority community such as African America.

No amount of scapegoating can shift to Whites the duty of Black leadership to help Black people.

Tony Brown has argued similar ideas as well as the need for Black leaders to do a better job of serving the Black community.

Brown is right in bringing the subject back to the leadership. We cannot blame other people for our failure of emphasis—not for the most part. *We* have to take the blame for our own wellbeing. No amount of scapegoating can shift to Whites the duty of Black leadership to help Black people. Please do not take this to mean that I am not an advocate of affirmative action, poor programming, and even reparations; I do not let the larger society exit their longstanding duty to compensate Blacks for what we have suffered in this country. This is the shoestring that we must have. However, no group in this country has risen from compensation over self-initiative. So, what we do for ourselves has to come first. Unfortunately, Brown's work does not tell us how to do this. His work is devoid of a precise plan for self-investment. Still, Brown, like Graves, points us in the right direction.

For instance, 10% annual growth for 15 years will quadruple economic output! This does not even measure our health, education, and relationship gains. Our money alone will quadruple—think about it!!!

THE POWER OF 10

The Banking Rule of 72 is the formula for how to ensure our economic expansion. The Banking Rule says "divide any rate by 72 and one will know how long it will take money to double at that rate." Our target every year is 10% growth. If through our plan Blacks meet or exceed 10% growth annual then over the years we shall grow exponentially.

For instance, 10% annual growth for 15 years will quadruple economic output! This does not even measure our health, education, and relationship gains. Our money alone will quadruple—think about it!!! Take the modest Black community in Seattle as an example. Our $642.5 million in greater Black Seattle would become $1.25 billion. This is how we exponentially grow our resources so that we can build our own households, neighborhoods, and communities economically, socially, educationally, and in every other way.

If we were to maintain 10% growth for 15 years, our income will have grown to $2.5 billion. If we do not put this plan in place, then it is likely that the best the Black community would do is grow at the rate of the rest of society: 3%. At 3% our community doubles every 24 years. So after 15 years we would have grown by about 50%, or half. So if we were at $642.5 million, then in a decade and a half we would have increased to about $900 million. The difference between the two scenarios is not time; it is engaging an effective plan. So let me ask you: what would you rather do, grow by 50% or by 400%? Would you rather have $900 million or $2.5 billion?

IT'S FIRST ECONOMIC, THEN SOCIO-EDUCATIONAL, AND ULTIMATELY SPIRITUAL

The priorities of this plan change depending on which phase the plan is in. Truly, this plan is unapologetic about economics being the driver in the short term. Yet, the short term is only the beginning. In the midterm, educational and social development has to emerge in priority in order to sustain economic development. Blacks have to learn from the ethnic groups covered herein as case studies how to better stress and finance academic excellence. Enrichment programs for those at grade level, and remedial programs for those who are not, are indispensable to transferring the gains from this plan to the next generation. It is time to invest a greater amount and percentage of our resources into our own children's education.

Similarly, we are obliged to improve relations between Black men and women in order to promote and strengthen successful marriages. We have to strengthen the Black family. We need to double the marriage rate, and halve the divorce rate. We must make our relationships more civil and affirming. We will need help from our faith and our African brothers and sisters to do this. Next, we have to bring out brothers living on the down low. We have got to foster more responsible sexual relations. All these hold many benefits: increasing household income, providing more custodial childcare, facilitating healthier living, and promoting companionship. At a minimum folks, this will equate into many more households' resources, and the more efficient use of the community resources. It will as well mean that the quality of our lives, and those of our children, will improve. Lastly, it will put Blacks in a better position to serve as the conscience of this country.

I believe that Black spiritual synergy and its leaders are going to rise and play an even more crucial role in this country. Blacks are starting with an intact spiritual heritage, and we must come back to it to renew it. Taylor Branch was right when he said that the Civil Rights Movement was the most important phenomenon of the last half of the 20th century, and the Rev. Dr. Martin Luther King, the most influential leader (although the Reaganites would beg to differ). Yet, if we rest on the last half of the 20th century we will miss our destiny in the 21st century. So, in the longer term, this plan revitalizes

Black spiritual development. Should we loose this, we will in time loose all of the gains we have made and diminish our voice in the world.

How do we spiritually revitalize? We do this by rededicating our lives to God, increasing their participation in a religious institution, and advancing in good works to the point that the golden rule becomes the general rule. The spiritual leaders must lead the way. If they will not, then the congregants must rise to demand that these things happen.

In conclusion, there are seven areas that make up the fabric of civilization: spiritual, political, social, and economic; educational, medical, and artistic. In a perfect world, no one of these would be more important than the other—except maybe the spiritual area. Each of these is crucial to a Black renaissance. Still, in this world, in this country, at this time, economics must lead the way. No one should know this more than Black leaders of the 21st century.

ECONOMIC, POLITICAL, AND RELIGIOUS LEADERS MUST EFFECTIVELY LEAD

It is crucial that Black leaders get together and begin to bring Black people into a Black renaissance. We have to come together and stay together until the job is done. We will have to bury hatchets and get past our personal hurts as well as our personal issues.

All of the leaders in every area need to rally, but to do so with the realization that economics is the driver. The artistic and educational leaders must unify separately and together, determining sub-plans in their respective areas that are grounded in economic development. The medical and social leaders must do likewise. However, three types of leaders must particularly be on point and in communication. They are the economic, political and religious leaders. The professors, owners, officials, executives, and elders in these three areas have a unique duty given the nature of their areas and the vagaries of these times.

The economics professors should have gotten us to this level a long time ago. With one voice and in instructive ways, they should have helped Black leaders see that something like this is what has to be done. Most all of them clearly see the answer, however they have not effectively shaken us out of our slumber.

The Black politicians are also a group that should have, and that has to, see such problems and communicate the answers to the people. They may be our most experienced leaders in that they are public servants in government at the city, state, or national level. However, given their divided loyalties, understandable because they have to represent all of their constituents not just Blacks, they have been only reactive in their response to what ails the Black masses. They have not been proactive.

Black religious leaders, particularly the Christian clergy, are probably the most influential of the three most important groups. Every Sunday they preach to a captive audience of Black America. Because spirituality is so transformative, the preachers' words tend to move masses, even launch movements. With so many churches in the Black community, such a spiritual heritage, and the silvery oratorical skills of many of those in the pulpit, the religious leaders have held the prime place of power in the Black community. This is how it should be, given the size of the issues they teach on, their call to live for the benefit of others even over their own material gain, and the history that shows they have uniquely helped to bring Blacks over the troubled waters.

Nevertheless, it is time—no, it is past time—for the religious leaders to take care of what is wrong with this world while they prepare people for the next. It is especially past time for Black pastors to do this for their people. If ancient Egypt's (Kemet's) temples, ancient Israel's temples, and modern Jewish synagogues can double as the cultural, social, educational, and spiritual preservative of their larger communities, then the Black churches can do the same for their communities across this country.

What is the moral of these stories? People can lead themselves and can lead the leaders to lead better.

PEOPLE MUST ENSURE THAT LEADERS LEAD

But what if the leaders fail the test? What if even the religious leaders shirk their higher responsibilities concerning taking care of the people? Then the people themselves must somehow save themselves. It is tough to do, but not impossible. For a lesson in this regard, we can look to the Nigerians. Nigerians will not let Nigeria remain a military government. The people rise up and face down the bullets of the military if need be to restore civil government to their country. Mexicans can teach us something about this as well, as Mexicans rose up against over 70 years of one party rule to elect Vicente Fox to be their leader. It required mass action in a sustained way to accomplish this feat. The civil rights movement in the U.S. is also a model for us.

Yes, leaders like Martin Luther King and Fannie Lou Hamer stepped up to lead. Yet, it is also the case that thousands upon thousands of ordinary folk fought segregation themselves, often before the marquis leaders arrived, and without the protection of the mass media watching. What is the moral of these stories? People can lead themselves and can lead the leaders to lead better.

Even if we agree that the leaders have failed, surely not all of the blame can be laid at the feet of the leaders. The people play a role in this as well. When leaders do not lead and then the people fail to hold them accountable, the people are partly responsible. The people of whom I speak are the millions of adults in our community. Black adults are survivors, creative, savvy, and resourceful. We could not have gotten this far being anything less. People vote ineffective leaders into power. People tolerate ineffective leaders in office. People put unachieving leaders back into power. We are too brilliant to tolerate leaders who do not serve our interests.

So we come right back to Black Tulsa. When Black Tulsa built and ran its own taxis, stores, and other businesses it was acting in its behalf in the only way a capitalistic country rewards: capitalism rewards capitalists. Good Black leadership enabled this to happen in Black Tulsa and throughout Black America as late as the 1960s. Unified Black people in the thousands advanced what these leaders proposed. The leaders and the people worked together, and the result was that a backwoods community impressively built a Black civilization, and in the process picked itself up by its bootstraps. Black people there did this without shoestrings of assistance from the larger society.

Since then, they largely, and we, too, have lost it. We have got to get it back. What we had to do by default, we failed to do by design: integration led to Black disinvestment in Black businesses and Black upper class flight from Black neighborhoods. Our leaders have to help us do this. Alas, they are not quite there yet. To put things in street terms, our leaders are "slippin." For whatever it is worth, I wrote a poem about it. You will find it in the appendix, so named: "Slippin."

The people too, not just the leaders, have gotten distracted, fallen into pathologies like drugs or violence, and have not made the most of our great abilities. Nelson Mandela was right when he said that our problem is that we are brilliant beyond measure. Will we use our brilliance for our own good?

The people have not asked their leaders to represent their interests sufficiently. We are grown; we cannot afford to tolerate irresponsibility; to do so is irresponsible on the people's part. In sum, I remind us all that we are too brilliant to tolerate leaders who do not serve our interest. Pick leaders who will get the job done; and whatever they fail to do, do yourself. Every single person is needed for this renaissance.

The next two chapters pick up from these points regarding counsel and take the argument further. It is not just teachers like William Julius Wilson and entrepreneurs like William Graves, Jr. making the point, but the three main development works of the last decade do the same, as did the three main Black leaders of the twentieth century.

BETRAYAL, POWERNOMICS, AND THE COVENANT

There are three works that merit discrete attention. Each of these works is an attempt to address the major needs of the entire Black community. Each either contains a plan or calls for the preparation of one. Each has its great strengths and its weaknesses. It could be argued that each of these books is superior to this work because they proceeded it. On the other hand, because this work benefited from the strengths and weaknesses of the others, I think this work presents a more workable plan than even these fine works.

BETRAYAL: A CUTTING CRITIQUE OF BLACK LEADERSHIP

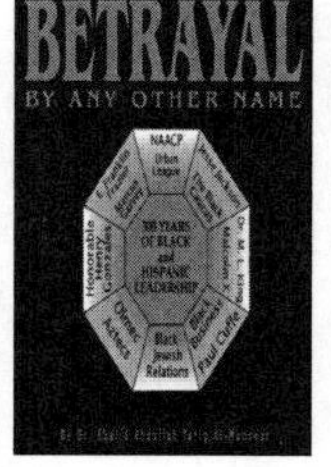

Dr. Khalid Abdullah Al-Mansour called Blacks to immediate action and offered the basics of a plan to act on in his work entitled *Betrayal By Any Other Name* (1993). Al-Mansour is an attorney and devout Muslim. He travels widely throughout the U.S. and the Muslim world. As a man about the world, he is involved in a number of pan-Arab and cross-cultural organizations. From what he has seen and heard, Al-Mansour is convinced that Blacks are drifting away from the developed world technologically and that our poverty may soon consign Blacks to the status of a permanent underclass caught in a caste. He wants to prepare Blacks here for their own survival in the 21st century.

Al-Mansour rightly emphasizes economics and education. He appeals to Blacks to build our own businesses and to teach ourselves afrocentrically. He feels that past leaders, personalities like Paul Cuffe, Martin Delaney and Malcolm X are the examples Blacks should follow. They were committed to Blacks as a people, they were economically engaged, and they were pan-African in their orientation. None of them, though, rise to the heights of Marcus Garvey in what they actually did for and said to Blacks. For Garvey led a movement that for established multiple businesses and brought tens of thousands of dollars into the greater Harlem area.

Incidentally, by 'Africa' or 'afrocentrism', Al-Mansour includes Saudi Arabia and the Middle East. In fact, I think that he means these places just as much, if not more so, than the continent proper. This is his religion speaking through him, which I understand.

The issue with Al-Mansour is that his plan is not detailed enough, although it properly emphasizes economics. It is more a warning as to why African Americans need to help themselves now, primarily economically and afrocentrically, and a history of those Blacks who understood this best.

Another concern I have is the asides to Islam and things Arabic. It is a sidetrack that has more to do with promoting Islam than with developing Black people. On the other hand, I feel that my work is also liable to a similar criticism, in that I am decidedly pro the church and Christianity.

POWERNOMICS: AN IMPRESSIVE MODEL PROBLEMATIC TO DETROIT

An even better work is Claud Anderson's, *Powernomics*. It is everything that Dr. Al-Mansour's book is and more. This book takes the Black Dollar Days concepts to another level. It provides a pretty good plan as to how to do this great work.

Claud Anderson is an African American who has a doctorate in education, and has done most of his writing in economics. He served as State Coordinator of Education for Governor Reuben Askew of Florida. I suspect his most meaningful assignment has been assisting Detroit as it has been grappling with how to incorporate many of his ideas.

An avid writer, Mr. Anderson's first major work was *Black Labor, White Wealth: The Search for Power and Economic Justice*. However, by far his most famous book is *Powernomics; The National Plan to Empower Black America*. On the ideas contained in his works, Anderson has lectured around the country and throughout the world. Farrakhan gave Anderson time at his Millions More March to do a presentation on the current efforts of the *Powernomics* national movement.

In *Powernomics*, Anderson advises that Blacks should buy from themselves and use their wealth to build their own institutions in every other area: health, education, politics, and the like. He suggests how this could be done. I laud Anderson because he gives first place to economics, and because he put his ideas in a usable, published plan. Too few Blacks are writing good clear works. Anderson is an exception.

***Betrayal*, *Powernomics*, and *The Covenant* are all must have books. They deserve a place in the library of any student of Black development.**

Anderson works to present his ideas, grounded in the importance of economics, in a historical context. This adds weight to the power of his ideas. He mentions Washington, Garvey, Hamer, and others. The discussion of afrocentric education and economic self-help are apt; however, his emphasis on reparations and staking claim to a section of town are, in my opinion, misdirected. Allow me to explain.

Anderson advises that Blacks push hard for a hefty reparations payment from the U.S., and that Blacks separately establish Africa Towns just as other groups have such areas as China Towns. Both of these measures are controversial. The reparations action I believe is something that will require a great investment just to force the larger society to consider it. I believe that it is unlikely that Blacks will get anything significant for the resources invested, most Whites being much more likely to heed the insular and selfish arguments of David Horowitz than to listen to the arguments of Anderson, NCOBRA, or even a progressive multi-ethnic movement. (Horowitz has written and argued to the effect that this Black generation is undeserving of reparations; and besides, as significant recipients of welfare payments, he argues, Blacks have already received a type of reparations.) I would push for reparations, but I would not invest a lost of resources in such an effort. Our dominant efforts must go to executing our plan to pick ourselves up by our own bootstraps.

As for Anderson, he hails from Detroit. Detroit Blacks moved to institute the *Powernomics* program in the early 2000's. Success has been checkered at best. The ideas on self-investment have proven useful. The Africa Town and reparations components have been problematic. In fact, many leading Blacks lost the courage to push the full program through, despite their demographic majority, given the angst over establishing an Africa Town sector of the city. I believe that a plan of Black self-investment should be advanced without such a declaration. I recall that Anderson believed that the Africa Town designation was related to receiving certain governmental grants or tax advantages. We are likely to get more without so marking our territory. Besides, our businesses and architecture, our homes and parks, our paintings and plays will provide all the markings we need.

Still, I commend Anderson for his forward looking, detailed and developed plan. His is a monumental work, misguided in a few parts, but brilliant for the most part. If Blacks had more leaders like Anderson it is likely that we would rise much farther, much faster.

I encourage everyone to purchase his book. It is must reading, and it commands its rightful place on every bookshelf that catalogues the works of Black liberation.

COVENANT: MAKINGS OF A PLAN, BUT STILL UNDER PLAYS ECONOMICS

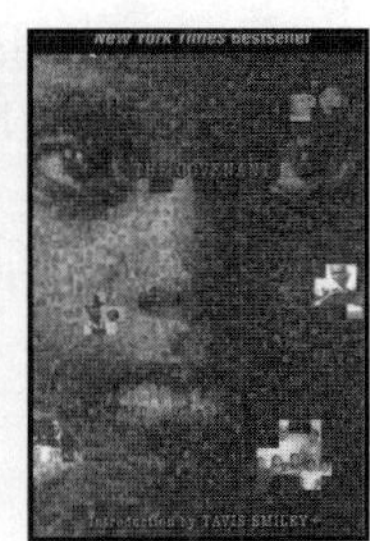

Broadcaster and television personality Tavis Smiley has been calling the Black community leaders together in a leadership forum ever since BET's Robert Johnson sold the company to non-Black interests around 2000. Wisely, while preparing the 2006 Black Leadership Forum, Smiley asked certain influential Blacks in a number of areas to write articles about where Blacks are suffering and what can be done to right things in each area. Hence, the book contains articles on every major area Blacks need to address for our comprehensive development.

No less than Cornel West, preacher at large and professor at Princeton, shaped the book's title and wrote with Smiley summarizing pieces that served as bookends for the work. West urged that such a book was not a contract in the Gingrinch sense, or a compact as in the case of the Mayflower. Instead, given our spiritual heritage, it was a covenant. Thus the name *The Covenant With Black America.*

In record time Haki Mahtibuti with Third World Press published the book and helped promote its distribution. *The Covenant* has been a resounding success, having won a spot on the New York Times' Best Seller List. It is good to see something so meaningful, and so urgent to our community, receive a profile so high. Much of the success is owing to Tavis Smiley, who, as of this writing, has a late night television show simply entitled *Tavis Smiley* that airs on the Public Broadcasting Service (PBS), a ten-minute slot on the nationally syndicated *Tom Joyner Morning Show* radio in the mornings, and a Sunday evening show on National Public Radio (NPR). All of this is in addition to his annual Black Leadership Forum.

The Covenant reads like a concise white paper on the Black condition in 2006. As such, it properly diagnosis the problem with statistics and cites. It also offers a prognosis or solution, albeit one in outline form. Still, it works well and is an informative read.

To me, it has one glaring problem of priority that I believe errs. It places economic development toward the end, and it treats the other areas as if they are equally important or more so. This runs against the bias of everything I am saying herein. If Smiley is right, then I am wrong. Conversely, if I am right, then Smiley is wrong. Well, I believe that I, Al-Mansour, Claud Anderson, and even the leaders in the next chapter are right in directing our people to economic development as the centerpiece.

Betrayal, *Powernomics*, and *The Covenant* are all must have books. They deserve a place in the library of any student of Black development. In some way, each has shaped this work somewhat, and for that I feel I am indebted to each of these authors. The point of including them is to note the consensus forming about the centrality of economics, and where we are still missing the point. It should be mentioned as well that each has something to say about where Black leadership is under-serving Black America.

MARCUS, MALCOLM, AND MARTIN: LESSONS FROM OUR LATEST GREATEST LEADERS

❖ ❖ ❖

There are three leaders who have special significance in the Black community, owing to what they did for Blacks at cost to themselves. Number one on that list is, of course, the Rev. Dr. Martin Luther King, Jr., for reasons too obvious to state. The second is Malcolm X, who experienced resurgence in the 1980s primarily incident to the rise of rap and rappers' need for a revolutionary leader. Finally, there is Marcus Garvey. Of late, those emphasizing economic development mainly from community initiative have rediscovered Garvey. Anything Marcus, Malcolm, and Martin stood for should have great resonance in the Black community. I contend that each one was moving heavily in the direction of the centrality of economic development.

MARCUS GARVEY AND UNIA

> *I have traveled a good deal through many countries, and from my observations and study, I unhesitatingly and unreservedly say that the American Negro is the peer of all Negroes, the most progressive and the foremost unit in the expansive chain of scattered Ethiopia. Industrially, financially, educationally and socially, the Negroes of both hemispheres have to defer to the American brother, the fellow who has revolutionized history in race development in as much as to be within 50 years to produce men and women out of the immediate bond of slavery, the latchets of whose shoes many a "favored son and daughter" has been unable to loose.* (Marcus Garvey qtd. in John Henrik Clarke and Amy Garvey's Marcus Garvey and the Vision of Africa)

In the 1920s, Blacks in New York had the most far-reaching, forward-looking movement the country had ever seen theretofore. It was a movement that was as much political as it was social. But beyond these, it was economic and ideological. Jamaican born, Marcus Garvey went to New York because he felt that African Americans were the "most progressive and foremost" in "the expansive chain of scattered Ethiopia." Garvey lamented the fact that Africans outside of Africa had no king or sovereignty; he determined that he would gain these for them. Where better to do it than in the United States of America, with African Americans. Where better to go in the U.S., than to New York's Harlem where over 100,000 Blacks made their home? New York was then and remains today the largest enclave of Africans outside of the Motherland.

Garvey held a high regard for American Blacks, although he knew they were in a struggle for justice. He said so:

> *Let not the American Negro be misled; he occupies the best position among all Negroes up to the present time, and my advice to him is to keep up his constitutional fight for equity and justice.* (Marcus Garvey qtd. in John Henrik Clarke and Amy Garvey's Marcus Garvey and the Vision of Africa)

At the high point of his movement, a movement called the Universal Negro Improvement Association (UNIA), the list of Black-owned endeavors UNIA was financing is impressive: a number of stores, teaching sites, trading companies, and two ships for doing high seas commerce with the Caribbean. These surely were major forays into economic development. Incidentally, Garvey chose the name 'UNIA' after Whites were forming neighborhood improvement associations (NIA) across the North and West. These NIA's brought realtors, legislators, and the police together to formulate local initiatives to either keep Blacks out, or to confine them to certain blocks in a city. Words that the larger society used for Black segregation, Garvey appropriated and revised for Black liberation.

Anything Marcus, Malcolm, and Martin stood for should have great resonance in the Black community. I contend that each one was moving heavily in the direction of the centrality of economic development.

Al-Mansour argues that Garvey was the most progressive African American leader Blacks have ever had. He says this because Garvey understood that the nature of the answer in the U.S. was economic development, and then he led Blacks at doing just that. Moreover, Garvey was afrocentric. He was part of the pan-African movement and was interested in building alliances as well as trading, Afro-Caribbeans with African

Americans. Garvey actually espoused African Americans returning to Africa where they would be respected and enjoy all the opportunity they could ever need.

It is Garvey's example that Blacks need to follow more than his words. Garvey's ownership endeavors, though incomplete, were accomplished in fewer than 10 years. If they could have continued in the way they began, think of how far they could have gone in 20 years. They may have owned buildings and shipping lines by then. Think of the jobs and contracting opportunities provided. Handfuls of people were enjoying new-found money that they did not have before, and that they would not have again after Garvey.

When Garvey provided the people such economic opportunities, he had their attention for all of the other things he wanted to say, and needed to do. Then he could instruct them about the urgency of forming families, of families helping their relatives, and of neighborhoods of families working together. Then he could teach them about Africa and Africans around the world. Then he could explain why Africans outside of Africa rely on Africans in America to help them rise. Common folk and business people alike found in Garvey someone who commanded their respect because he did more than talk or preach—he brought opportunity.

Now this is not to say that Garvey did everything right. Garvey's failure to properly oversee his staff, and his pomp, to the extreme of parading around in military gear, are illustrative of his errors. Garvey may have been too dictatorial, and he certainly trusted inexperienced people with complicated tasks that were over their heads. Garvey was a visionary but not as good at the realities and details of his endeavors.

It should also be mentioned, however, that Garvey had many enemies inside and outside of the Black community. Enemies in the camp make it hard to deliver on one's promises. The U.S. government was against him, the more successful he became. The government feared any Black leader who was independent minded and appealed to the masses. Black leaders were apparently jealous of Garvey. I write of leaders like W.E.B. Dubois, who turned his extraordinary tongue and pen against Garvey, using these stellar tools to discredit Garvey. Dubois went so far as to cartoonize Garvey, talking about him as if he were a ruffian and a knave. It is hard to build a successful movement with such leaders undermining who you are and what you are doing. Then with the government coming down on you, there is little left to do but leave the country—which is what Garvey did.

Nothing like what Garvey did has been done since, not by one charismatic leader trying to help the people in general. For this reason, Marcus Garvey is the model. He is the prototype. He is the example of what leaders should be doing for their people. Al-Mansour and John Henrik Clarke were right to praise him. Malcolm and King could have learned from what Garvey did.

MALCOLM X

When Malcolm Malik Hajj X returned from his spiritual sojourn to Mecca, he arrived in the U.S. with a new mindset and a renewed mission. He had a mind to discard racist views of Whites, and a mission to devise a plan for Black development. Malcolm X never got the chance to complete his work as he was felled by an assassin's bullet within a year. This was to the great loss of the Black community and the wider world.

For Malcolm was a great student of learning and of the world. As any student would, X sought out accomplished people he had access to who would instruct him. These people became his teachers. In jail he looked to the Hon. Elijah Muhammad. Muhammad inculcated in Malcolm the spiritual bindings that reigned in the gangster, awakened spiritual discipline, and gave him a call to live for higher than himself. His learning continued.

As he became spokesperson and fully appreciated his lack of historical awareness, he sought out John Henrik Clarke and was taught by this great Black historian. As he made the change toward the development of a platform, he looked to Africa and its transformational leaders like Ghanaian President Kwame Nkrumah and Kenyan Premier Jomo Kenyatta. They helped him see that an appeal to the United Nations may give his movement an international airing that could embarrass the U.S. to action; but that he needed to move in a direction similar to where the Rev. Dr. Martin Luther King, respected world wide, was going. Malcolm was moving toward King before he died. Where King was going, Malcolm would not have been too far away.

On the day of Malcolm's death, he held in his hands the proposed platform of the Organization of African American Unity. Days before, he had announced the name and the basic purpose of this new organization. At that time, he promised to speak in greater detail later. The day of detail was the very day of his death. X never got the chance to elucidate the items on that page. His assailants executed their conspiratorial scheme shortly after Malcolm greeted those assembled, which included his wife and little girls.

The following is the list of items on the sheet he intended to speak from. We can only speculate as to what he would have said about each item:

Restoration: relations with African Americans and Africans,

Reorientation: role in the world and with Africa,

Education: Afrocentric education from our own day care centers to our own schools,

Economic Security: freedom from economic slavery of every type, one way of which is by establishing a technician bank of African Americans or Africans, and,

Self Defense: encouraging law abiding behavior but demanding the right to defend ourselves from oppression, even police brutality.

Notice that economic security is on this list. Malcolm went on to propose eight standing committees, one of which would have been the Economic Committee.

It is likely that Malcolm would have been the greatest modern leader Blacks ever had, as he was such a quick study. From a prisoner to a disciple of the Nation of Islam, Malcolm X's learning curve was intense. From disciple to spokesperson for the entire movement, his on-the-job education was extraordinary. Who could doubt that his journey from spokesperson to independent leader would have been equally filled with quickly acquired instruction?

MARTIN LUTHER KING AND THE POOR PEOPLE'S CAMPAIGN

Negroes have irrevocably undermined the foundations of Southern segregation; they have assembled the power through self-organization and coalition to place their demands on all significant national agendas. And beyond this, they have now accumulated the strength to change the quality and substance of their demands. From issues of personal dignity they are now advancing to programs that impinge upon the basic system of social and economic control. At this level Negro programs go beyond race and deal with economic inequality, wherever it exists. In the pursuit of these goals, the white poor become involved, and the potentiality emerges for a powerful new alliance. (Rev. Dr. Martin Luther King, Jr., Where Do We Go From Here 19 [emphasis added])

It is generally believed that the greatest Black leader past and present is the Rev. Dr. Martin Luther King, Jr. His leadership through segregation, north and south, provided Blacks political liberation. We are now in position, because of him and those of his generation, to obtain economic development and everything it supports.

This chapter opens in celebration of Marcus Garvey. Notwithstanding his significance, in some ways our celebration of Garvey is premature. For Garvey was after economic development before achieving political liberation. This is out of order, and history shows it did not work. This was also the oversight of Booker T. Washington. It brings us back to the syllogism of this work set forth in a box on page 27.

Whereas Garvey missed this, King was right on point. Singularly, he led a movement that attacked segregation, the label of our political bondage. The Civil Rights Movement won for all Americans, not merely Blacks, the 1964 Civil Rights Act, and the 1965 Voting Rights Act. These were the acts that would take over the heavy lifting to pull Blacks up from the abyss to the starting point of liberation.

By 1967 King was already writing that the problem was, and yet remains, economic. He saw this as early as 1965, and spoke publicly on it by 1966. The quote that introduces the section on MLK is from his last book, *Where Do We Go From Here?* In it, King makes unmistakable that Negro programs must now deal with economic inequality. Then King took this the next step.

King began to ponder with his leadership team a major economic initiative. The consensus formed around going to Washington, D.C., with people of every race and camping on the grounds there, one million strong, until Congress passed comprehensive legislation uplifting the poor. The trip to Memphis to help the garbage workers was a tune-up for treating poverty and means of showcasing America's economic mistreatment of its people. King would not get out of Memphis.

The *Poor People's Campaign* was a seminal event in the ministry to King, this time, to the nation. As he planned this event, King traveled through the deepest part of the South compiling first-hand information about unsung poverty. He heard stories of the lack of running water and of inadequate bathroom facilities. He heard accounts of freezing in winter and sweltering in summer. He heard himself mothers recounting their fears about where their children's next meal was coming from. He witnessed the unsanitary conditions of their daily travail and dire ramifications of their going without pre- and post-natal health care. It was as if King were in a college of a different kind, taking courses in a life King really never lived.

King grew up the son of a well-to-do Black family in Atlanta. His father was a respected pastor making a salary significant enough to afford a nice two-story home that still looks "bourgie" today, a home open to all as a national historic site. King did not grow up like the average Black American in the South. Those were the days of Jim Crow segregation, meaning that the average Black was, or was only a couple of decades removed from, either sharecropping someone else's land or subsistence living as the owner of a small farm. In an upper-middle class neighborhood in fancy Atlanta, one of the, if not the most, developed cities of the South, King could shield himself from all of this privation.

In the Poor People's Campaign, King immersed himself in the throes of the bereft life. He did not run from it; he ran to it. He returned to his roundtable of inner circle comrades, who could have used a college-level immersion into poverty themselves, King was illumined and focused on the need for economic development. He had visceral knowledge from which to work. It is within this context that we should understand the 1967 quote above on the importance on "economic inequality."

King clearly foresaw that it was time for economics to lead. Yet, neither the Black community in general nor the Black leadership in particular sees this. We especially do not see that the answer is about capitalistic answers given that we exist in a capitalistic setting causing us capitalistic problems. Since this is where King was, it is likely that X would have not been too far behind . . . had he lived.

Incidentally, I began this work with the most poignant quote I know imploring, beseeching Black leaders for a good plan for the people's advancement. It is from Ossie Davis' speech to the Congressional Black Caucus, a meeting of the kinds of leaders who in short order should be able to come up with the most instructive material. If you forgot the quote, here it is again:

> *Give us a plan of action. . a 10 Black Commandments; simple, strong, that we can carry in our hearts, and in our memories no matter where we are and reach out and touch and feel the reassurance that there is behind everything we do a simple, moral, intelligent plan that must be fulfilled in the course of time even if all of our leaders, one by one fall in battle, somebody will rise and say 'Brother!! Our leader died while we were on page three of the Plan. Now that the funeral is over, let us proceed to page four.* (OSSIE DAVIS, FIRST ANNUAL CBC DINNER 18 JUNE 1971)

Mr. Davis made this appeal just three short years after the death of Martin King, and six years after Malcolm X's death. His reference, "even if all of our leaders, one by one, fall in battle," referred to King and X. By the time of Davis' words, Garvey had long been dead, and his work in the U.S. ended with his banishment from the U.S. in 1927. So, our greatest leaders of the century had fallen—their work prematurely ended. Thus, Davis called the leaders to formulate a plan so that we would know what to do in the event that forces outside of our community extinguished leader after leader.

Yet, the CBC did not devise a relevant, detailed plan for a Black renaissance. To this day, African Americans still do not have a comprehensive, clear, development plan from which we are working. The Congressional Black Caucus came up with something, but it was not a comprehensive, clear, development plan by any stretch of the imagination.

Malcolm X was formulating a plan when he was killed, and Martin Luther King was re-formulating his plans along economic lines. I am unaware of a comprehensive plan of Garvey, although his example is all the plan I need. If we were to quiet ourselves and listen well, listening with our inner ear, the ear that heard the ancients guide us through the Middle Passage and slavery, the ear that perceived our forbears speak us through segregation and lynchings; if we were to hush enough past the sounds of materialism and individualism, then we would hear the chorus of three men, this time, beckon us to where they had ended up; we would hear three of our latest, greatest leaders bellowing that our answer is primarily economic and that our bootstraps are strong enough to pull ourselves up on. I hear Marcus, Malcolm, and Martin calling. Do you?

A BOOTSTRAP

A bootstrap is no flimsy thing. It is a solid strip of animal skin, fabric or synthetic. Bootstraps have holding power, as they are sizeable. They fit well in the hand. A shoestring is no bootstrap. Bootstraps are much wider and tougher than a mere string.

Bootstraps are usually sown or riveted onto a shoe. They derive their strength from the integrity of the shoe—the areas and levels of it. I have Nike's with a shoestring and bootstraps. The bootstrap is really an afterthought, a design feature making the shoe stand out from the rest. Yet when buckled, the bootstrap still adds remarkably to the integrity of the shoe. I like to buckle the strap tight when the better players shoe up at the gym when I am playing. The strap lies at the center of the shoe.

I want to see our community get to a place to where we are not longer reliant on the government for subsistence and emergency assistance. Where such help is unavoidable, no one should disparage a person for taking it. However, we must work like Navy Seals to help ourselves. We have to get beyond living on shoestrings. This is where our leaders past and present have fought us. This is the place from which we can address every area and level of our community. This is the solid place of our integrity. We must come to this place wherein we may have shoestrings, but we rely on the holding power our bootstraps afford.

AREAS AND LEVELS

Freeing yourself was one thing; claiming ownership of that freed self was another.
(Toni Morrison)

People have multi-faceted needs that they seek to meet in a multi-dimensional environment. Our needs are naturally economic, but they are social too, because we prefer to exist in relationships. They are medical, but they are also artistic, as we are given as much to beauty as to pleasure. Our needs are truly multi-faceted.

The complex nature of our needs drives us to find differing environments that meet our multiple needs. The household is one such environment, a more private one that affords us more control and intimacy. Yet, people find it needful to go beyond their homes for the greater resources of the neighborhood and still greater facilities of the community. The home, neighborhood, association, city, and state are many of the levels humans have established. Certainly, our environment responds with different levels to address the different areas in which our needs arise. Complex beings in complex situations require complex solutions.

Accordingly, one should expect that any plan for the development of a people or an ethnic group would be complex. For African Americans, such a plan would have to be usable where we find ourselves: in our families, our many associations, and our extended communities.

I call the various aspects that this plan must address simply "areas." I refer to the different arrangements in which Blacks place themselves as "levels." We go now to a short discussion on areas and levels so that you know that we are not fixated on economics or on a community approach.

CONCERN ABOUT THE NON-ECONOMIC AREAS: POLITICAL, SOCIAL, MEDICAL, EDUCATIONAL, ARTISTIC, AND SPIRITUAL

Economics is not everything. Although it is central to what Blacks must concentrate on now, it is really only one of seven areas in which we must work. It does complicate matters to bring up other areas, but we have no choice. Promoting a Black renaissance in Seattle means addressing all the lagging areas. The six areas: political, social, medical, educational, artistic, and spiritual. They are not listed in order of importance; they are all important. Our leaders in all of these areas are right to make sure that we understand the importance of each.

Because this is a plan for the total development of the community, there is a chapter for each of these areas towards the end. All of these areas, though, need to tie into and relate back to the economic area.

NEED FOR A POLITICAL PLAN

Politically, African Americans leaders must unify and move to forge a plan. The area is too important to all of the others not to, for the political level is important for protection, protocol, and provision. It does not really exist for itself: it protects, orders, and provides for all of the other areas so that the people can live the best possible lives.

Specifically, protection is needed because of enemies from within and without. When the police do not secure our community, then we need to do something for ourselves. After petty criminals and predatory businesses, our communities need protection from uncaring politicians. Public officials from the local to the state levels have exploited, under-funded, over-regulated Black communities from Seattle to Miami. Freeways have been cut through the heart of the Black core, schools serving Black children deteriorate for lack of capital improvements, while extra police are given orders to each make manifold arrests on the beat in the "hood".[1] Our community has to find a way to rise up as one, so that together we can do what individuals working alone cannot do for themselves. Such protection is political.

Protocol and provision go together. Protocol has to do with arranging our property, people, and practices in such a way that things work as well as can be expected. It is working out bottlenecks, disputes, and regulation so that things happen faster, better, and fairer. Provision, on the other hand, involves the community coming up with the resources that are needed to get our people through emergencies or downturns, or just to assist with the projects necessary for development.

Protocol and provision are the items even more important to this work. We are usually good at protection because mostly it is a matter of reacting to events. Protocol and provision have more to do with policymaking and problem solving. All of these aspects of politics require our community to elect leaders who are smart and have the interests of the community at heart.

Economics is not everything. Although it is central to what Blacks must concentrate on now, it is really only one of seven areas in which we must work.

What will the agenda be? Within the community it will be the plan that is contained herein. When our political leaders are serving in the general community, it will be an inclusive plan that supports the interests of the middle class and the poor. They will struggle with protection, protocol, and provision, and continue to do so until their leaders provide policy and policing in appropriate ways for their polity. This is what politics concerns.

NEED FOR A SOCIAL PLAN

Socially, Black leaders need a plan as well. The social area has to do with promoting healthy relationships and caring for those who cannot physically care for themselves. The relationship arena concerns loneliness, dating, shacking, marriage, civil unions, parenting, and divorce. Caring for the needy entails services to children, addicts, alcoholics, the disabled, the disruptive, and the aged.

Of all of these items, marriage and family counseling and resources are crucial. Marriage is the foundation of society. It is the first institution most religions speak of God creating. This is definitely the case with Christianity, Judaism, and Islam. It can be said that as marriage goes, so goes society. We need to learn and re-learn how to live together. We particularly need this in ways that speak to differences in gender but fairness in roles. We need teaching that focuses on the way people believe, behave, and belong. We have to do this in ways that are not sexist, androgynous, or homophobic. Men and women, and Black men and Black women are far too distrustful and combative, perhaps more so than any other ethnic group. This is a clear and present danger to the fabric of Black society.

When marriages suffer, single parents—usually mothers—are left to raise the children. Without the other partner in the home, it is especially tough to raise children well. Boys particularly become impossible for many mothers to discipline. Too many of these young people make poor choices about their homework, school, gangs, and the like. These single parents, heroes to whatever degree they are holding their families together, need more community assistance from a relevant plan.

People in the various social areas need the necessities of life, parenting, mentoring, counseling, friendship, and education. When a people are poor, then they are prey to pathologies. They developed substance abuse and behavior problems. Their family life suffers and they lose the ability to manage their own lives.

As more people fall into these problems, the social safety net is taxed, at times beyond the breaking point. People are under-served or disserved. Deviance and abnormalities become policing matters by default. This criminalizes the problem, as the police are not sociological professionals. As more people are incarcerated, the problem gets worse. Too often society's answer is just more police and prisons. So, Blacks must develop sociological answers to their problem and to put these ideas into practice. It will require bringing sociology professionals together. It mandates more resources devoted to solving these problems.

It should become the goal—if not the norm—that Black couples enjoy loving relationships and raise their children in healthy families. They should reside in communities that are holistic villages, catering to the elderly and serving the disabled. At every age level, Blacks should be in associations of their choice that provide them recreation, fun, and community service. These are social concerns, concerns that have an indispensable place in a development plan.

NEED FOR A MEDICAL PLAN

Medically, African Americans need a plan. The aim of all of this must be to decrease infant mortality and disease, while simultaneously increasing pre-natal care, quality of life, and life expectancy.

The medical plan must address preventative care, primary care, specialty care, and alternative care. Preventative care is the patient doing the following things for him or herself: eating a well-balanced diet, exercising, lowering stress, resting, self-testing, and engaging in safe behavior. Primary care involves a family physician that conducts annual check-ups, regular examinations, and basic in-office procedures. Specialty care is the examinations, diagnoses, surgeries, and other procedures a specialist performs. Alternative care involves naturopathic, chiropractic, massage, and far eastern health care.

People generally need a lot of preventative and primary care, and some specialty and alternative care as the primary care physicians approve. In fact, of all of these items, Blacks need preventative care the most. No less than Dr. Ben Carson, the number one brain surgeon in the world, said in a meeting at which I was in attendance that preventative care is the most important health area of poorer communities. I trust his medical opinion about us. We need a plan that addresses what we can do to help ourselves, from how we eat to how we sleep.

To provide this for an entire community, we will have to study affordable health care, HMOs, community clinics, mobile examinations, and especially more doctors and hospitals committing to serve the under-served. The plan has to bring more doctors to Black patients. We need resources to make this happen and an appeal to civic duty to fill in the gap where the resources run short.

NEED FOR AN EDUCATIONAL PLAN

Educationally, African Americans need a plan without a doubt. This plan will have to do with pre-school, academic, and vocational education. Pre-school education is everything from pre-natal up to kindergarten schooling. Academic education is primary, secondary, college, and graduate instruction. Primary and secondary schooling these days include public, private, charter, home schooling. Collegiate education is public or private. Vocational schooling entails blue and white collar certificated and licensure programs from construction work to cosmetology. Here I would like to include the military, although it is not really vocational education. I propose that every graduating high school student be told to go either to a university, community college, vocational school, or the military—but staying home is not an option.

Black children in the U.S. are the lowest performing of all groups SAT, IQ, and WASL tested, and have been so since such tests were devised. In a system that purports to be a meritocracy, in which education is the primary way of upward mobility, this is a wall preventing our advancement. It is totally unacceptable. It demands the uniting of educational professionals to resolve the disparities. We must learn from how the case study groups—Jewish, Vietnamese, and Ethiopian Americans—emphasize education. Then we must do likewise.

Incidentally, West African students in the 1990s were some of the very highest performing college students in Western Europe. Moreover, anecdotal evidence suggests that Ethiopian and Eritrean American students perform not at the bottom but towards the middle on SAT and Assessment of Student Learning tests. What does this suggest? It suggests that it is not nature that causes African Americans to score lower but nurture. To put it differently, it is not that there is something wrong with us, but instead something wrong with our society that causes, what Jonathon Kozol labeled, these "savage inequalities." We know this. We have to prove it. We have to make what poet Gwendolyn Brooks described a thing of the past:

We Real Cool

We real cool
we skipped school
we lurk late
we strike straight
we thin gin
we sing sin
we jazz June
we die soon

Of all of these things, Blacks need a plan that deals with family involvement and public schooling. Parents and other family members simply have to get more involved in their relative's education. At the same time, Black children will mostly have to attend public schools. Most will not be able to go to charter or private schools. They will not be able to home school. We have to make public schools work for our young people.

WE NEED AN ARTISTIC PLAN

Believe it or not, artistically, we need a plan. The arts concern the dramatic (i.e., plays), literary (i.e., novels, poems), musical, kinesthetic (i.e., dance), athletic, oratorical (i.e., rap, spoken word), and visual (i.e., paintings, sculptures) categories. What the arts do is entertain, inform, and inspire. They tell us who we are, teach us about our world, allow us to escape the throes of reality, and point the way to where we need to go. The arts are a major part of our culture and are so important to us that we pay hefty sums at times to experience what they have to offer.

Without major support of the arts, art will still happen. It will just be diminished, rougher, and will convey the values and sentiments of the lesser resourced. In many ways art will rise triumphantly ethical. In other respects, too much in fact, it will go amiss. When they are amiss they can miss-inform, miss-direct, or lull a whole people to sleep. For instance, there is a major debate ensuing about whether gangster rap and its prolific use of the "b" word [that rhymes with "witch"] is a negative or an innocuous influence on the culture. This area is crucial.

If every other area addressed thus far were right, but only the arts were wrong, then in time the arts alone would work to undo all of the gains in every area. This is the power of the visual arts and the spoken word. We need a plan that supports the arts and funds its informing, inspiring along the lines of the plan. We must do more to support our artists and to direct them toward serving our development.

WE NEED A SPIRITUAL PLAN

Now we come to the last but far from the least area. No plan would be complete without addressing the area that has been the most important to the protection and care of Black America. We need spiritual leaders to unify enough to forge a spiritual sub-plan. Whereas as the political area is the purse umbrella covering the areas, the spiritual area is the golf umbrella that covers even the political area. The spiritual area has to ensure that all leaders, even themselves and the crucial political leaders, serve the people with character, competence, and courage.

Like no other, the spiritual area gives answers to the major questions of life: who we are, where we came from, why we are here, and where we are going. Religion helps us with timeless core and community principles from which flow our ethics that determine our behavior. Of these principles, no universal principle is more important than the golden rule: loving others as one loves one's self has to be central to the plan. Good neighborhoods and good nations are built on nothing less.

Christianity, Islam, Buddhism, Africanism, and Theism comprise the main beliefs of African Americans. Of these beliefs, none has been more important to Black American survival than Christianity and Islam. These are the faiths that remind us of the importance of loving God, of the golden rule, and of something like the Ten Commandments. These are the faiths that are strongest in the Black community. Thus, the plan must primarily deal with these two beliefs. In the South, where over half of all Blacks reside, Christianity reigns supreme; it has been the strongest faith, the longest time. Throughout the Black community the Black church has had an historic and a symbolic role. It has been the most convenient and effective house for programming. Its speakers have been the most eloquent spokespersons for the community. There are two laudable exceptions to the eloquence examples: Malcolm X and Louis Farrakhan. These two are among the handful of greatest speakers Africa has produced in America.

Religious institutions and their leaders should not be used, and will not be. So, the plan will have to promote, as it pulls from, the churches and mosques. It has to add to the membership rolls without taking too much away from the financial coffers. It has to support the religious mission without taking too much of the time of its members. It has to be that good.

Now, to be sure, African Americans need help in every area. We are languishing in different ways, across the board. We need advancement in every area. Economics may be first but it is not everything. Let's summarize what we need across the board:

THE SUMMARY OF THESE IMPORTANT AREAS IN THIS COMPREHENSIVE PLAN:

We suffer economically: We must re-invest the black dollar in black businesses in order to become a prosperous people.

We suffer socially: We must renew our relationships and thus restore our villages.

We suffer educationally: We must excel at investing in our own and our children's education in order to maximize our potential.

We suffer medically: We must improve the way we eat, exercise, and rest under the guidance of caring health professionals for our healing.

We suffer politically: We must support those who support us and sanction those who sanction us.

We suffer artistically: We must encourage art that informs Blacks of who we are, where we came from, where we are going, and how to get there.

We suffer religiously: We need courageous conversations around Christianity, Islam, Judaism, Buddhism, and other religions that have proven themselves worthy in the marketplace of ideas, and that have a moral code that all nations can be built upon. Even if no other people will, we must believe and speak prophetic truth to power to help the U.S. be as good in the world as it is great.

Surely, we have to be concerned about every area, not just economics. I trust it is clear by now that this book is calling for the formulation of a comprehensive plan.

LEVELS OF THE PLAN:
PERSONAL, ASSOCIATIONAL, AND COMMUNAL INVESTMENT

From the "areas", it is time now to address "levels." The levels are personal, associational, and communal. These are different from the spiritual, political, social, economic, medical, educational, and artistic areas. For any community plan to work—and work well—it has to address all of the levels that inhere in a community. Having outlined the seven areas, we come now to the three levels a comprehensive plan should address.

PERSONAL LEVEL INVOLVES HOUSEHOLDS

The personal level has to do with the person, the family, and the extended family. This is the level of the households and clans. Households are made up of people living alone, or any combination of them living together: single, single with children, roommates, married, married with children, or extended family arrangements. The clan is the extended family. It is your aunts and uncles, nieces and nephews, and your cousins, first, second, and third.

One level of this plan has to do with getting it into each household and doing so in a format that is easy to use. Members of each household must understand it and know how to invest in itself and in the Black community. One or more family members must step up to see to it that each family member is given the chance to really live, rather than the entire family ignoring members who are barely existing.

We can change our community one household at a time.

We come back to Seattle as an example. There are about 47,000 Blacks in Seattle. There are approximately 15,000 households. All of us must prod the direction of these 15,000 households in a positive way for the good of each family and our entire community. We need a plan that is given to, and understandable to, 15,000 households here, as we do in all of Black America. The plan in every community should attempt to serve every Black household.

I believe that what is good for the household is good for the whole. The household is what the community is to ultimately serve, and it is what the community is made up of. The community exists on the foundation of the households. If this plan were to fail at the associational and communal levels, the households alone can keep the Renaissance going like a thousand invisible hands working independently. For it is from the household that the community is formed, it is at the household level that the largest number of financial transactions directing Black wealth are made, and it is there that our people are housed. Surely, households make communities. Besides, it is in the households that the children are raised who will finish whatever we start. Thus, households have the greatest generational impact.

In other words, we can change our community one household at a time.

ASSOCIATIONAL LEVEL

Another level concerns associations. Churches and mosques, fraternities and sororities, organizations and businesses have the most vital role to play. Such organizations do more than provide an outlet for our people. They are a means of unifying us; they help to provide our political structure for helping us get our act together as a people; and they multiply our voices into a symphony of power for speaking to those outside of our community.

The 1000 associations, coordinated in the six categories of the preceding sentence, will help unify our 35,000 plus people enough so that we can work as one.

There are 100 or so Black associations in greater Seattle alone. Each must receive this plan in a way that is turnkey: tight, right, and ready to go. Then each organization must help its own members and the larger Black community grow in wealth and in health in all of the seven areas. Our associations must promote all of these things we have to do for our own selves.

This plan calls for individuals and whole families to join Black associations of their choice. We must encourage our people to be in associations. This is much, much more than a payback to the associations for their community assistance. This is how the community unifies, given that we are a minority spread out around this country, a minority that cannot form a separate government. Our associations will serve as an amalgamated government. The churches and mosques, fraternities and sororities, professions and trades, organizations and businesses will do this as they are in communication, and some level of support, with each other. In Seattle, the 1000 associations, coordinated in the six categories of the preceding sentence, will help unify its 35,000 plus people enough so that they can work as one.

Our communities need each association to abandon living entirely for itself. Each association has to live partly for the community, for that which helps all of us. No association should do these things more than the local Black church. The Black church should, and can, do so much more. The church must take the lead, as it is the most pervasive, has the greatest heritage, and is the best resourced of institutions in the Black community.

COMMUNITY LEVEL

Obviously, there is the community level. It is at the community level that the plan is chosen, distributed, supervised, and overtures to the outside community are made. The community level is a combination of the leadership team, public meetings, and the coordination of Black associations. In all honesty, the folks that make up these groupings are really only a small segment of the entire community. But this is how it always works: those who show up in meetings open to all have the right to act in the name of all. The last half of this book contains the details of the community level plan.

I suppose that the real magic of this plan is that it is geared to the personal and associational levels. Of these two, associations play the indispensable connecting role. In other words, the 'community' is really a leadership team shrouding our associations investing in the community. This, I hope you will agree with me, will ensure its success.

THE NEED FOR A PLAN

At all of these levels and in all of these areas, Blacks need a plan. We need to have action items written down on which we are working. Remember the maxim with which I began: you cannot help a people as a people who as a people do not help themselves. In Seattle, Blacks lost many assets such as our bank because we did not help ourselves as a people. Blacks will be "unhelpable" if we remain without a plan. We will not be able to support a renaissance business corp, build renaissance schools, patronize renaissance arts, or launch renaissance clinics. The money will leave the community almost as fast as it enters. This is what I was referring to in the chapter on capitalist development when I labeled such a community "porous as a sieve," and its own worst "fiend." We need a plan.

In the absence of a plan we are mutually using, our community will remain at the bottom in terms of political and social clout. As mentioned, many White groups have over the decades figured out how to unify enough to rise to equality and empowerment. I have shown that Jewish Americans are now leading in this regard, and that Vietnamese and Ethiopian Americans are rising now right in front of African Americans. Groups most respected in this country are the ones at the top and those gaining on them. Those groups who still languish, who act as though they do not have a clue, are not so respected. Thus I say, until a people seriously work from a plan for its development, it remains a joke to the peoples who are seriously working from a plan for their development.

This is how much of a joke we are. Blacks are the Democrats' most reliable constituents, but we receive relatively less support from them. In Seattle, a Democratic city, the Black community struggles to save elementary schools named after its most important civil rights leaders and centers that house the elderly. We are rarely able to get the city on federally supported public works projects to provide local Blacks jobs amounting to one third of our percentage in the community. This is disrespect. To be sure, we will continue to be disrespected, a byword, and a joke until we engage a plan. I am ready for a plan. How about you?

GET MY STRAP

The phrase "get my strap" can mean different things in the Black community. When my parents said "get my strap" about something that I had done, I knew then that I was in trouble—big trouble. By this they obviously meant that they wanted someone to retrieve the belt for some corporal punishment. Some of the belts were so thin that they were like, or were actually, a barber's razor strap for sharpening blades. Such straps were to enforce the rules of the house, and they were quite useful for that purpose. I know that this is tantamount to child abuse these days, so I will not defend a strap being used in this way. I simply want to remind folks what the term has meant. I am over forty years old and still when I hear the statement "get my strap" I have flashbacks; in fact, a cold chill goes through my body.

The statement has a newer street meaning. This meaning also concerns a type of justice and enforcement. The term means that a person is requesting a gun, which can be held in a leather holster that can strap about a person any number of ways. This has to do with street justice, and taking the law in one's own hands. Again, I am not endorsing this meaning; I am just recounting what is a meaning of the term.

Well, a strap in this book means the self-help of a plan that is first economic. We need a plan. We need it for protection. We need to get our strap. We also could use a good whipping for not being more self-reliant and self-sufficient in capitalistic ways sooner than we have. Thankfully, it is not too late. Get our strap—our bootstrap. So, we need a detailed, thorough economic plan. Around economics we need to engage a plan in every other area. We need a plan.

THE PLAN

THE PLAN

It must be borne in mind that the tragedy of life does not lie in not reaching your goal.
The tragedy of life lies in having no goal to reach.
(Benjamin E. Mays)

I declared at the Black Dollar Days Task Force annual meeting that they needed a plan. It has been a tragedy that we have not had a clear goal to reach, to put things in terms that the great Morehouse president Benjamin Mays used above. One cannot get much clearer than putting goals in a writing that also explains how to achieve the goals and why in a plan for all of the people. This is such a plan, in answer to the challenge of the board of the Black Dollar Days Task Force.

No obstacle can withstand a people acting on a plan.

Yes, it is true that one cannot help a people as a people who as a people do not help themselves. It certainly is true that without a vision, a people perish (Proverbs 29:18). These statements call a people to help themselves and to do so with a plan. A people without a plan to succeed are a people with a plan to fail. It is conversely true that no obstacle can withstand a people acting on a plan. The Bible says that when a people are united, nothing is impossible to them (Genesis 11:6). As we go forward with a visionary plan nothing can stand in our way, and everything is achievable.

If we devise the proper plan and then carry it out with dispatch, then we will rise like other groups in the U.S. Our success could even parallel Jewish and Cuban Americans, as unbelievable as that may seem to some. We can make this our century of emergence. At worst, we shall rise to the level of doing at least better than we have done; at best, we will become the capable conscience of this country and deliverers of the dark continent.

I am talking about a people stepping in this life with large bootstraps, bootstraps for tugging on every time we need to rise after falling to a knee. This is how we strap ourselves for a ride into the clouds, people. Shoestrings are helpful, but we need straps instead of strings to do this kind of heavy lifting. If this works for you, then we could say a similar thing through the use of the names of the leading Black magazines: through action on a plan that emphasizes *Black Enterprise* first, *Ebony* Americans can *Jet* into living life *Upscale*.

This plan makes our goals reachable, in the sense that Dr. Mays understood. This section leads with the economic portion of the plan. It is so important that I give it two chapters. It then goes into the political and social portions, the educational and medical portions, and finally the artistic and spiritual portions. This is a plan in which all of the community must participate, but which the leaders must facilitate. So, this section ends with a call to the leaders to convene, and then get busy.

Having said all of this, what follows is what we should do in all of the key areas, and how we should do it in all of the necessary ways. Let's read, and then get busy.

Prosperous, educated, and healthy,
Lovers of ourselves, our neighbors, and our deity,
Shall African America be,
By the close of the twenty-first century.

(LIVINGSTON, BLACK COLLEGE STUDENT FAIR BREAKFAST SPEECH, 1998)

ECONOMICS:
BUILDING BLACK BUSINESSES AND HONORABLE-WAGE JOBS

What you need if you want jobs are small and medium sized enterprises, local initiatives, labour intensive work, community development, service providers and the like.
(SUSAN GEORGE)

Susan George gave a keynote address at a conference dedicated to exploring how the few have mostly benefited from economics worldwide and how to help areas needing development despite this. Her advice is sound: give the people jobs by funding the businesses that provide the jobs. She encourages those who care to push economics first, and to remember the importance of small- and medium-sized enterprises in so doing. Smaller businesses spur more growth than do larger ones. This advice was sound then, and it is sound now.

In a way that would show Susan George she was heard, *Shoestrings & Bootstraps* is a plan to achieve 10% decade economic growth for the Greater Seattle area Blacks, and to use this economic productivity as a platform to develop politically, socially, medically, educationally, artistically, and spiritually. This will garner mass support precisely because it promotes profits for businesses and jobs for the people. The one who provides these is the one the people will follow. This chapter and the next provide greater detail about how this is done economically.

This plan applies in related ways to the three different levels discussed earlier: the communal (macro), associational, and personal levels (micro). At each of these levels it advocates owning instead of owing and investing more inside instead of outside the community. At the personal and associational levels, the leaders will provide this plan to every Black association and household. Moreover, leaders must facilitate every association and family doing much more to help their own members into family ownership and community investment. This allows associations to play their connecting role, unifying us into a working whole.

The community strategy is a modified application of two "third world" development strategies: *import substitution industrialization* and *export led industrialization* explained in this chapter and in the appendix. The agreed target that all must be dogged about exceeding is growing the Black community 10% annually, treated mainly in the next chapter.

THE PERSONAL LEVEL

The foundational level of this plan is the household. We can develop our community one household at a time by getting the plan to every family, encouraging a family member to convene the family around this plan, urging owning instead of owing, and directing family money in greater support of Black businesses. This means developing a family program to become debt free while instituting a family investment plan.

Each household is to get the plan in a format that is easy to use. Members of each household must understand it and know how to invest in itself and in the Black community. I still believe that the most important learning occurs in the family. We need our mothers and fathers to model and teach the plan to their children and speak to relatives about it. Most of our households with children are single-parent headed. Single parent families can do this, as can same-sex families notwithstanding that the paradigm family is a father, mother, and one or more children connected to their extended family.

Each extended family has at least one person who is the matriarch or patriarch for the extended family. This is the person who is senior and most respected. This person needs to help get this plan to all family members and to talk up its importance and implementation.

However, if the patriarch or matriarch does not do so, then someone has to. Each family needs a person who will step up to reach out to the entire family with the ideas contained herein. If you love your family, then it is time to get past the frivolities and partying, to move away from indifference and individualism, and to endeavor to move the entire family to a higher existential dimension. Help your family members really live, rather than ignoring them in their bare existence. If no one else steps up to the plate, then you do it. What is the first step? Get the plan to each family member.

The next step is to call a meeting around some fun activity, and then take about 30 minutes to outline and explain the basics of the plan. Allow those who want to leave to do so. Linger with those more interested for further discussion.

The third step is to demonstrate earnestness regarding the plan's goals by starting two different kitties: one for helping family members personally own and the second for instituting a family investment fund. If we are to instill the principle of owning instead of owing, then our people are going to need more than words—they are going need handholding. Home ownership is the main way that a person retires with wealth. The personal ownership fund could be change brought to "Big Mama's" house one Sunday a month for the family meal. You would be surprised how much can be saved from everyone putting their coins in the hat for a good cause.

Every time the kitty reaches, say, $2,000 a family member could be chosen, and the money used for down payment on a condo, house, business equipment, or a car. The aim should be asset ownership or business establishment.

Expect that the lessons of minimizing debt and maximizing assets to take time, with family members falling behind before they surge ahead. For, debt spending is hard to control in our Madison Avenue designed, commercialized, corporate world. The world is geared to get people to spend what they do not have and then to blame the debtors for the debt they were lured into obtaining.

Work with all family members about financially destructive behavior: using predatory lenders for quick money, gambling, alcoholism, smoking, over-eating, and drug problems. As the family goes, so goes the community. Put another way, the habits that rob the people in our community rob the community of our people. Unhealthy financial living leads to unhealthy financial communities.

The second kitty is for the investment fund. If the family has mechanics, then the money could go to buying fixer cars for servicing and selling for a profit. If the family has carpenters, then it could go to buying a fixer house for a similar end. If a family wants an easier, hassle-free investment, it could then simply purchase a mutual fund from the list of high performing funds on *Money* or *Forbes* magazine's annual list. Every month family members could put in what they can afford, with just one dollar afforded being respected. Two people should keep track of what is invested in cash. If a person puts in labor instead of cash, the family can determine the value of the services contributed. Then the family should determine if they want to make decisions equally or according to the amount invested.

Although this is a way for the family to make money, this is not the first purpose of the investment. The first purpose is education. Some family members would never do such a thing on their own without other family members showing them the way. Seeing the investment through to profit statements and cash in hand will show everyone in the family, including the children, how to make money work for, rather than only against, the family. This is a lesson in itself.

The education is complete when family members are empowered to own individually. Every person should own what each person uses. Buy clothes that are timeless and make them last. Build a relationship with a quality person and make it last. In this way we can have shared living instead of so much solitary living. But nothing is more important financially than the major purchase of any household: a condo, a home, or a mobile home. Mass home ownership is paramount to our renaissance.

The habits that rob the people in our community rob the community of our people.

Ownership is about more than controlling expenses. It has as much to do with increasing income. We have to help each African American get a living wage job and then enhance their skill set and knowledge base. This may mean attending vocational school, college, or a university. Almost always, the classes will seem tough, the finances too high, or the time required too much. The key is to transcend the difficulties by preparing and, if necessary, taking the risk of failing. True failure is not work undone but instead refusing to try.

We also have to get Black households to spend their money with Black businesses, at least at the same rate that other ethnic groups do. Family members should explain to other members the significance of this. Then something should be devised to encourage every family member to do this more. Perhaps the meal at Big Mama's house could begin with appreciation going to the family member that most supported Black businesses that month. The family could also have a meeting at a Black restaurant or resort. If so, make it worth the establishment's while by ordering sufficiently to help the business (and leave a good tip for the server).

At the household or microeconomic level, each of us, no matter your income, must work to do the following:

THE FAMILY PLAN

Facilitator: allow one family member in every household to organize the family around this plan.

Work: work hard, starting a little early and staying a little late; but work 5 days for the "man," and 1 day for yourself.

Debt: decrease unsecured debt at least 10% annually.

Income: increase your ability to make money (get vocational training, become more highly educated, consider starting your own business).

Ownership: Increase ownership by 10% annually (own a home, a personal mutual fund, and start a family investment fund).

Community: Buy at least 10% more from Black businesses.

Platform: Incorporate all the others areas of the plan on to this economic platform.

Reunions: Hold a family reunion every other year or so, and share these ideas there.

Associations: Encourage members to be in at least one religious and one non-religious association.

Every member should do every one of these things for the success of the entire family.

If you cannot get this entire book to your family members, then copy the box above on the front, and the one-page plan in a summary on the back. Give family members the double-sided copy and challenge them to live to show they value the gift.

We have to be realistic: not every family, not even most of the families, need work with the plan completely in order to see success. However, we do need many to do so. We should take what we can get.

THE ASSOCIATIONAL LEVEL

The pivotal part of this plan is associations. They are crucial to connecting households to the community, and vice versa. We can develop our community by channeling people into associations and by getting associations to take better care of their members.

This is necessary in order to unify our community into a working whole. This section presents these items as the associational part of the plan: every association must get the plan for its members, call members together around the plan, urge owning instead of owing, funnel associational dollars into Black businesses, prod members to reach their family, and communicate with other associations.

First of all, make sure all of your members get the plan. The chief executive officer of the association should see to it that this occurs. Albeit, if that person is unable or unwilling to do so, then someone else in the association should work through the proper processes to bring this before the associational body.

Next, call a meeting with your members with this plan as the sole agenda item. Is not this important enough? Outline and explain the plan. Discuss it. Start the same funds mentioned above that family should start for family members.

Third, every association needs to provide some kind of program, no matter how small, to encourage its own members to get out of owing into owning. They can have a small fund to help one member a year buy the kind of assets discussed above in the family section. They should have a mutual fund, or some kind of investment, for their members to contribute to. They should teach their members about the importance of owning. In fact, the association should work to own the place where it meets.

Some may read this and wonder whether I am including their bowling or pinochle club in this list. The answer is a resounding yes. Herein I am referring to every one of our organizations. That means every fraternity and every sorority; every association and every affiliation; every church and every mosque. If you love your members, then take care of them. Don't just give them a spiritual word and then take their material money and get in your material car and drive to your material house. Give them a spiritual word and material help too. This is what Jesus did. While he was with his closest followers he said that they did not need a purse or a sword because he fed them, he sheltered them, and he protected them. Likewise, King helped us spiritually, politically, and economically. Where would we be had the Rev. Dr. Martin Luther King decided all he could do was help Blacks and the poor spiritually?

Fourth, associations need to support Black businesses very well. They should begin meetings giving small awards to those who support Black businesses the most. They should have annual meetings at African American-owned establishments, catered by an African American.

Associations need to add to their communication, unification. Associations of a feather should flock together.

Fifth, associations have to help their members' families. If possible, they should supply members with plans for their family members. Every organization must help its members—your members—out of owing and into owning. The pull of the world's ads and its credit card convenience are such that you will have to help them with teaching, with encouragement, and with money. Do not expect them to do it alone. Then make sure your organization's members—I'm talking about your members now—do all of the non-economic things well. If we cannot help our own family members and members in the association of our choice, then it is unlikely that we will do anything community-wide that will matter. The members should get their association to reach down to their members' families while simultaneously reaching out to every other association.

Your members who need to increase their income will need your assistance. In order to help Blacks get their fair share of living wage jobs, we are going to ask our associations to help their own members with letters and contacts. In order to assist their training we will need associations to advocate for their own members.

Last, we must encourage our people to be in associations. The more Blacks are in associations the more connected they will be, and the more potentially connected our community will be. It is also a small gift back to our associations to encourage everyone to be involved. How involved should Blacks be in their associations? Well, I feel each person should be in a religious organization, and still be in one or more other associations. Thus, each person should be in two to three Black associations minimum.

Our associations will serve as a pseudo government. This happens as the churches and mosques, fraternities and sororities, trades and professions, organizations and businesses all communicate with each other to a sufficient degree.

Associations need to add to their communication, unification. Associations of a feather should flock together. Churches should meet with other churches, and mosques with mosques. Fraternal and soriorital associations should do the same; and so on. The way to ensure this occurs is by the two largest associations in a given area taking the lead in this, joined by two of the more committed but smaller associations in an area. In this way, four would come together of different sizes in order to bring on board the rest of the associations in an area. So two of the largest corporations would meet with two smaller ones to determine how to bring the rest of the corporations on board for the purpose of playing their unique role in the development of Black people. This is the "have four get more" plan.

We particularly need the churches in order to make the difference. What other institutions have the history, are on nearly every corner, and meet with more people? Any religious institution can fit this bill; the traditional ones are likely to do it best. Not every religious institution needs work with the plan completely in order to see success—not even most of them. But we will need many to do so.

Our little church tries to help a member every few years with a down payment on a home. If our little church can do this, something we started with less than 75 active members, then I know that your religous association can do the same. If every church would just help well their own members from owing to owning, then Black communities would have a renaissance. Pastors should make sure that those who serve them are taken care of well. At the same time, Pastors should have a program for their average member's economic development. Pastors should judge their leadership not by the size of their building, or by their salary, nor even by their high profile members; instead, Pastor's should judge their leadership by how well the average member's lives have improved spiritually, mentally, and physically. The physical arena includes finances. Judge that. This is how we make people and their communities whole.

THE ASSOCIATION PLAN

Leader: either the elected CEO, or else someone on the executive committee or board, must propose that the association adopt this plan.

Resolution: approve a specific resolution in support of this plan and put it in writing.

Convey: get this plan to all of your members.

Incentives: devise ways to recognize your members who most invest in the Black community.

Debt: set up a fund to help your members out of debt and a pledge that they will decrease unsecured debt at least 10% annually.

Buying: increase buying and contracting with Black businesses.

Connecting: link up with other community associations.

Ownership: try to own what the associations rents, to rent spaces (including for functions) from Blacks, and encourage your members to increase their ownership by 10% annually .

Community: buy at least 10% more from Black businesses and encourage members to do the same.

Platform: Incorporate all the others areas of the plan on to this economic platform.

Every member does every one of these things for the success of the entire community.

Black associations are needed as the base for the community's replacing goods or services provided by those outside of it with goods or services offered by those within the community, as I mention in the paragraphs follow. The plan as well uses associations as the platform for, on the other hand, launching Black businesses outside the community to provide goods or services to those outside of it. Of all associations, none is more important than the Black church to do all of the items outlined here, especially the tandem measures regarding goods and services at the community level.

THE COMMUNAL LEVEL

What should be done at the community level? We must build our own community through an economically-centered comprehensive plan as Claud Anderson and the Black Dollar Days Movement propose. A core of leaders must gather to commence this work and then see it through to periodic completion. The goal has to be providing inside what we had imported from outside the community and then helping more of our businesses better compete outside of our community. Through goals and enforcement, we can double our economic output, and then double it again. This is the path towards meeting and then exceeding the development in place in the 1970s.

In other words, where Blacks need to go is where they have been. In Seattle, the Black community used to have at least two supermarkets; it needs at least one Black supermarket again. It had general contractors who could bond multi-million dollar jobs; it needs at least three such contractors with an expertise in steel again. It had a number of jazz and dance clubs; it needs at least two clubs again. It had a Black bank; it needs a Black bank again, and to make greater use of the Black owned credit union in town. It needs to do this in order to spawn businesses that make for a vibrant business core, and to double the wages Black workers bring to their households. What does your community need?

LEADERSHIP CORE

Every Black community across this nation needs a team of leaders to come together. This can happen in a thousand different ways. The associational leaders could come together, particularly the main four in each area. The pastors of the churches united could rally the community together. The Black politicians and business owners could do it. The Black press could convene a community gathering. The Urban League and the NAACP could call the leaders to a general meeting (and then at the gatherings urge that exclusively Black organizations lead this cause). The students of the black student unions could do it. Then the people in general could assemble, agitating until leaders resolve to do this great work. It can happen any number of ways.

This effort will require leaders from across the spectrum to become actively engaged for the long haul. No effort this large and broad can be accomplished by a few folk from one or two associations. Such an endeavor community-wide will be a grand test of the caliber and grit of this generation of Blacks, and especially of its leaders. Do we have what it takes to do it? Despite how dour things look, I believe. Do you believe?

IMPORT SUBSTITUTION COMMERCIALIZATION

Our job is to provide inside of the community what Blacks have been spending money on outside of the community (import substitution commercialization); it is also to market Black goods or services outside of the community so that Blacks gain the kind of share of the larger economy that other successful groups have (export led commercialization). These ideas are adapted from two development approaches Southern countries, such as Brazil, used from the 1950s onward. As I stated in the introduction, in the process of preparing to teach a new Political Economy course I discovered them. The official names of these strategies are *import substitution industrialization* (ISI) and *export led industrialization* (ELI).

Simply put, African Americans need to spend more on businesses owned by African Americans. Then Blacks need to promote businesses within our community by investing within them so as to prepare them to compete outside the community. These ideas carried out throughout the community will double the dollars put in Black businesses, which will cut in half our unemployment, and then lead to a doubling of Black assets.

Import substitution may be the logical place to begin since it mostly entails many smaller buying decisions. As a community Blacks can do all this without having to first raise sizable seed money. They start by taking an accounting of the amount and types of money they are spending outside of the community. Housing is the biggest expense, then comes food, automobile, insurance, entertainment, gas, utilities, telephone, hair care, charity (mostly offerings to churches), and so on. Then Blacks should adopt a strategy of which area to substitute based on likelihood of success.

We should begin with something easier to achieve like doubling the receipts of an existing African American owned beauty supply company (or establishing one). Our study would show that Black communities have the beauticians, barbers, and customers in need of such products. So the demand is there. Seattle's Black community, for instance, needs a campaign, including affordable incentives, so that a community beauty supplier receives more like 30% of the Black dollar, rather than 15% (a percentage that has been declining over the last few decades).

Next, Blacks in every local community can then encourage patronage of a list of Black restaurants. Blacks are not doing a bad job of supporting Black restaurants, but they could do better. The third move would be to a gas station or grocery store, if there is a Black store in place. Seattle may have one Black gas station currently in business, but does not have a Black supermarket.

What will this do? It will increase profits, perhaps doubling them. It will lead to businesses being able to buy in larger quantities, which should decrease per unit costs. It should cause the hiring of employees. It may lead to the upgrading of the facilities. It will ensure the survival and even thriving of these businesses over the long haul if sustained.

Next, buy into one of the major stores to capture that part of your dollar. Build up your gas stations to increase that part of your money. Build up your construction contractors. Start with the easier areas and then go from sector to sector. You can do it with your pennies and sustained efforts.

IMPORT SUBSTITUTION AREAS

1. COSMETOLOGY
    - Support existing beauty/barber shops
    - Invest in a large beauty supply company
    - Invest in a large full-service solon
    - Own the building(s) that house these businesses

2. RESTAURANTS
    - Support existing restaurants
    - Invest in specialty African and African American Foods
    - Develop Black ownership of non-African restaurants
    - Own building(s)

3. GROCERY STORE
    - Support existing grocers
    - Invest in a supermarket (i.e., Stock Market)
    - Invest in a mega-market (i.e., Costco)

4. GAS STATION
    - Support existing
    - Establish other ones
    - Own station real estate

5. ENTERTAINMENT
    - Grow large music stores
    - Invest in a night club
    - Own buildings where such businesses are housed

6. AUTOMOTIVE SERVICES
    - Support existing
    - Establish full service Car, Battery & Tire Repair shop

7. INSURANCE
    - Support existing
    - Establish other ones
    - Own buildings from which the businesses operate

8. CONSTRUCTION
    - Support existing
    - Provide them technical assistance with computers
    - Establish other ones companies
    - Own buildings from which the businesses operate

9. MORTUARIES
    - Support existing
    - Establish other ones
    - Own buildings from which the businesses operate

10. INFORMATION / COMPUTERS
    - Support existing
    - Establish other ones
    - Own buildings from which the businesses operate

11. BLACK PRESS
    - Invest in towers of radio stations to increase strength
    - Retool Black print media equipment
    - Own buildings within which the businesses operate

12. BLACK ARTS
    - Support existing performances and companies
    - Establish other ones
    - Invest in television documentary and film production
    - Own buildings from which the businesses operate

EXPORT LED COMMERCIALIZATION

Export led commercialization must occur nearly simultaneously. This requires a greater investment of community resources. After local Blacks incubate such businesses within our community, they will then launch them with our pennies to compete in the larger community. This is using the incubator and the accelerator. There is nothing more powerful to a community than combining import substitution commercialization with export led commercialization.

The two areas to begin this work are in food and construction. With regard to food, Blacks should support restaurants in venture opportunities outside of the community. Seattle's Blacks should support restaurants like Catfish Corner, Ezell's Chicken, Kingfish, and Casuelitos in the opening of stores or franchising outside of the Central Area or Rainier Beach, Black enclave areas. This means that Blacks country-wide will need to raise capital to assist businesses in this.

Construction is an area ripe for expansion. Many cities and towns have large scale public works projects in progress. Seattle has the Sound Transit Light Rail project in place as of this writing. Its Black community has to capitalize on this public opportunity with the billions of dollars of governmental funds being spent. African Americans have been taxed too to provide these funds; they deserve an equal share of the contracting pie. The construction industry, a symbol of the emerging power of the Seattle African American community in 1970s, is on the ropes now, and there is no general contractor in the city able to bond million dollar projects as a prime.

Promoting our designers, contractors, and consultants who work in construction involves a different investment depending on the type of potential project owners. If the owner is the government, then it will mean making full use of Blacks in government and of caring non-Blacks so that DBE requirements are written into the bid documents, Blacks get their fair share, and then are protected on the job through compliance officers who are competent and engaged. If the owner is a non-profit organization, the endeavor is similar. The challenge is that fewer Blacks are in position to help on the inside, and there are not the laws or regulations applicable about diversity or disadvantage. On the other hand, non-profits generally try to be sensitive to such issues, so there is a decent chance that Black businesses will get significant work.

If the owner is a private developer, Blacks stand the most difficult challenges when it comes to getting construction contracts. Private owners developing for profit are "old boys" who like the "old boy network." They have been historically intolerant of diversity and have viewed it as wasteful or incompetent. Private developers have spent billions of dollars building most of downtown Seattle over the past thirty years, and they have used only a handful of legitimate Black businesses. It is a travesty.

Blacks need to out this injustice, for this has been going on since the days of segregation, and is in fact a vestige of it. We cannot allow this to continue. This will require writing about, using political suasion, and some direct action.

EXPORT LED AREAS:

Community helps fund Black businesses in larger community that have proven successful in the Black community in the following areas:

1. RESTAURANTS

2. CONSTRUCTION
This area will require more than funds; the community will have to bring pressure to bear to open the larger community to Black designers, consultants and contractors in the public, non-profit, and private sectors.

3. RETAIL (clothes, music, jewelry)

4. AUTOMOTIVE SERVICES

5. ENTERTAINMENT (rap, vocals, instrumentals, arranging, publishing, studio)

6. BLACK MEDIA
This area too will require more than funds; the community will have to bring pressure to bear to open the larger community to Black print, broadcast, and on-line media in the public, non-profit, and private sectors.

7. PROFESSIONAL SERVICES (law, medicine, accounting, information), This area as well will require the community to bring pressure to bear to open the larger community to Black professionals in the public, non-profit, and private sectors.

Our import substitution and export led endeavors will build businesses and wealth in our community. Bates makes clear that this comes with many rewards:

Moreover, the presence of business success stories lures younger, better educated blacks into self-employment, and this further promotes economic development. Similarly, existing firms in less profitable lines of business are motivated—by the success story phenomenon—to reorient their operations toward products and services that offer greater profit potential; once again, economic development is promoted. Most important for members of the ghetto community, if business success increase in their area the resulting economic development will tend to reverse the drain of resources that exacerbates their poverty. Profitable operations build up additional capital and reinvestment, greater ownership of businesses by local residents strengthens the flow of income within (rather than leakage out of) the ghetto, and capable business people are retained in the community where their enterprises create income and jobs. (BATES, BANKING ON BLACK ENTERPRISE XXII)

In other words, success begets success. Economic development promotes further economic development.

We need a group of leaders to arise who know about economics first hand, and who are focused on the development of the community just as they are interested in their personal development. We have had such leaders in the past, we potentially have them now, and we will have them in the future. An example of the kind of person Black communities need is in order. Paul Cuffe was such a person, and he lived hundreds of years ago. Had Blacks kept his example ever before them, they would not be in this position today. They need the return of his spirit.

PAUL CUFFE

It was the work *Betrayal By Any Other Name* that introduced Paul Cuffe to me. I am embarrassed to admit that my early education had not exposed me to his life, literature, or legacy. It is as Carter G. Woodson stated as summarized in the title of his work, I suffer from the *Mis-education of the Negro*. Since being exposed to him, I have been keen to learn more about him.

Paul Cuffe was born in 1759, the son of an Ashanti Father and a Native American mother. A smart student, by the age of 18 he had learned enough about reading, writing, arithmetic, and the maritime industry that he decided he should try his hand at building a boat.

During the Revolutionary War, he made money smuggling goods past the blockading British Naval ships. Saving his money, he now had the capital to do something entrepreneurial. In time he purchased a dock and ship maintenance facility. There he could build sturdy whaling vessels of his own. Cuffe become a successful whaler, joining his crew to do this dangerous work along side of them. It keeps productivity high for an owner to be involved in the work of the business.

It was not long before Cuffe become the wealthiest African American in the new United States of America. Cuffe's success in business allowed him to purchase larger vessels and hire more skilled mariners and whalers. Cuffe acquired or constructed a class of high sea-worthy vessels on which he could traverse the Atlantic. With one of his ships he even rounded the horn of Africa. Cuffe diversified and purchased a 200-acre farm as well.

Cuffe did not stop with making money for himself. He was concerned about how African Americans were faring. Cuffe authorized the first document of its kind lobbying the Continental Congress to free Blacks who were enslaved. He grew increasingly disenchanted with a country that could treat people like him, or him, as second or third class citizens. Cuffe thus worked against slavery and favor of the "Back to Africa" movement. The difference was that Cuffe was the only African American who could directly do something about the situation.

Paul Cuffe was a very successful maritime businessman during the de-humanizing days of slavery. Cuffe determined that Blacks would be better off in Africa where they could rise to be a people. I think that Cuffe was right and wrong. He was right to value the freedom of being on the motherland. He was wrong to approach this in terms suggesting Africans were not already a people. His language and perspective were too close to the Blacks who would leave the U.S. and "found" Liberia, acting too similarly to how Europeans and Arabs had done on the motherland. Secondly, Cuffe should have been as involved establishing a strong, financially successful Black community in the U.S. as he was trying to do this in Africa.

Cuffe died September 9, 1817. His example makes clear that Blacks need to be about their own economic development just as they work for their political liberation and our afrocentric education.

When Blacks devote themselves to a plan like this they will find many non-Black allies. I have no doubt that money will pour in from outside by those impressed with activity that is capitalistic and has a good return. Blacks must be happy to work in league with everyone who wants to genuinely help them whether they are Black or non-Black.

Alternatively, all money is not good money. Blacks must leave on the table money that has strings attached, strings that are against our goals. Take the money without such strings, but do not become dependent upon it. Use it each year as if it will not be renewed. It is the only way to be free and to be true to this plan, which is as much about wealth development as it is about community empowerment. We need self-determination in order to be truly free. We need to follow Cuffe's example.

We have covered the main points that concern the crucial economic development piece of this plan. However, the target, special measures, and controls have to be explained in greater detail in order to view the power of how it can all be done. This is done in the ensuing chapter.

ECONOMICS: MAINTAINING TEN PERCENT PLUS GROWTH

The so-called "small business" sector can also be a route to wealth and social status. The Census Bureau keeps count of the number of firms owned by black men and women. Its most recent survey found 425,000 such enterprises, numbering about 2.4 percent of the country's corporations, partnerships, and sole proprietorships. By and large, the black businesses are local concerns, with annual receipts averaging around $50,000, and they deal largely in products or services oriented to black clienteles. Indeed, only 70,000 of the 425,000 have any paid employees. In other words, almost 85 percent are one-person enterprises or family-run firms. Of the 100 largest black-owned manufacturing and service companies, only 10 have as many as 1,000 employees, and 33 have fewer than 100. Taken together, the 25 biggest banks under black ownership hire 1,740 people, compared with the 85,500 employees of one leading white-owned bank.

(HACKER, *TWO NATIONS: BLACK AND WHITE, SEPARATE, HOSTILE, UNEQUAL* 113)

The above Andrew Hacker quote spells out why Blacks are so under-employed in our mostly capitalist country. It is because in the arena that comprises about 60% of the economy, the private business sector, Blacks own only 2.4% of the businesses. They should be at least 12%, given that we are in excess of 12% of the nation's population. It gets worse. By a higher percentage than the larger economy, Black businesses owners cannot afford to pay an employee full-time wages to assist with the work of the business. Effectively, this means that Black businesses provide an even smaller part of private sector employment than 2.4%.

Is there any wonder why this "route to wealth and social status" has helped too few Blacks? The businesses most likely to hire them are seldom in position to hire anyone. Our job is to turn this around. It will take great action on a good plan to do this grand work. This chapter outlines more of the points that make this plan good. The last chapter sets forth the main points that concern the crucial economic development piece of this plan. This chapter details the target, special measures, and controls of this plan.

POWER OF THE BANKING RULE OF 72

The target is to grow Black productivity—in fact, to double it and then double it again. To be sure, our folks must be reconciled to advancing this plan beyond the annual target for the long haul: if so, the results will be small at first, significant after a few years, and then impressive in just a handful of years. Specifically, with sustained 10% growth, Blacks can double our productivity every 7.2 years. The banking rule of 72 states that anything growing at 10% doubles every 7.2 years. If Blacks can stay on the plan for 15 years, the Black community will quadruple in economic output alone! Let me add some dollars to this discussion.

Black Enterprise and the National Black Chamber of Commerce report that at least $500 billion passes into and out of black hands nationally. I estimate that in Seattle the number is $642,445,303.50 (see the econometric model in the appendix). The doubling of Black productivity would take Black Seattleites from about $642,445,303.50 to $1,284,890,000 in new wealth, money Blacks generated themselves by using the principles of economics in their favor. In less than a decade they would have $1,284,890,000 in our community, for our community. What would this do for our community of more than 47,541 people? The doubling twice of Black productivity nationwide would carry Black America from $1 trillion to $2 trillion dollars—$1.5 trillion in new wealth. This would dramatically increase Black income and greatly reduce Black unemployment.

The first doubling alone will allow Black businesses to better survive and to thrive. This will be a boon to these businesses. It will equate into more income than most of our businesses have ever seen. With such capital, they will have the ability to increase inventories, purchase necessary equipment, and to upgrade their services. It should also assist their paying off burdensome start-up loans, start-up investors, or high-cost creditors. This profitability should mean more money with which to buy from Black contractors or suppliers, and for the hiring of Black employees.

The doubling of Black productivity would take us from about $642,445,303.5 to $1,284,890,000 in new wealth, money Blacks generated themselves by using the principles of economics in their favor.

In 15 years Blacks would have $2,569,780,000 in Seattle and $2,000,000,000,000 in the U.S. The business growth will be staggering, and the demand for Black labor at this point should mean enough jobs for all, at a decent wage for all. This is how Blacks exponentially grow our resources so that they can build our own households, neighborhoods, and communities economically, socially, educationally, and in every other way.

Please know that 10% growth is doable. Developing nations of promise expect this kind of growth. The "Four Tigers"—Taiwan, Hong Kong, South Korea, and Singapore—achieved this from 1971 through 1985. China has experienced at least 8.5%, if not 10%, growth annually since 1980! This is how a people rise! China, particularly, demonstrates that a large country, with complex challenges, can do it. If they can do it, then African Americans can do it. South Africa has made its target 8% growth annually over the next decade. It is likely that subsequent studies of Jewish, Vietnamese, or Ethiopian Americans will substantiate that they grew for numbers of years at 10% plus. The Four Tigers, China, and South Africa show that 10% sustained growth is not only doable, it is being done. Besides, this is the kind of target serious leaders work toward in order to bring their people to a place of respect in the global economy in relatively short order. Where are our serious leaders? For, Blacks could use a dose of respect in the U.S. economy, which is the leader in the global economy.

If Blacks do not put this plan in place, then it is likely that the best their community would do is grow at the rate of the rest of society: 3%. (Often the Black community lags behind the rate of the larger community, so 3% is being generous.) At 3% our community doubles every 24 years. So after 15 years Blacks would have grown by about 50%, or half. So if they were at $642.5 million in Seattle, then Blacks would have increased to about $950 million. Nationwide we would increase to about $800 billion. The difference between the two scenarios is not time; it is the execution of an effective plan at a higher rate of growth.

So let me ask you: what would you rather do in the time you have? Would you prefer to grow by 50% or by 400% over the next 15 years? Would you rather have in the same amount of time: $800 million or $2 trillion? Would you rather have $300 billion in new income or $1.5 trillion? This is $1.5 trillion more, or five times the new income, than Blacks would have received without this plan. So, following a plan like this for 15 years translates into 350% more growth, expanding our total income 3.5 times, and increasing our new income by over 5 times the amount they would have received without a similar plan. This is the power, the sheer transformative power, of growing by 10% over a significant period of time. I rest my case.

The Banking Rule explains why 10% growth is essential to a renaissance. The rest of this chapter explains how to achieve the 10% plus growth. We do it by what I call the "10, 10, and 10 Plan:" at least 10% increase in Black personal equity, 10% increase in Black investment in Blacks, and 10% increase in non-Black investment in Black businesses. All of this is required to achieve at least 10% annual growth in Black America productivity (GBP: gross Black product), and to keep this occurring for decades. This is the target that will cause the renaissance. Blacks will engage soft and hard techniques in order to see to it that Blacks properly execute this plan. There are no two ways about it: they have to quality control Black support of Blacks, both in terms of buying Black and excellent Black service. As this money pours in, Blacks must also give their businesses technical assistance for the proper management of their growth.

This is a "10, 10, and 10 Plan:" at least 10% increase in Black personal equity, 10% increase in Black investment in Blacks, and 10% increase in non-Black investment in Black businesses.

10% INCREASE IN PERSONAL EQUITY

Every African American household needs to set a 10% target for the annual growth of household wealth. By doing the five things noted in the last chapter with the help of the other parts of this plan, Blacks can experience such an increase in personal wealth. Recall that the five items are these: (1) decreasing unsecured debt, (2) increasing employment skills, (3) owning assets, (4) buying more within the community, and (5) incorporating the health and other non-economic parts of the plan as a lifestyle. This will usually begin by making a budget, and living by it. I know how tough all of this is; I struggle with it myself.

Every household is to try to live below its means, invest the difference, and support Black businesses more. Blacks have to get most Black renters into a condo, mobile home, or home. Even a trailer home is better than renting for years. Add up all of the money wasted and you will see.

Every Black household has to have a retirement, which all too often they will have to provide for themselves—fading are the days in which they could count on our employers or the government to provide such plans. Hopefully, you will put enough in the plan—whether you get your own individual retirement account, or your employer provides the plan—so that after 10 years you will have at least $20,000. If so, then after 20 years you will have at least $75,000; after 30 years, $200,000; after 40, $500,000.

This does not include the value of your house that you will obtain, if you have not done so yet, as a consequence of this plan. Increasingly, as they retire, the value of their homes will reach the half a million dollar mark, houses are appreciating so. This means that our retirement accounts, along with the house, will mean that each Black household could be worth at retirement at least $1,000,000. Per chance if you cannot reach this yourself, you can do so in your relationship (hopefully a marriage), as you two combine your assets together.

Consider even your hobbies and habits. If what you do at your leisure is a big financial drain, you may want to reconsider it. Do you really need to travel all over the world now? Could you do a little traveling now, and wait a little later in your life to do the grand junkets? Do you really need to get your hair and nails professionally done every week? Could you try doing it every other, or every third week, and do them sometimes yourself? Some of our hobbies can get very, very expensive. They can become so expensive that they consume our future prosperity. Do you have to smoke a pack of cigarettes a day? That can addup to over $1000 a year.

The converse could pour money in rather than draining it from your coffers. Consider hobbies that may generate money: cooking, baking, horticulture, landscaping, doll-making, speaking, wood-working, interior decorating, consulting, or computer programming. If you have thought about writing, then write. Do things you enjoy that add to your resources.

You track the degree to which you are building wealth by 10% annually. This is to your credit, redounds to your benefit, and means money in your pocket. Hence, you have every reason to do this. Just know now that the community is rooting on your doing it as well. The better Blacks do individually, the better they should do communally. Our communal wealth is tied to your personal wealth. It has always been this way; African Americans are only now beginning to quantify how much it matters. Consequently, every association should do what it can to prod all of its members to achieve this personal target year after year.

The Four Tigers, China, and South Africa show that 10% sustained growth is not only doable, it is being done.

10% GROWTH IN COMMUNITY SELF-INVESTMENT

While achieving a 10% increase in personal net wealth, this plan pursues 10% growth in business profitability. On the associational level, particularly with respect to their businesses, Blacks have to decrease debt as well as expenditures on non-appreciating assets while greatly increasing income and ownership. Loans need to be paid, equipment purchased over leasing (unless buying is counterproductive), and space should be purchased over renting. Customers and clients have to be professionally served to such an extent that they become the best advertisers of the association.

Encourage your members to learn to invest in their own community. The jobs they need come from this pool—and the money is there. While money in the white community circulates 5 – 6 times, in the black community it circulates only about 1.5 times. This is what is known as the "multiplier effect." Incidentally, each time the money circulates, a portion of it is lost. With money that comes into the Black community only circulating 1.5 times before it leaves, the $500 billion only multiplies to about $750 billion a year that can be used to build businesses and family wealth.

If this same money could circulate at 5 – 6 times, more than $3 trillion would multiply in the community in total capital. In other words, just as our lack of home ownership robs our families, so our buying mainly outside of our community robs our communities. How much does it rob our community? Blacks deny their own selves about $2 trillion dollars per year (they have $750 billion multiplying when they could have had $3 trillion). Thus, every Black person and every Black organization not addressing Black Dollar Days like investing is failing our community to the tune of $2 trillion dollars per year! Do you hear me? This we do to ourselves. The Ku Klux Klan is not doing this to us. That is why we need to pick ourselves up by our own bootstraps: no amount of government assistance can do for us what we can do for ourselves. And the converse is equally true: no outside force can rob us like we rob ourselves.

To further ensure 10% communal growth, the community needs to help launch smaller and larger-scale development projects. The projects will provide more businesses in which Blacks can invest. With Blacks doing the design, construction, bonding, and labor, these projects will pour billions of dollars of revenue into the community. They will also provide millions of dollars in income to be used in the households of Black workers.

DEVELOPMENT FROM SMALLER-SCALE PROJECTS

We need to help launch with community funds small business projects funded as well by Black private investors. The community should particularly so invest where the businesses will be near Black enclave areas and bring wealth to Blacks who have business experience or education. These projects must be owned by blacks, funded by Blacks, designed by Blacks, built by Blacks, bonded by Blacks, and moved into by Blacks. No group is going to build our community for us. We have to build it ourselves, one project at a time, starting with our own pennies, and using our own labor. Every three to five years Blacks should be launching a new smaller scale project for our development.

The first project could be a smaller task like building ornate architectural corner markers in an area in which there are Black businesses. They could be made out of brick, rock, or plaster. An architect with the help of an artist makes sure that the work is done in a way that adds value to the corner, brings more customer traffic, and is aesthetically pleasing. I am not as big a fan of this one as I am of what follows.

Blacks can do business endeavors such as these: expanding a beauty supply business, assisting the establishment of a gas station, and promoting the franchise of a Black restaurant outside of the Black community. In the last chapter I provided a list of import substitution and export led endeavors. We could, if we wanted to, work from those lists. The aim remains making a dollar multiply in the Black community closer to the number of times it circulates in the White community.

DEVELOPMENT FROM LARGER-SCALE PROJECTS

One of the prime catalysts of this plan and a symbol to keep the program before the people is the funding of certain larger-scale projects to build up, beautify, and create jobs in our community. Projects over $3 million are larger scale. In order to coordinate this happening in a sustained way, they have to build Black communal infrastructure, especially the economic infrastructure necessary to keep things going. They need a Black-owned gas station, supermarket, and office building. They need more Black housing. At a minimum this means tripling the size of the Black credit union, re-establishing the community development corporation, and regular meetings of the economic advisors meeting to ensure that the plan is being properly engaged.

Please, please do not get caught on directing most of the capital improvement funds to building of non-profit facilities like community centers and recreation areas. These are so vital, but they do not build ownership, nor do they keep on giving financially. A park when it is done provides our kids wonderful places and gives to them outlets to keep them off of the streets. This can have a financial impact as it keeps them from getting in trouble, which costs money. On the other hand, when they build an office park it provides a business site, jobs, and rent for as long as it is around. Besides, we already have a lot of parks and ball courts, although we still could use more. What we have to have now are jobs and assets to own. If we build enough business complexes then we will more easily be able to construct parks and "rec" centers ourselves.

We can also build an apartment complex or do a condominium conversion. It is equally important that we invest in the restaurants, hair care establishments, and media companies that have been fixtures in the community and are in need of renovation. If they have ownership of their site—all the better. For instance, let's use Catfish Corner as an example. It is a restaurant with a history of good service and food.

In the event Blacks were able to get, say, Catfish Corner to rebuild the spot it occupies into a four story building, this could be a major project that would bring millions of dollars into Black hands. How could this happen? Let's say that the building would cost $4 million to build. The architectural and engineering work, generally 10% - 15% of a project, would constitute at least $400,000 that we should ensure goes to Black businesses. The bonding and insurance, another 5% - 10%, comes to $300,000 and would as well go to another Black consortium, if not a single businesses.

The construction would total $4 million and provide about $400,000 of profit to a Black general contractor. If we can find Black mechanical and electrical sub-contractors, this could be another $500,000 in profit back to our community. Then comes labor, approximately 30 jobs paying at least $20,000 that would go to Black workers. This constitutes another $600,000 that would go into Black hands, but this time to a number of Black young and middle-aged adults desperately needing work, as they are the last hired and first fired.

Then there is the money to the owners. Catfish Corner's owners should make $50,000 from each of three condos sold. Their rental income on the second and third floors could be another $100,000 per year. The total amount of money from this transaction in Black hands would be $2.45 million, an amount that only came to be from the foresight of this project. Now these are numbers from my own estimates looking at these from a distance. But I know a bit about Seattle real estate and so the numbers are based in reality.

I provide this detail because this is the only way that the community can come to see how everyone benefits from making sure all of us support deals like this. Still, the benefit does not include the equity the owner would have, or any increased sales from the larger, brighter, newer space to house the restaurant in. Nor does it include the value to the community of a nice, newer, afrocentric structure in the historic Black community. Everyone wins, but only when we duplicate such deals all across the country. A $2.5 million dollar project done in the top 20 Black communities nationwide would mean an extra $50 million in income. $50 million multiplies into at least $75 million and perhaps as much as $150 million depending on how soon we really begin to act like real capitalists we love those like us.

So, we have to do what we can to get consumers, other businesses, and the government to buy Black, and then to technically assist Black business growth so that the increased demand is properly accounted for, invested in, and staffed out. When it comes to staffing, we must monitor hiring to ensure that Blacks continue to receive employment to the same degree they did before the increased demand.

10% GROWTH IN NON-BLACK INVESTMENT

I do not want to make the mistake of African American leaders in the Civil Rights Movement of the latter 1960s and early 1970s. They so blackened the movement that they gave too small a place to well-intentioned and well-meaning non-Blacks to remain. The speeches of Malcolm X and the rise of the Black Power Movement led Black leaders to make sure that Blacks dominate their own organizations. This makes sense to me. Blacks need to lead Black organizations, but all of this needs to be tempered with godly concern for people inside and outside of our community.

The problem was that these leaders came too close to communicating that they wanted the Whites to have no voice in the respective organizations. Progressively being denied a voice in the movements they had supported, Whites moved away from key civil rights groups in particular, and some moved away from the movement in general. It started with Malcolm X answering a White woman's question with the words that there was nothing she could do to support the Nation of Islam. It burgeoned in Malcolm's indictments of the NAACP as White led and controlled. There were discussions around this very point in the Student Non-Violent Coordinating Committee (SNCC) meetings. It extended through the speeches at public meetings of H. Rap Brown and Stokely Carmichael, Southern Christian Leadership Council, and the Black Panther Party for Self-Defense.

Perhaps Whites left too early; maybe they over-reacted. To the extent this is true, then it was unavoidable and thus they bear some of the blame. Whatever the case, it is clear that this zapped the movement of resources, as Whites have many items to offer, given that they are the majority of the population, and the supermajority in the power structure. It also sapped the movement of some of its resolve, as some of the Whites that had been involved were committed to the point of laying their lives down for the cause. Who can forget how the White and Black students offered their bodies to integrate Alabama and Mississippi in the Freedom Rides of 1960. Who can forget Chaney, Schoerner, and Goodman, two Whites and a Black, working with others in Mississippi for Black voting rights. Clannish scoundrels brutally murdered them in 1964, history that is now the subject of cinema.

I want whatever non-Black support we can get for the movement that this plan envisages. In fact, I revised some of this work in the third person so that readers of any ethnicity would not feel they are not excluded. Originally, I wrote this work as if the only audience was African Americans. However, it seemed to me that this jeopardized obtaining a shoestring for Black people.

I want whatever non-Black support we can get for the movement that this plan envisages. In fact, I revised some of this work in the third person so that readers of any ethnicity would not feel they are not excluded. Originally, I wrote this work as if the only audience was African Americans. However, it seemed to me that this jeopardized obtaining a shoestring for Black people.

We need a target as well for the level of investment we need from outside of our community. Blacks must have at least shoestrings from the larger society. This we have to go about securing intentionally and unashamedly. This plan merits societal investment.

The goal should again be 10%. We have to have this in order that we can be assured of meeting our overall 10% goal. Thus, we need a 10% increase in the amount of capital invested in this plan from private business, government, and the non-profit sector. The aim should be increasing the profitability of the businesses that hire Blacks by the larger percentage.

A number of these communities are being neglected by city and county budgets. Governmental budgets have money for enhancement of parks, lighting, planning strips, and related public spaces. Eddie Williams explains how disinvestment in Black communities breeds illicit activity.

> *Clearly, it is not good enough to plan for national economic growth while abandoning struggling African American urban communities to a downward spiral of vanishing jobs, skills, diplomas, and capital. We have seen how quickly violent crime and illicit drug trade rush in to fill that vacuum.* (Williams qtd. in Bates, Banking on Black Enterprise iv).

This plan addresses the governmental, private, and non-profit sectors separately. In each of these sectors we seek contracting, consulting, employment opportunities. This will require political astuteness. Because political pressure needs to be brought to bear, I say more about what should be done and how in the Political chapter that follows. Yet, commercial construction, aerospace manufacturing, and software designing are areas that demand discrete attention.

MORE GOVERNMENTAL, PRIVATE, AND NON-PROFIT EMPLOYMENT

Black leaders have to think of ways to get money from outside the community, inside it. This is what economists call foreign investment. One way is to make the community attractive to outside investment by lowering crime, cleaning things up, establishing enterprise zones, and opening opportunities to outsiders to buy things in the Black community. This has been happening, mainly through gentrification.

There is another way to do it. African Americans need to push for all of the programs that pour money into our community: affirmative action, poverty programs, urban renewal. There are certain specific things we can do as well. First, we have to set up community development corporations that Blacks control.

Second, we have to entice corporations to do business with African Americans and to invest in the Black community. One way to do this is through working with the major area banks that have disadvantaged community investment programs. Some of these programs set aside millions of dollars with which banks will extend favorable loan terms on projects in such areas.

In the recent past, banks have done many of these kinds of transactions by selling investment credits (tax breaks) that the U.S. government gives to projects in such areas. The banks sell the tax breaks to outside corporations. Corporations buy the credits because they make money off of them. The bank uses the money the corporations give as the down payment on the loan (and on the principle if there is enough left over). Then there are programs like the Community Reinvestment Act. Bates spoke to this as follows:

> *The Community Reinvestment Act may therefore be a useful tool in the 1990s for prodding banks that are reluctant to finance minority borrowers.*

(Bates, *Banking on Black Enterprise* 116)

If the bank in the area wants to give hundreds of thousands instead of millions to such a cause then Black leaders will have to step up the demand for fairness. This is only right given that the Federal Reserve controlling these banks ordered the banks in the latter 1980s to invest in disadvantaged areas after studies showed that banks were still redlining and/or discriminating against blacks in lending (even when Blacks applied for mortgages for home ownership). These programs were set up as a means of making amends.

Since the mistreatment cost Blacks hundreds of millions—even billions—the remedy should help us in the same way. Demand an accounting of the funds spent, the projects they went to, and the amount of money that stayed in the community (as opposed to going to people who live outside of the community). Bates states that governments can investigate such things.

States can successfully demand information from banks on their lending practices. It is the states, after all, that charter many of the commercial banking institutions. If they care to, states can also outlaw discriminatory lending, and they can back up these laws with nontrivial sanctions. Banks that redline can be barred from opening new branches...by focusing public scrutiny on the activities of redlining banks, cities and states have a powerful tool for encouraging nondiscriminatory bank lending practices. To date this tool has been underutilized. (Bates, *Banking on Black Enterprise* 116)

If states can demand such information, then why cannot our community.

My guess is that the banks will not like this kind of scrutiny and may be more willing to work with Black interests, particularly if the businesses advantaged have long track records of being in business, if they will put up at least ten percent of the down payment, if they can afford to pay the loan payments, and if the community (particularly the pastors of the largest churches) are behind the deal.

In the appendix is an e-mail I sent to certain leaders in the Black community about getting a significant piece of a large public contract after Blacks were denied a fair share of the contracts and were in other ways suffering discrimination. The e-mail suggests one way to get compensation on a cash-strapped project on which the governmental officials were reluctant to do anything for us. The idea was to get the governmental officials to award a contract extension (a change order) in excess of $3 million to a Black general contractor and at least one major Black subcontractor. To make the deal work more reliably, I asked Black leaders to pressure the government to get the general on the main contract to be one of the main subcontractors on the Black-led extension contract, and to force the general to disclose the original bids received on the work. In this way, the general will be invested in the contract extension and remain on the job to minimize sabotaging the new Black general.

We need to ask for the kinds of investments that will really build wealth in our community. In the e-mail mentioned above, I was asking our community to do much, much more than ask for a few jobs or small subcontracts. Ask for a general contract in a change order so that you can lead a piece of the project. This provides opportunities and builds businesses at the same time.

We want our fair share of governmental and Fortune 500 (or better, Russell 2000) company employment. We need to pressure landlords to offer properties to our people at a fair price. We need to demand that our people have their fair percentage of jobs in public, private, and non-profit work –we have to demand it. We have to assist our people in doing franchising, remodels, and new construction through political pressure on those who have the money where we do not have the money ourselves. We have no choice. We have to get started now. We cannot wait.

> *The ratios …make it clear that black Americans get jobs only after white applicants have been accommodated. In periods of prosperity, when the economy requires more workers, blacks who had been unemployed are offered vacant positions. But as the last hired, they can expect to be the first fired. In bleak times, the jobless rate among blacks can approach 20 percent, as it did in 1983. Since 1975, unemployment rates for blacks have remained at double-digit levels, and they have not fallen below twice the white rate since 1976. Even more depressing, the gap between the black and white figures grew during the 1980s, suggesting that the economy has little interest in enlisting black contributions.* (Hacker, Two Nations: Black and White, Separate, Hostile, Unequal 108)

We have to change the dynamics that Hacker describes above, and it will take more than qualified individuals acting in their own interest to do so. The community is going to have to stand up for our workers seeking employment opportunities outside and inside of our community. We have to deal with our compatriots who have struck a dastardly bargain: bringing in illegal immigrants who are treated like third-class citizens, in order to have a workforce that keeps them from having to deal with the structurally unemployed who are largely Black and are treated like second-class citizens. Hacker stated this as far back as 1990.

> *Exacerbating the situation today is the fact that millions of jobs are being filled by legal and illegal aliens, largely from Latin America and Asia. Few of the positions they take call for special skills, so the question arises as to why these places haven't been offered to native born black Americans. This issue is not new, since it has long been argued that immigrant labor takes bread from the mouths of citizens. In most cases, though, immigrants acquiesce to wages and working conditions that black and white Americans are unwilling to accept.* (Hacker, Two Nations: Black and White, Separate, Hostile, Unequal 109-110)

In 2006 Americans witnessed Latinos/as, from all parts of Latin America, participate in mass rallies advocating for amnesty and worker certification. As much as I supported their cause and hoped they achieved their ends, I could not help lamenting what this would mean for unskilled and semi-skilled African American would-be workers, particularly the structurally unemployed. Where are the leaders advocating for them?

Neither is there an effort to ensure that Black businesses are hiring Blacks to the same degree as non-blacks are hiring those of their ethnicity. We are not effectively holding our businesses under employment inspection. It is a recipe for poverty that extends from one generation to the next. Remember this principle: *You cannot help a people as a people who as a people do not help themselves.*

When an entire community does not help itself then all that is left is helping a part of it, such as certain of its groups or individuals: those who are ready and able to seize the opportunity. When a community does not support its own businesses, then it cannot be helped as a whole. This is the plight of a community ill-informed about what it is doing to itself, and how to change its damaging behavior.

> *This study clearly shows that in hiring practices, white owners of small businesses continue to exclude minorities; black owners, by contrast, consistently hire minority workers. This pattern holds up regardless of the firms' location. White owners employ a predominantly—and often entirely—white work force even when their businesses are located in inner-city minority communities. By contrast, black-owned firms in the same communities utilize a labor force made up overwhelmingly of minority workers; only 3.2 percent of these firms employ a work force that is 50 percent or more white. Even outside minority neighborhoods, black owners continue to rely largely on minority workers, whereas most white-owned businesses have no minority employees at all.* (BATES, BANKING ON BLACK ENTERPRISE XVIII)

We need the Urban League, the NAACP, and similar organizations around the country to research the workforces of the major businesses, for profit organizations, and the public employers in order to locate where the under-hiring of our people is occurring. This is where we must apply pressure to get Blacks in the door, and once in, promoted. We need the leadership committee of these same organizations to support African Americans getting higher profile government, business, and non-profit positions. The employment of African Americans is vital to healthy Black communities.

Particularly rapid growth areas for this emerging group include wholesaling, general construction, and skill-intensive service industries, particularly finance and business services. The construction industry—certainly not a new line of black enterprise—is also evolving into an emerging line of business: growth in construction has been most rapid among the large-scale firms that do not rely primarily on minority clients. Opportunities offered by special corporate procurement and government minority business set-aside programs have also contributed heavily to the growth of these emerging entrepreneurs. (BATES, BANKING ON BLACK ENTERPRISE XVIII)

While our community cannot rely on affirmative action any longer, we can make use of any programming in the following areas that Bates lists above: manufacturing (i.e., aerospace), construction, skill-intensive service, recreation (i.e., the cruise industry), and business services. These are areas in which we have already demonstrated proficiency, they are growth areas, and they are not too difficult to train for. With more training and leverage, we can get Black employees into Microsoft and other more skilled employment that employers are going abroad to find workers for.

The aim is to provide a wealthy and healthy life for every African American in each household. Since the best welfare program in the world is a good job, this plan is focused on the provision of good-paying jobs for Blacks. But jobs do not just fall from the sky. In order to have good-paying jobs, we must direct money into Black businesses while we pressure businesses outside of our community as well as the government and non-profit sector to hire Blacks. We have to change the low demand for Black labor, the dynamic of Blacks being the last hired and the first fired. Such demand comes from one of four places: consumers, other businesses, non-profit organizations, and sometimes the government.

The following are the additional measures to safeguard our achieving the 10% goal.

Safeguard Meeting the 10% Goal By These Means:

1. Trust Fund
2. Technical Assistance
3. Soft Measures, including buy-in from those benefiting most
4. Development Week
5. Hard Measures
6. Better Black Business Bureau

A discussion of each of these items immediately follows.

FUND FOR THE COMMUNITY

The community needs a fund raised to launch community development initiatives. Everyone should try to give something to it. The small sums that individuals, families, and associations raise for the community would go to this community fund. Although we may feel that our dollars look like pennies, pennies united become dollars. Moreover, those with larger sums within the community will give to the effort as they see it going to efforts that truly bring development. On this score, those outside of our community, those desperately waiting for private sector initiatives, responsibly managed, and targeted to do good, will also kick in monies. All of these investments—pennies from those first engaged, large sums from those who give later, and even larger sums from those outside of the community—will grow the fund to an impressive degree. A lot can be leveraged from pennies.

In fact, our political leaders can help us lobby the larger society to in fact steer monies to this fund. We have a handful of ways to pour money in. With the right efforts, we can raise a community fund that becomes sizeable.

We can also set the fund up in such a way that we steer into it resources people wish to give at death. It would be a good idea to encourage people to do this, as the cause merits it. How so? Well, we could have seminars that show people how to will anywhere from 1 – 10% of their money to this plan. For those who want their principle to be retained, and only the interest to go to development, we can set up a trust. I rather like the idea of a trust better even though it is much less use of the money available. In the short term it is frustrating to see the interest looking like a dwarf, while the need is giant. However, in the longer term, the money raised continues perpetually to give to the cause, even in the years in which no new principle is raised for the trust. It becomes the gift that keeps on giving.

One-third of the fund could go to the smaller-scale projects, and two-thirds to the larger ones. The community's leaders would decide this. Finally, we will have dedicated funds of our own for development projects.

TECHNICAL AND EDUCATIONAL ASSISTANCE

As business revenue rises, even more assistance should be invested in our business owners to promote their long-term profitability in the ever-changing, global market place. Studies have shown the following to be true.

> *Entrepreneurial ability is highly correlated with both education and income levels: successful business operators tend to be above average in both categories.* (Bates, Banking on Black Enterprise xxii)

Continuous training and professional development are a must, given that knowledge is advancing, techniques are upgrading, and laws are changing. Attorneys have to attend continuing legal education courses, as do doctors, accountants, engineers, and every other kind of professional, for business occurs in dynamic and innovative markets. The static business falls further and further behind.

Our business owners need help catching up and keeping up. One of the most instructive areas along these lines is construction. Contractors who try to do sizeable work will find that they have trouble with the new requirements. Jobs now require computer-aided designing, computerized shop drawings, computerized estimating, electronic bidding, critical path method scheduling, teleconferencing with specialty suppliers or regulators, language interpreting, training in specialty products and equipment, as well as more applications for off-hours work. Increasingly owners and general contractors are adding liquidated damages provisions to penalize contractors who finish the work beyond the contract completion date. The laws are progressively making it tougher for small contractors to survive. The work demands periodic re-training, new equipment, and systems upgrading.

In the various areas like construction, the community will need those more abreast of the advances to train those who are not. We have to find such ways to get our people up to speed, and to keep them out of court—bankruptcy court, civil court, or criminal court. Time in law court is time away from the jobsite. We cannot do all of this work to launch businesses and then fail to do the work necessary to help them survive and thrive.

Every business also needs a business analysis: a professional evaluation by someone who can access future profitability and analyze how to make the business more profitable at various levels of income. Some businesses can afford to pay for this; others will have to secure the services of non-profits or graduate students for help. If no one is available to assist, then we will urge owners to analyze themselves. Every business needs this, and from this to develop their own business plan for the next ten years of growth. Where we cannot do this on an individual basis, we will hold seminars in order to give entrepreneurs the analytical tools en masse.

SOFT MEASURES

This plan includes soft and hard accountability measures to give it teeth. Such is necessary for the accomplishment of the community target of 10%. Soft measures include asking each group to begin its meetings by recognizing their members who that month most supported Black businesses (i.e., have everyone stand, then ask those to sit who do not have a Black barber or beautician; repeat this asking about a doctor, accountant, computer tech, insurer, attorney, loan officer; then go to buying from Black store, gas station, etc.).

Soft measures are such things as incentives for workers, making more demands on those making more from the plan, and holding an annual development week. Sweeteners for laborers will give them the incentives to take the first jobs offered, though menial they may be. Using the captive audience means asking the businesses and workers making the most money to be the models of all of the aspects of the plan that apply to them. Finally, a development week will give us the opportunities to not only celebrate our success, but to provide our talented artists to creatively express what the plan is all about.

Also, if Detroit is instructive, other communities will be concerned about this being separatist, divisive, or protectionist. We will need to have answers for the outside community to speak to their fears. With regard to being separatist, this is our doing for us. Capitalism requires capitalism. These are our own capitalist measures to build ourselves in a capitalistic world. We will also celebrate that part of the plan that gives those outside of our community a role. They can help us with this plan. There is room for everybody, as long as they promote the plan. If they are not really helping us with this plan, then they are not really helping us.

INCENTIVES FOR HARD TO EMPLOY WORKERS

This plan as executed has to bring hope to every Black person, even those coming out of jail. Our overall plan has to bring the light—the true, achievable light at the end of a tunnel of reasonable length—to everyone who is part of the Black community. Here is what I mean.

This plan has to increasingly provide decent jobs to more of our people, including those who have felonies on their record. The outside community does not want to hire them, so we have to. Some of our adults have $50,000 or more in back child support by age 30. Others have fines totaling in the thousands that they are obliged to pay at the risk of re-arrest. A program should be put in place to lower the back child support and fines of workers who continue in this plan for numbers of months. Such a program is already in place in Seattle. With Black attorneys and judges assisting, we need to ask more of it and make it part of this plan.

If there are court costs and fines to pay as part of parole pursuant to a felony conviction parole, then such a person's voting rights will remain withdrawn. Those who will work with us need our help. We need to restore the voting rights of those who have completed a couple of years in the program.

Many African Americans, especially the males, have no home of their own. In fact, too many do not even have an apartment of their own; they go from girlfriend's apartment to momma's house, and sometimes grandma's house. We have to establish housing assistance for those who have been in the program for a few years. As soon as they can demonstrate that they can pay rent on time for over a year while controlling their debt, this should mean to us that they are ready to buy at the same monthly amount their rent was. What our program would do is help with the thousands that have to be saved for the down payment, money that could push the actual purchase date off years, perhaps forever. Keep in mind, a house that's paid for is the number one way to retire with a nest egg. If all we did for the masses of our people were this, we would still be lifting a generation out of poverty.

The learned know that learning is life-long. Our people must never stop enhancing their skill set and building their resumes. We should and can do this. For our people are brilliant beyond their board scores or their school grades. This remains true even in the case of our youth who have dropped out of school, or our adults in prison. Accordingly, we must grow scholarship chests for vocational or university education for those who have been committed to this plan for years. Sometimes students are more ready to learn at 28 than they were at 18. All they need is someone to believe as they do and to give them half a chance.

We have to help our people help themselves. We must win for them lives of hope and promise. No longer can we consign them to such a perilous and, in time, abysmal existence. By default we participated in leaving them to such an austere fate, and by design we can all work to brighten their course.

GETTING WORKERS WHO BENEFIT TO BENEFIT THE PLAN

This plan fully utilizes its captive audience. The captive audience is both those who are the first to receive business or personal income from the plan, as well as the leaders espousing it. Those who benefit financially from this plan will have an incentive, and will in fact be urged, to make use of the education, health, and other non-economic parts of the plan. The immediate beneficiaries are the businesses targeted to receive community patronage, and then it's those from the community who receive jobs as a result of the new money these businesses receive. With regard to the businesses enjoying increased capital, the leaders will go to them to urge them to do what they already are inclined to do: follow the economic, the educational, and all of the other initiatives progressively outlined in the community plan. Such businesses will be the greatest proponent of the plan; they will be more than happy to do whatever they can to make the plan a success.

However, the leaders cannot wait for inclination to do all of the work. We will go by and check to *see* that they are working the entire plan. If not, then the leaders should remind them where the extra money came from. That should do the trick. On the other hand, in the event that a business is still enjoying the people's extra money without serving the plan that is for the people, then leaders should meet with the business owner and convey in no uncertain terms that the money can be shut off just as easily as it is turned on.

A BUSINESS RECEIVING PLAN INCOME SHOULD
BE MORE THAN HAPPY TO DO THE FOLLOWING:

Provide excellent goods or services.

Continue to hire African Americans as your company has in the past.

Contract with Black producers, suppliers, consultants, and contractors.

Advertise in the Black media.

Communicate plan information to everyone in the company.

Contribute financially to the plan efforts.

Promote the plan's educational, social, medical, political, spiritual, and artistic initiatives.

Encourage company employees to participate in the plan.

Urge company employees to get out of owing and into owning.

Set up a kitty, no matter how small, of management and employee money for employee down payment assistance.

Be involved in a spiritual and at least one non-spiritual Black association.

Get a business analysis and work from it.

This similarly applies to the workers getting jobs as a direct result of this plan. As a condition of their employment they will need to agree to pay their child support, read about Black history, and work on their relationship issues—doing all parts of the comprehensive plan that apply to a person. As hard as decent jobs are to come by, employees should be more than eager to follow the parts of this plan that empower themselves and lift their community. On the other hand, there are always some who think they are entitled to what comes their way, or who like to buck authority. In either case, they need to be reminded that their job came from this plan. This should be enough to get these workers to do what they need to for their own betterment. However, if this is not enough, then they should be told in unmistakable terms that their jobs can go as fast as they came. These jobs come with conditions for the comprehensive development of Blacks. They will get the message, or else they will lose their jobs and have to reapply at the end of the line.

Most employees will be all too happy to work all aspects of the plan. They will see that this plan aims to pick them up and get them a foothold in society.

A DAY IN THE LIFE OF A GUY WHO RECEIVED A JOB UNDER THIS PLAN

7:30 a.m.	Arrive early to work to do reading (i.e. John Hope Franklin, Maya Angelieu, John Henrik Clarke, Alice Walker, Marita Golden, and Charles Johnson)
8:00 a.m.	Begin work
12:00 p.m.	30 minutes of exercise (basketball at the job, running, or pilates)
12:30 p.m.	Lunch (reading book again)
1:00 p.m.	Resume work
2:15 p.m.	Boss talks to workers for 10 minutes about owning instead of owing
4:00 p.m.	Leave work
4:30 p.m.	Pick child up from after school program. Meet with child's counselor.
5:00 p.m.	Talk with child about school and life over a salad and juice
5:30 p.m.	Drop child off. Pay child support
5:35 p.m.	Few Minutes of down time for Dad
6:00 p.m.	Check on brother and sister. Call mom.

6:30 p.m.	Pick up my Lady; Get some food and then go to church
8:45 p.m.	Discuss with members my progress working the plan
9:15 p.m.	Talk through problems with Beau and a trusted friend as facilitator
11:15 p.m.	Get home; review my goals for the week
11:30 p.m.	Lights out

This may not sound like much, but picture this person doing this early into his first job, after having come out of rehabilitation, or fresh out of jail. Think of someone doing this who is not college degreed, did not grow up in a middle class family, and who may not have had a father figure on whom to count.

What is unique about the schedule above is the time for monitored reading, exercise, and discussions, as part of this plan. The plan, as well, encourages our folks to do what they already are inclined to do: parent children, keep up with family, and be in supportive relationships. It is important to be realistic though: these are a lot of activities to cram in one day; moreover, this father is not doing the lion's share of the child rearing by only spending an hour with his child.

On the other hand, he did spend some time, did check with the counselor, and did pay his child support. This is more than the typical non-custodial father is thought to do. Perhaps the average father, even the one doing a plan such as this, will not spend such daily time with his child. Still, if he is keeping current with his child support, and spending his court-ordered visitation time with the child, then he is part of the solution.

Remember that this part of the plan discussion is occurring in the economic plan section. The plan still has social, educational, and medical structures to ease this person into. The aim is to re-connect people to their own families, renew in them a sense of dignity, lift their heads to dream again about their purpose, to enhance their relationships, to make marriage more attractive while making those marriages healthier, and to link these people better to their community. All of these things develop along side of the growth in this person's financial knowledge and ownership. So although the slice of just one day may seem a small beginning, the Bible warns us thusly: "Despise not the day of small beginnings." For a long march begins with one step, and grand things launch from modest beginnings.

So, the leaders will not have to be the examples to the rest of the community alone. Those who benefit will be examples as well. In other words, we will have a growing captive audience of benefactors and smaller core of leaders to assist with getting the entire community to live the complete plan.

DEVELOPMENT WEEK

Another measure to focus the community's energies on this plan and to showcase those making it work is through devoting a week just to the plan. I call this the "Week of Recognition" (Development Week). This is the week that will tie this great work to the calendar as well as providing a way of motivating those expending so much goodwill for the community.

The week could begin with reports from various area professionals on the state of Black Americans in the city in their area. Medical professionals might present one day; educational professionals, the next; social professionals, the following day; and political professionals, the last day. The hardest, most verifiable numbers may come from 2 – 3 years before, with anecdotal information and inferences concerning the year just ended. This will add to the relevance and immediacy of action on a plan.

Wednesday could include workshops and other events to bring first generation African Americans together with African Americans who have been here a while. Africans from Ethiopia all the way over to Sierra Leone, recently removed from the Motherland, need to be closer linked to Black Americans, long removed from the Motherland. By virtue of our skin and heritage, we are still voyagers in the same boat when in this country. Consequently, we have to forge greater ties for the survival of us all. Whatever resolutions we come up with would become part of the published work on the week.

Thursday is the day to lighten things up. Sometimes a good laugh is the break that we all need. Thursday could be for a comedy show with the best area comedians making us laugh and think about what is going wrong and right with the plan. The best (and cleanest) jokes should be part of the work on the week. This will be a glorified Def Comedy Jam.

Friday could be the time set aside for spoken word: poems, short dramatizations, and speeches on development. This will be a particularly rich night, with apt contributions from a number of people. The best ones could be part of the published work on the development week. This will be reminiscent of Russell Simmonds Def Poets.

Saturday around one in the afternoon could be a play someone has done on development. Saturday night could be the recognition banquet with a keynote that will bring the house down about development. At the banquet the community leaders who have led this plan should be recognized. The volunteers who have given the most to this effort should also be recognized.

Sunday at 3:00 would be a preaching circle as about three preachers teach on development. It is fine if believers of different faiths hold separate *3 Sermons at 3:00 Services.* One of the speakers should come from an ethnic group that has risen well in the U.S. Perhaps one of the speakers should be from a White church to which a connection could be made to promote this plan; to be sure, many such pastors could benefit from being "baptized" into a progressive African American Christian experience in which they are going to listen and clap more than they are going speak and orchestrate. At least one of the speakers should be one of the most accomplished Black speakers (with something to say) to take the people "on up high to calvary," while still speaking on biblical development. Sunday night would conclude things with a concert. None of this should be about form or fashion; all of this is to focus the community on the goal of staying united and motivated on the plan.

DEVELOPMENT WEEK

Mon-Tues	Wednesday	Thursday	Friday	Saturday	Sunday
School & Misc. Group Events	African & African American Day	Comedy Show	Spoken Word, then later, Dance	Play, then later, Community Banquet	3 Sermon Service, then later, Gospel Concert

I would suggest that Development Week be right after Martin Luther King's birthday, then it will serve as a grand lead in to Black History Month and all that it entails. The old calendar year will have ended, a natural ending of the development year. Then we will have a few extra weeks to compile and prepare. Incidentally, the work to determine who will do the reports, speak at spoken word, do the play, etc., should be decided by the end of September in a fair way so that people are prepared and ready. The biggest church of the community needs to take the lead in housing the events Sunday, if not the others.

This will be a powerful week that focuses the community on the gains achieved and that launches it into an even stronger year. It also serves as a means for our artists to display their rich gifts in a way that inspires as it informs. Development Week: the most entertaining strategy week of the year.

HARD MEASURES

A renaissance is not going to happen on its own. It absolutely requires concerted action and supervision. Once the plan is launched there will be natural inertia because it is a new idea. There will be the "Rebuild the Community Fatigue" I discussed earlier as a result of former plans promising to do the same thing. Then there will be the challenge of sustaining the effort. Big in this regard is some kind of enforcement measure that is tougher than the soft items mentioned above. Yep: I thought about that too.

Firmer measures will include putting cards on the window of those frequenting non-Black businesses, cards that teach of the impact of their money going outside of the community.

PLEASE SUPPORT BLACK BUSINESS OWNERS

Community leaders supporting the Black Development Plan have asked that we place this card on the windshield of the cars of African Americans who frequent non-African American establishments. This is not to embarrass or to harass you. Instead, it is all in an effort to encourage mass community investment—and our businesses and community at large need every dollar.

Did you know that African Americans buy from their businesses to a lesser degree than almost any other ethnic group? This keeps us under-developed and unemployed. We need the help of all of us working together in order to have the Black renaissance that our development plan is targeting. Will you help us more? Support Black businesses every time you can. Thank you.

We would appreciate if you would leave this card at your church, or another Black associational meeting.

Firmer still might be articles in the Black newspapers about those who are not supporting Black community businesses, like the articles by Clingman in the *Facts* about the same in Detroit and around the nation. We can also use the Black media to chart progress towards the goals of the plan and to critique those black businesses providing inferior goods or service. Finally, our leaders can visit businesses that are not acting in accord with the plan. Associations can check their own members. Family members can hold other members accountable.

Earlier I raised the subject of the captive audience. We may have to confront some of our own people. We may have to recommend that outside agencies and firms not rehire or work with some of our own people who while in place disserved the community. We may have to work against politicians who hurt the plan. We may have to direct our people away from our own businesses that work against us or are recalcitrant.

With regard to this being separatist or protectionist, we should provide the material about how much other communities support their own businesses. Given that Blacks fall below Jewish, Asian, and now many new-arrival African Americans, we should be exempt from criticism for starting as we shall. Until our support of our businesses exceeds the rate of other groups supporting their businesses, no one should have the right to criticize us. We have to have this information and use it.

If Black businesses do not serve well, then we will have something to hold them accountable. Can you say "BBBB"?

BBBB: BETTER BLACK BUSINESS BUREAU

As I discuss using and relying more and more on Black businesses, fear is rising in the hearts of some of my readers. "Been there, done that; don't want to do it again," may be the response. Some have been burned by Black contractors who performed poorly the work they promised to do. Others have had Black consultants drop the ball on an important part of a project that left you and your team reeling to recover. Some felt they were accosted by Black service providers who gave them sub-standard service, and then tried to "cuss them out" when they registered a complaint. Still others simply do not want to hire a mostly Black workforce as they believe that they have had problems getting them to do the work they were hired to do.

The first thing that has to be said is that most people who speak like this are referring not to hundreds of times something like this happened, but instead once or twice.

Of course, even one such occurrence can be hurtful, even traumatic, depending on how bad the failure was. Still, the point is that even the best of businesses or workers will disappoint a customer now and then. Even the best of persons can make a mistake or have a bad day and take it out on others. In fact, any person, of any ethnicity, can do this—so if perfection is what you cannot live without, where will you go to find it? The fact that some Black business owners were sub-standard does not mean that all or even most Black businesses are as well. If we are not careful, we will run afoul of the old sayings Blacks grew up with like, "Some Blacks think White folks ice is colder." Beware or else we will find ourselves discriminating against ourselves just as Whites used to do to us.

The second point is that if we do not help ourselves as a people then we will never rise. We will remain as we are: broke, busted, and disgusted. Moreover, the help that we need has to be about building Black businesses into bounty. It means we have no choice but to find Black businesses in which to invest our money. So we come full circle: even if our businesses perform in an unacceptable way, the only way to our renaissance is to work to improve their service and products while continuing to patronize them. This is what groups like Jewish Americans did.

Yet, there are some things we can do to get our poorly performing businesses to shape up. We can devise something like the Better Business Bureau. We have to find an agency that can provide a message line and play the role of a library and clearinghouse of consumer complaints. This agency can catalogue those complaints. Then we can develop a rule as to when a type or number of complaints rise to the level of public notice of the complaint. We can contract with one or more of the newspapers to have a column just for these complaints. For the protection of the business, the column can begin with a legend that reads thusly:

> *Business complaints are not atypical, and in some areas they are customary. Furthermore, a complaint does not mean that the business is guilty of the facts alleged. These complaints are published because of the number or nature of the complaints against the business listed.*

Then the complaint would run as it is written or edited. The column may garner such attention that it becomes a point of interest for the newspaper, making the column information valuable enough to make a newspaper want to pay to have it.

This publicity in and of itself should be enough to get the business to improve its ways. If not, though, we can take it to the next step. Annually, we could compile the data and then send it to the leadership to consider how to approach the business owner on behalf of the community. If the owner is hard-headed, then we can fund another business to compete with it. That should get the owner's attention. Besides, we should not have any sector with merely one Black business in it. This is too conducive to poor service. We could call these efforts by the acronym, the BBBB (Better Black Business Bureau).

Such is the economic component of this plan. This is the way to increase Black support of their own businesses, expand more of their businesses into the larger community, and to woo more investment inside the community from investing sources outside of the community. This is the 10 – 10 – 10 Plan to achieve 10% sustained growth for at least a decade and a half. Upon this platform, all of the political, social, medical, and other measures will fit just fine.

LETTING GO OF WHAT YOU NO LONGER NEED

I don't wear dress shoes with strings any more. This applies to formal and business shoes: before and after 5:00 wear. One of the wisest men my age I know, Larry N. Scruggs, told me in law school why he wears slip-ons almost exclusively, "They are faster to put on and show more of the shine on the shoe, especially when seated." Larry is an attorney and an accomplished real estate developer. His time is committed—almost every minute. He further confided that he prefers to not have to hassle any more over knots or worn strings.

All of this made a lot of sense to me. I graduated from Notre Dame Law School with Larry. I have seen him go from being a college student of modest means to becoming a multi-millionaire. I am also witnessing him come to terms with Christianity in earnest. He is a success on many fronts. So when he shared these gentle sentiments, I was all over it. It is primarily because of Larry that I do not wear dress shoes with strings.

On the other hand, I will wear shoes with a buckle or a strap. I wear slip-on dress shoes. My sandals have a strap or buckle. When I quickly don my shoes without needing to tie them, or see someone else's worn strings, when I admire the full shine on the top of my shoe or peer at the lack of this on someone's laced shoe, I think about how good it is to let dress-shoe strings go.

Likewise, it is time for our community to move on from some things. It is time to let go. We need to let go of poverty and get to ownership and investments. We need to let go of foolishness and begin to operate from a comprehensive plan. We have to let go of government reliance and graduate to launching and patronizing thousands of businesses of our own. We need to let go of political indifference and demand governments to support our agenda. We need to let go of competition and better work together for our social, medical, and educational health. It is time to let go of some things. We need to let go of reliance on strings. From henceforth, let us rely mostly on our straps.

POLITICS:
ASSOCIATION, AGENDA AND COALITION POLITICS

Somebody has to take responsibility for being a leader.
(TONI MORRISON)

The urgency of the hour calls for leaders of wise judgment and sound integrity—leaders not in love with money but in love with justice; leaders not in love with publicity, but in love with humanity; leaders who can subject their particular egos to the greatness of the cause.
(REV. DR. MARTIN LUTHER KING, JR.)

Dr. King is right to bring us to the subject of leadership. For, King led us through segregation and into the new opportunities and challenges under the southern strategy—all of which are economic and then political. Politics is about leadership. Leadership takes responsibility and then responds with solutions. In the Black community it is time for the leaders with the titles to take the responsibility that the term demands, as Toni Morrison urged.

Because politics is all about solving problems, political leaders worth their salt could lead themselves the movement for which this plan calls. In fact, the ills plaguing Blacks should have long ago called leaders so concerned to formulate and move on such a plan. Nevertheless, what is past is history. Besides, a plan is now formulated. With this plan, these leaders can show what they are made of to those in their community. Those who care about the Black community and who serve as public officials, lobbyists, consultants, and professors should keep their day job, but donate one or two evenings to using their unique problem-solving skills to save the community that serves them.

It is time to think about doing more than something beneficial in the community, such as "late night" sports programs or "just say no to drugs" campaigns. While these things are good, they are not enough—even taken together, they cannot solve the problem. It is time to approach this problem in the way that political leaders face any big challenge (i.e. crime, crumbling infrastructure, or disaster relief). Capable political leaders regularly tackle such problems, at times solving them for a generation. It is what they do; their jobs demand it.

Well, the circumstances demand something be done in Black communities. Capable political leaders who know how to solve large challenges need to turn their attention to the challenges in Black America. It is time to do more than serve the problem; it is time to solve the problem. So, this is a call to the political leaders to rise to the challenge, if you have to do so yourselves. Do for your own what you are uniquely trained to do; do for those like you what you do for those different from you.

Political leaders must help call the community together to select leaders who will oversee the selection and carrying out of the people's plan. Many of the political leaders should serve on the umbrella committee that will do this oversight work. Political leaders must go one step further. They are urged to connect with the community and its umbrella committee so that through them the community can have access to government at the local, state, and federal levels. So, political leaders can help the community with its own political leadership overseeing the plan inside of the community, and they help with points of access into government in order that the community may be realize better governmental representation. This is your call to action; your community implores you to do better what you do so well. It is an inside and an outside strategy to further the plan of the people.

We endeavor to move the people to pick themselves up by their bootstraps, and then to position our people to be the conscience of this country, and the advocates of Africa. In other words, it is time to become organized inwardly, influential outwardly, so that we can be mobile upwardly. Our political leaders can help us with this.

It is time to do more than serve the problem; it is time to solve the problem. So, this is a call to the political leaders to rise to the challenge, if you have to do so yourselves. Do for your own what you are uniquely trained to do; do for those like you what you do for those different from you.

POLITICAL DEVELOPMENT INSIDE THE COMMUNITY

Whereas economics is about creating the resources to fund a renaissance, politics is about the leadership needed to do the renaissance. This leadership is inward and outward for needed work inside and outside of our community. First, we have to work inwardly. Politically we must, first, build leadership within the community that develops and enforces policy consistent with this plan. Our community is so fractured and wounded that we will only be able to do this partially, but doing it in part will be enough. Then, second, we have to work with and through governments (city, county, state, and national) in order to get what we are now owed as citizens, or should have received over the centuries as the objects of discrimination. More on this second part later.

We begin by launching study groups to set the climate for a new type of mobilization. Once we get enough people thinking about the type of plans that can move us forward with power, we take the next step of action. We must then call our community together to launch this effort, but even more where the leaders in various associations formulate and institute the plan for our development. Leaders will need to adjust the policy from time to time in ways that better help the people. What we have to do inwardly is set forth below.

POLITICAL STEPS TO ORGANIZE THE COMMUNITY

- Launch plan study groups.
- Call leaders together.
- Develop Linking structures.
- Confer on an overall plan.
- Call leaders together in areas (medical, educational, etc.).
- Adopt specialized area plans.
- Agree on an overall plan.
- Develop implementation strategy.
- Call the community around the plan.
- Execute the plan.
- Institute Development Week.
- Ensure 10% economic growth.
- Make planned progress on the other areas.
- Develop the 'Outside the Community Plan' and employ it before election.
- Nurture future leaders willing to sacrifice and honored for it.

Within the community we have to call the community together to agree on a plan and on the leadership structures on which to execute it. It begins by a call to bring the community together. This will be a community forum, at the heart of which will be folks from the key associations. It should stand to reason then that the leadership will come mainly from these same key associations. We need structure.

The community will need leadership structures to keep things organized. The leadership consists of associations, area committees, and an umbrella committee. The base is associations. For, there is no Black government in Black America. Churches and mosques, organizations and businesses, trades and professions, as well as fraternities and sororities need to figure out what their members really need that they can help to provide, and then they must get the job done. In order for this to happen, Blacks will need to become more involved in their groups and their leaders will need to step up their leadership. To make the base strong, associations must be linked. We shall group like associations together and then link the groups together, as has been explained already. As a service to them, and to enhance this base even more, we need to encourage all of our people to be involved in a number of Black associations.

Then we should have area committees. These are made up of key people in the areas of religion, politics, social services, business, health care, education, and the arts. These leaders will have to meet as our plan is comprehensive and will need expert minds to expertly shepherd it from beginning to end. In each of these areas we will need the governmental, non-profit, educational, and business leaders to meet in order to figure out what our people need in these areas, what they need in order to better prosper, and what is needed to encourage more of our people in the area. Besides, folks in these areas should have been regularly meeting to support themselves a long time ago.

Those in the meetings will know how to reach the rest of our people in their specific area. Then quantify the contracts, patronage, jobs, grants, and other resources our entities in these, and our people in general, are receiving. Employ best practices ideas to help each other, without concern about selfish motives. No more time for the crabs-in-a-barrel mentality. Force the government to provide statistics to each group so that we do not have to do this costly work with our limited resources. Encourage the government to study governmental, non-profit, and commercial entities alike in terms of what they are doing, or not doing, for Blacks. In the meetings, they should challenge each other to do excellent work to further these aims, and to commit their ideas to writing. We have been talking and arguing far too much, and studying and writing far too little.

Produce a report, publish it to the people, and get it to the umbrella committee in a timely fashion. We need every kind of report. We must have spiritual, political, social, economic, medical, educational, and artistic analyses of our local situation. Do not worry that the first ones will be a little crude in substance or studies. We will build from report to report. In time they will be weighty and conclusive about how we are faring and about what more needs to be done. Some areas like health and education will have places—hospitals, schools, and agencies—to assemble more easily a thorough study. Other areas like art and religion will have to do everything from scratch. No matter the difficulty, we must get through every barrier to accomplish the task.

The goal for each plan should be the same: 10% improvement annually in each area. It will be left to each group to determine how to measure it and to accomplish it.

We need these reports no later than every three years, each report containing a solution with milestones. Every year the area committees should produce a status report as to what progress has been made on the milestones. The solution should have *most* to do with how we our going to help ourselves, and *much* to do with how others will help us. We must not get twisted who will do the *most* and who will do the *much*; it's bootstrap time. These reports will become sub-plans. When presented to the community-wide committee, they will be evaluated for incorporation in the overall plan.

The umbrella committee formed is at the center of it all. Our most competent, caring, and committed leaders should be there. They will need to be competent enough to bring the key players together in every area; competent enough to assist areas with their tasks, even their reports; and competent enough to access power and to galvanize the people to act. They should be caring enough to have the community at heart; caring enough to feel the pain of the people; and caring enough to be driven to do something now. They should be committed enough to sense a call to solve the problems of the people; committed enough to give this effort the proper priority in their lives; and committed enough to bore through the distractions that get in the way. With regard to length of service, some will serve for only a year, some for a few years, and some for over a decade. We have to take what we can get.

WHAT THE LEADERSHIP SHOULD DO WITHIN THE COMMUNITY

The umbrella committee needs to develop the overall plan, the implementation strategy, and carry out both effectively. Development and implementation bring the plan to, from, and through the people. This includes devising ways to hear from the people so that the plan can be adjusted where necessary.

The previous 10 items apply to the first years. After the plan is in place, it is the last 5 items that matter. It is all about different forms of development. The following box is what we do next.

POLITICAL PROGRAM INSIDE THE COMMUNITY

Development Week: hold Development Week annually.

Development Goal: ensure 10% economic growth annually.

Inside Development: make planned progress on the other areas.

Outside Development: update and employ the "Outside the Community Plan."

Leadership Development: continue to nurture future leaders.

We must institute Development Week. It will focus our efforts annually. We have to commit to the goal of 10% growth—more on this soon. We have to engage the inside and outside plans. Then we have to continue to nurture leaders so that this effort will have continuity.

POLITICAL DEVELOPMENT OUTSIDE OF THE COMMUNITY

If the inward work is the right arm, then the outward work is the left; and we need both arms to fight for our renaissance. Besides, a one armed person is dysfunctional, and we do not want to be that. Outward work is what we do in the larger society, where we have to be much, much more influential. This means working with governments, businesses, and non-profit organizations. How do we do this?

This forces us to have our plan in place and then communicate what we need to candidates and business executives so that they will know how to support us very specifically. So, we must develop the other part of the two-fold plan. Here are six steps concerning our community and candidates plan:

PRESENTING OUR CONCERNS TO CANDIDATES

Agenda: prepare an agenda that promotes our plan.

Call: call politicians to the agenda in the major races; publicize it for the smaller.

Money: raise some money for those who support our agenda.

Vote: vote for those who support our agenda.

Accountability: hold the candidate accountable to what they promise.

Sanction: sanction those who renege on the agenda by our votes, press conferences, money, and direct action.

The agenda should always include **policy**, **particulars**, and **personnel**. What do I mean by this? Policy is the larger, generalized matters that will help lift the entire community in a big way. Affirmative action, educational disparity, the educational achievement gap, restoring voting rights, getting more jobs on a large municipal contract are all policy examples. Before meeting with any politician, always clarify the issues on which support is contingent.

The particulars are the specific businesses, programs, or persons who are large or high profile enough that the larger community should assist. The loss of contracts to a significant Black business, the drafting of a subsidy to protect an entity losing funding, the unfair regulation of a non-profit, the harassing of a high level government official are particulars. Let us be clear about why we go to entities like the government with our demands. Bates helps us know why we should do this. He stated these things:

> *City governments have at their disposal numerous ways of promoting minority business development.* (Bates, Banking on Black Enterprise 94)
>
> *The mayor's appointment powers are one of the most powerful tools for assisting minority business development.* (Id. 94)

Like Bates, Hacker said this about various groups outside of our community, and the pain of budget cuts:

> *As has been noted, public and nonprofit organizations have become havens for much of the black workforce. Over a third of all black lawyers work for government departments, as do almost 30 percent of black scientists. Blacks account for over 20 percent of the nation's armed services, twice their proportion in the civilian economy. They hold almost a fifth of all positions in the Postal Service and have similar ratios in many urban agencies. Unfortunately,* **this makes middle-class blacks vulnerable to public budget cuts.** (HACKER, TWO NATIONS: BLACK AND WHITE, SEPARATE, HOSTILE, UNEQUAL, 121 [EMPHASIS ADDED])

Hopefully, it is clear now why we need an inside and outside political plan.

Before meeting with any politician, know which policies merit placement on the agenda, and keep the number around three items or less. The list of particulars may be a lot longer—maybe five items long. By the way, because the policy benefits the entire community, it should take precedence over the particulars. Do not let the politicians agree to the top two particulars and reject the rest of the agenda, unless you know that this is the absolute best that can be garnered because the community's political influence is so meager.

Personnel has to do with our always providing politicians and executives a list of the qualified people we would want to see them select from in their appointments. If they intend to listen to us as they signaled when they asked for our vote or for our business, then they need to strongly consider hiring from the list that we suggest to hold a close staff or cabinet position. This helps us importantly. First, it provides us people on the inside to present the community interests to the public or private executive. There is nothing like being part of the policy making from the formative stages. Second, it is a means of communication with the Black community. For politicians, it can help them understand what is being done in a more complete way; for our community it is a means of conveying what we want in a more complete way. For us it can actually be an early alert system, affording us the privilege of learning long in advance of things that will have an impact on our community.

Third, it is special access. Few things are worse than having a Black person in power who joins the powers that be in not responding to the concerns of our community. This happens way, way too often. Part of the reason why is because the community did not participate in putting the Black appointee in position to begin with. The Black appointee feels independent of the Black community, nearly estranged from the community of his ethnicity. How many times have I called on Black people in a governmental administration and been ignored when on high-level community business. Not just me: many leaders in the community with much greater clout than I have also been rebuffed—not by the non-Black powerholder, but instead by the Blacks they selected acting in their name. I am talking about Blacks who have chafed in the day of opportunity, and have even chided the community at the time we needed them the most. I will say more on this later.

POLITICAL PLATFORM FOR OUTSIDE THE COMMUNITY

African Americans definitely need Blacks serving in the larger society to represent their interests. Too often, such Blacks do very little to bring Black issues to the table at which they have some influence. Sometimes it is because they fear that their status is so tenuous that they cannot afford to risk this kind of resolve and representation.

THE POLITICAL PLATFORM OUTSIDE THE COMMUNITY

I. Extend the American Dream
   A. Extend Worker Power
   B. Extend Worker Income
   C. Extend Worker Ownership

II. End the American Nightmare
   A. End Housing Under-Supply
   B. End Educational Disparities
   C. End Health Care Insurance Disparities
   D. End (Structural) Unemployment
   E. End Criminal Enforcement Disparities

III. Mend Affirmative Action
   A. Mend Set Aside Programs
   B. Mend Remedial Hiring & Promotions Programs
   C. Mend Remedial Enrolment & Funding Programs

The spine of the platform is simple: there are three things to extend, five things end, and three things to mend. Outside of our community, we have to help all of America in our effort to help African America; we have to grow the pie for all of America to have enough funds to grow African America. So, with respect to things to extend, we must increase worker power. What gives workers more power, also gives them the ability to obtain greater benefits. In a top down approach, it means promoting employer sensitivity to, and inclusion of, workers in their business decisions. Worker inclusive managing at companies like Google and Ben & Jerry's serve as models. The main way to empower workers, though, is by a bottom up approach: promoting unions.

No entity has done more to support worker rights and benefits than unionization. With the rise of unionization the country witnessed the greatest increase in workers' percentage of the national income. With the recent decline in unionization the country saw the concomitant decline in the worker share of overall income. If we make workers generally more powerful then we position African American workers to share in this power, given that most Blacks are workers. Incidentally, workers have to be discouraged from the kind of coercive tactics that poison company profitability. For, if we hamstring the companies that provide the jobs then we cripple the workers who need the jobs. The solution has to be a delicate balance. Blacks will have to be vigilant to keep union members from discriminating against Blacks as such members have historically done.

Then, we have to increase worker income. Workers deserve a living wage, no matter whether they are uneducated or illegal. No one in the U.S. should have to work at wages that risk their nutrition, expose them to unreasonable risk, or make it difficult for them to function as a responsible citizen. This requires re-assessing the minimum wage to ensure that it is high enough. It also means updating the poverty level index so that Americans know the realistic measure of those below the poverty line. In most communities this includes factoring into the calculus the ownership of a basic car, and what all that entails; this is a must for a mother with children in a commuter society.

Increasing worker ownership has to do with much more than saving Social Security. It involves restructuring work so that workers are owning more of Wall Street and finding ways to connect workers to the vote to which their shares entitle them. Workers need the kind of investments that wealthy people have. The problem for the average worker is not how much they make as much as it is how much they invest. If workers could save more of their income and invest it where the wealthy do, workers would live when they retire more as the wealthy do. But to really empower workers, we need to get the retirement and mutual funds that hold the workers' billions to vote in the interest of the workers.

Some of these fund managers holding predominantly worker funds control 30% of the shares of a company, which means they control 30% of the shareholder votes. The next largest owner might have only 10%. As a result, the fund managers with the workers' money could decide almost every major issue of the company, because of rules of how companies are run. In other words, workers could control the major decisions of the company if the fund managers would vote the way the workers would. Yet, these fund managers will either be silent parties at shareholder meetings, or else they too often side with the other wealthy shareholders. For instance, the workers could be pressing for better wages at the company; the management might present to the shareholders a vote on whether to raise wages; all the while, the fund managers are standing by as if they do not have a dog in the fight. Workers need to have the votes their money entitles them to on Wall Street and on the Chicago mercantile exchanges. If this is done, workers will control both Wall Street and the Mercantile Exchange within a generation. I am sure that you can imagine why big money is uninterested in doing this for workers. For, on the day that this is done, the U.S. will more truly have a democracy. Remember, we have to help all of America in our effort to help African America; we have to grow the pie for all of America to have enough funds to grow African America.

I will not spend as much time on the other areas. Suffice it to say, all Americans need their nightmare ended in the areas of housing, education, health care, employment and criminal enforcement. We must end the improper disparities in these areas and promote home ownership, excellent education, comprehensive care, employment, and equal enforcement across the board.

Then we have to mend affirmative action in all of its aspects. Affirmative action is the remedy in the present that Americans owe certain groups for the injury caused by Americans in the past. Where there is an injury, there has to be a remedy. I will say more on this below. This is how we advance a plan that helps all of America in our effort to help African America; this is how we grow the pie for all of America to have enough funds to grow African America. This is the outside of the Community Plan.

HOW TO ENFORCE THE POLITICAL PLATFORM

We have to move to get people to listen to our agenda, moving like we are serious. We mentioned this earlier in terms of supporting those who support us. Supporting those who support us means helping supportive Black and non-Black candidates get elected. They will surely need our vote; until we fix the system, they will need money too. While in office they may need a friendly public letter or tangible recognition of some kind, like an award. In turn, we must work to get these officials to appoint community friendly Blacks and non-Blacks.

Sometimes we will have to carry a big stick. When our supporting does not work, we will have to shift to sanctioning. Sanctioning those who sanction us is first explained by clarifying what a sanction to us is. Anything that makes it more difficult for us to move forward on our plan is a sanction against us; acting so as to make it difficult for them to remain in office is a sanction against them.

We can start by meeting with them to let them know that we are not happy about their performance and intend to move against them politically or economically. We can send a public letter to them or give them an award of disapproval. If these actions do not work then we have to really make our presence known. Sanctioning those working against our plan will require more than marching: it entails studying, discussing, writing, contributing, campaigning, voting, and then cajoling (including marching, suing, and civil disobedience). Protesting and even civil disobedience in the modern era should come after working all of the other pressure points first.

We certainly can vote against them. We can support their opponent financially and with volunteers doing phone banking, door-knocking, placard holding, mass mailings, and so on. We have to show those in the larger society that we mean business. We are serious and astute now.

Do not vote for the party officials that will not support our plan. Do not buy from the businesses that will not support our plan. Use your ballot and your dollar as tools and weapons. All we have to do is bring a realistic agenda to the Democratic, Republican and Green parties. It will only take us once or twice voting as a block for the Greens or the Republicans in select races in order to get the Democrats to take us seriously.

On the other hand, I do not advocate giving people a long time of delay in addressing our concerns; nor do I support allowing powerholders to dictate the schedule as to when they will respond. King already addressed such things in his *Letter From a Birmingham Jail*; in it, King detailed poignantly why we cannot wait. Hence, we should present a schedule that starts with talking and ends in civil disobedience; that schedule must always be on our timetable—and when we say we will do the next thing, then we should do that thing near the date we first said, unless those we were opposing did the best that they could do (in our determination—not their estimation). Thus, if we said that we will start direct action in three months, then on the 90th day we should start marching and be already preparing to sue. I hope you hear what I am saying.

ECONOMICS AND THE 10% TARGET

Notice that this agenda above includes every area: spiritual, political, social, and economic; medical, educational and artistic. Why are all of these areas included in the political agenda? Well, political leadership must not exist by itself, for itself. It has to help our people medically, educationally, and especially economically; it has to work with key Blacks across the board, particularly work with pastors. This should have been clear as well in the area of the inside plan. From the calling of leaders together in various areas to the employment of the plan, the aim is to bring every aspect together, with economics at the center.

In fact, we need political leaders who have a keen awareness of the importance of all of the areas, but especially economics. Economics is only going to lead our development if we understand how it works, and if we appreciate the primacy of it now in our struggle. For too long we have had political and spiritual leaders who are economic novices. We must have the reverse of this from here on: our political leaders must have a keen understanding of economics, of capitalism, and of development in a mainly privatized world.

These leaders have to thoroughly grasp that knowing these concepts without knowledge of how they affect a people is not knowing enough. Thus they have to be convinced that you cannot help a people as a people who as a people do not help themselves. They must advocate that a people without a plan to succeed is a people with a plan to fail. Then the political leaders need to understand the power of owning instead of owing and of investing within the community as we do outside of it. We must insist that they know how money multiplies and how other groups have used their pennies to develop themselves. This is how economically savvy the new Black leaders must be. If our political leaders are not convinced of these ideas then we will never proceed on a comprehensive plan like this one. If they understand and advocate these ideas, then they are more then qualified to lead the development of our people. No obstacle can withstand a people acting on a plan.

Next, we have to know what our target is. Our strategic target, for down the road, is to get our fair share of the resources from and protection of the government and outside businesses; our tactical target annually is 10% growth.

There is one major way to evaluate the performance of the umbrella committee in the first couple of years. It is this: did it devise, adopt, and implement a comprehensive plan? Likewise, there is one major way to evaluate their performance after a few years. It is this: is it achieving at least 10% growth in the Black community and folding into this development all of the other areas of the plan? It is this simple; it is this serious.

If the non-black political leaders cannot deliver on what is truly due us if the government were to give us what is right, then at least our political leaders have to get what we absolutely have to obtain so that we open another spigot that helps us achieve our economic target.

Blacks must get their share of construction and commercial contracts; if not, then we absolutely must have 10% more each year than we have ever gotten. We must be involved in construction from the design, to construction and compliance, making sure that a fair share of the total goes to African Americans. Then we have to examine where the government is contracting with vendors and get this work from professional services, to blue-collar services, from supplies to food, from security to art. This includes open bid, qualified open bid, and exclusive contracts. Allow none of these to be exempted from reporting to the Black community or bids from Black contractors. Of course, we have to bundle within this 10% target the other goals of the plan as well, especially the educational and medical goals relating to governments and business. This is a must and, I feel, a test of the worth of the folks who are supposed to be leading us.

The 10% target will consistently be a challenge. As mentioned earlier, we will not have precise measurements, but we must strive to get an objective measure for our productivity. The countries today that set such targets for themselves do not even have bulletproof measures. They estimate, extrapolate, and approximate. If they can proceed without 100% reliability, then we can proceed with less as well. It is crucial that we have a target however. We must have a goal against which we will judge our efforts, no matter how difficult to calculate. It is our standard. The more we fail to account for substandard performance, the farther behind we will be. We have to earnestly strive for the goal.

We have to gain our fair share of governmental services, contracts, and positions. For instance, if we are 8% of the jurisdiction in numbers then we want at least 8% of the resources set aside for Black communities and at least 8% of the governmental jobs. We usually receive such a small percentage of the largess—often less than 1%—that just getting close to our fair share will be in excess of an 10% increase.

On rare occasions, we will press for our percentage so effectively that we will exceed our percentage in the population. In such situations, have another benchmark for ourselves. We should then seek to achieve the over-representation of power of Jewish Americans countrywide and Cuban Americans in Miami. Perhaps we can get it. If not, we will settle for our proportionate share. Again, we have been receiving such a small portion merely getting our proportionate share will be a boon to us, one that is long overdue. Then, we have to force the government to protect our people and businesses from illegal or unfair activity.

ALL POWER IS LOCAL

Former Speaker of the U.S. House of Representatives Tip O'Neill said something quite profound: "all power is local." I had to learn this lesson all over again later in life. I was one of two spokespersons for a group of Seattle area pastors that had private meetings with state congressional officials on African American Legislative Day at the Washington State capitol. For a number of years many of the Seattle area pastors had ignored this day. In the run up to the meeting, the main spokesperson for our group, another Black United Methodist Pastor, had learned of a large appropriation of money that the Seattle area Black community had missed because we did not have lobbyists at the state capitol advocating for us and because our leaders were not well representing us. We should have received at least a million dollars; we received thousands of dollars. The difference was more than tenfold.

I thought about how many times during that session this was repeated—once, twice, thrice? I pondered how many times it had happened at the county and city levels. Then I estimated how much money was lost over a ten-year period. My math suggested that Blacks were missing millions of dollars in governmental assistance annually, well over ten million for the decade because we are not actively engaged in lobbying for budget inclusion. At least ten times this number is lost through failure to press for the contracting and hiring of Black businesses and employees on governmental projects. Keep in mind, I am not referring to the national or federal government here—I am talking about state and local money.

It occurred to me that every Black community has to be powerful locally. The local institutions and their leaders are closer to us. They are more accessible. They come by more often. Moreover, they are more susceptible to our power. This is especially so if we will do the things stated above.

Becoming more powerful locally makes us more powerful nationally. This connects us back to Tip O'Neil. For what O'Neil was revealing is that national power is based on broad affiliations of local power. Voters in a thousand locals elect national leaders to office. National leaders thus have to go to a thousand local hamlets to have the local powers raise the national candidate's hand in support.

Even the billionaires of the world are sensitive to local power, for they have to live somewhere, and that somewhere is local to wherever it is. Billionaires like to travel. Wherever they go, they will have arrived at another locale. Billionaires are much, much more insulated from local authority than are national politicians; and national politicians are more insulated than are local people of wealth; local people of wealth are more insulated from local power than our local politicians. Local power is not a panacea. Being powerful locally does not make a people powerholders everywhere; it does make them more powerful than they were otherwise. If we are powerful locally then we will build our communities faster, get help sooner, and be more powerful nationally.

AFFIRMATIVE ACTION

There are certain specific issues about which we have to be adamant. One is moving criminal laws back towards rehabilitation and equity, and the other is affirmative action. With regard to affirmative action, we have to know that this remedy that has helped us greatly is slowly being eroded. As I wrote in 1996, affirmative action is on trial in the U.S. Truthfully, it is experiencing a slow death. Unless the civil rights community acts with uncommon valor, it will end in the U.S., probably within the next 20 years. Though a longer remedial period than the Reconstruction, it will be another shorter remedial period when viewed against the longer damaging periods of slavery and segregation. Given that the Southern Strategy is a few years older than affirmative action, the affirmative action era has actually had a damaging cancer at work on it, older than it, and that may exist longer than it if the civil rights community does not act to end it. The Southern Strategy is discussed in this chapter.

Blacks need to be more proactive in protecting and promoting affirmative action. We have to evaluate candidates according to their track record on minority hiring and contracting, and we need to do the studies and make arguments on discrimination from 1970 to the present in order to provide the necessary basis for remedial programming. Today's conservative justices on the U.S. and state Supreme Courts are increasingly taking the position in their decisions that real discrimination ended with segregation. They believe that only isolated incidents remain, incidents so isolated that they are not significantly hindering African Americans in any of the areas: educationally, medically, economically, socially, politically, artistically, or spiritually.

They are getting so bold in these assertions, that they are now saying that unless such proof is provided, there can be no constitutional basis for granting a racial remedy to

Blacks for being Black. They are basically saying, "If you think that racism still significantly exists, then prove it and you can get or keep affirmative action." This poses a tough challenge to our under-resourced communities. Yet, what choice do we have? If the courts are increasingly demanding it, all that is left is providing the proof or else watching affirmative action slowly die. So far we have seen it dramatically limited in education in the Michigan case (2002) and in bussing (2007). By initiative or board action, it has ended in California (1996), in Texas higher education (1998), Washington (1998), and Michigan (2006). How much more do you want to see?

I wrote an article that the *Howard Law Journal* published in 1996 about this. It is entitled, "Affirmative Action on Trial; the Retraction of Affirmative Action and the Case for its Retention." In the article, I argued that Blacks need to institute a nation-wide campaign to save affirmative action. We must make a type of national case for it whether we like doing it or not. The Supreme Court is giving us no alternative.

When the state of Washington was preparing to bring affirmative action to a vote, the Washington State African American Affairs Commission launched the kind of study and polemic of which I am speaking. In three pamphlets on affirmative action in contracting, education, and public employment, they studied the issue and made arguments. They concluded that women benefited most from affirmative action. They calculated the true verifiable percent of the remedial programming Blacks received. They showed that the loss of affirmative action would have a profound detrimental affect on the women and minorities. This was an excellent start. This is the kind of research that serves to provide a warrant for affirmative action programming.

An even better place to go is to the numerous studies that schools, governments, and corporations did in the 1980s and early 1990s in order to provide a minimal showing of discrimination for their programs after the *City of Richmond v. Croson* (1989) case. Find the studies, try to get the transcripts of any hearings. Put all of this information into one comprehensive document in your jurisdiction. Link this information up with what professors have added in their research. Find court cases and claims of discrimination. Add them to the mix. Then finalize the analysis. In this way we will be fighting to save affirmative action for subsequent generations. In this way we will be quantifying our own history from jurisdiction to jurisdiction. This is another way of picking ourselves up by our own bootstraps. Consistent with the conservative practice of finding a Black mouthpiece for their anti-affirmative action movement, pro-affirmative action advocates should resort to proven White advocates like Tim Wise. Wise has traveled this country making a compelling case for affirmative action.

When making the case, I urge those supportive of us to use the report of Gunnar Myrdal entitled *An American Dilemma* (discrimination not communism is plaguing Black populations in the U.S.), the Riot Commission Report (discrimination not communism is the problem in Black communities), the Moynihan Report (warning that unemployment particularly of Black males was leading to the untying of the Black family), and the 1994 Civil Rights Commission Report (White privilege remains a problem in the U.S.). As a quick history to cite as a reference, employ multi-edition classics such as John Hope Franklin's *From Slavery to Freedom*. Franklin was the chair of the 1994 Civil Rights Report.

So, we need to make out our agenda and move public officials and corporate executives to promote affirmative action. We have to later sanction them should they fail to do so. Thus, affirmative action has to be on the outside agenda.

POLICING, INCARCERATING, AND DISENFRANCHISING

Another specific issue about which we have to be adamant is fairness in how the criminal laws are applied. If political science is supposed to ensure protocol, provision, and protection, then there is something amiss about how the country is ensuring that protection. It is as if the country has a vendetta against African Americans, or that they have decided to fix a social problem through incarcerating a healthy portion of a people. Protection brings us squarely to policing and to the over-representation of Blacks in U.S. jails. It is a problem of the first order in the U.S., and the Black diaspora. I think that the country should re-consider its abandonment of rehabilitation in favor only of retribution. This is a political problem.

If it was not clear before 2006, it surely became so by the close of it: the U.S. has become the most incarcerated industrialized country in the world. Black political leaders must lead an effort to change the structure funneling Black males, particularly, into the criminal justice system, and then diminishing their opportunities further from the point of their first brush with the law.

The fact that the U.S. is the most incarcerated industrialized society is not a good thing and has been traumatic on the Black community. This country has arrived at a place now where 2.2 million citizens are incarcerated as of this writing. About thirty percent of this number are African Americans. Blacks, then, are three times more represented in the criminal justice system than their numbers in the population. Tellingly, there are almost two times more Black males in prison than in college. In the state of Washington, the number is approaching three times more Black males incarcerated than in college. In Washington State, Blacks are incarcerated at 5 to 8 times their percentage of the population. This means that Washington, my state, is worse than Mississippi in how it incarcerates African Americans.

This has bloody ramifications in the Black community. A tremendous amount of labor income is removed from the community. A great amount of money is invested in attorneys and other legal costs. Children have to go significant stretches unable to be in a healthy relationship with their fathers; women go similar stretches without these men in their lives. Moreover, with a record, sometimes a lengthened one, women prefer to opt out of being in committed relationships with these men primarily because of their diminished earning capacity. These men leave prison more knowledgeable of criminal behavior than gainful employment. They also leave with diseases, not the least of which is HIV. It is a scourge on the community. It is especially so given the brilliance of many, if not most, of these men. Go to the prisons and speak with them; meet them when they return to the community: you will discover a mind with perceptive analytical ability. It is one of the great wastes of human talent going on in the world.

Finally, these men get out and find it hard going. With less opportunity and love from their families by virtue of having less to offer them, they turn back to crime with a vengeance. It has much to do with why the leading cause of death of Black men between 18 and 30 is homicide. Surely the ramifications are bloody. This affects Blacks worst, but does make its way outside of the Black community. Thus, it should be beyond clear that this is a costly, expensive, deadly travesty that the country needs to deal with. Whether they do so or not, Blacks have to; these are their fathers, sons, uncles, nephews, and cousins. How did we get here?

It had to do with Broken Windows policing especially Rudolph Giuliani style, the former mayor of New York City. It had to do with get tough policies of the conservatives, much, much more interested in retribution and restitution than in rehabilitation and reform. Punitive people gave us punitive laws: three strikes and you are out, truth in sentencing, weed and seed, life without parole, and for a time a 100:1 disparity in crack and powder cocaine sentencing. Punitive people then gave us punitive policing: SWAT teams, beefed-up patrols, controlling the point of encounter, dragnet surveillance, the right to frisk at street stops (called *Terry* stops), and the use of overwhelming force. Then there was the belief that at-risk communities require aggressive policing, tickets and arrests prove effective policing, discretion in charging used against at-risk communities, and when one officer discharges a weapon, all discharge.[2]

This is the cause of the greater incarcerating of Blacks. It is certain that this is so when one learns that most are in prison as a result of small amounts of illegal drugs that Blacks neither make nor import into their communities; it is doubly evident when one learns that studies suggest that Whites use illegal drugs at the same or a higher rate than Blacks. This is a political issue of massive proportions.

We need to change the laws that full-court-press our Black youngsters into jail. We need to equate, or hopefully lower, crack and powder cocaine sentencing laws. We have to end three strike laws and the death penalty, given its racially disparate application.

Also, we need to visit these people. They are human beings who are lonely and missing contact from the outside. Are there no spiritual leaders teaching all of society the importance of visiting the shut-in or locked-up? The closer we get to them, the closer we will be to the problems; the closer we get to the problem, the more likely we will craft solutions.

In terms of policing, we need true community policing, in which officers are not only known by the community, but listen to them. Of course, they need community involvement in enforcement. One hand has to help the other. We need more Black police officers doing this more sensitive community policing, although we have to watch them too. Black elders, most of which are senior women, have to become the chief enforcement officers even to the police. It was a Black under-cover cop who shot the Black young man in New York on the day before his wedding. These Black cops need to be re-connected to their own communities. Their selection and training is such that it makes these officers about as bad as those who are insensitive to Black rights and interests. This must change.

We have to change the culture of accumulating stop and arrest numbers in "high crime" communities. We need another measure for success. I believe that measure is the amount of crime itself. This is the only reasonable number to judge success. Another may be the number of people incarcerated. If the crime numbers stay the same, or dip slightly, but the incarceration rate has doubled, this is not a success—it is a failure.

In jail or prison, we need enrichment programs in addition to work for these inmates. They are human beings. Have not our spiritual leaders taught us that all of us have sinned and fallen short, and that each should be given a chance to repent and reform? Our jails and prisons have to be places of reformation.

Then, when these folks get out, there should be a lot of assistance helping them get decent shelter and a job. Their fines and costs should be small enough that they can start again and do well. Those that have to register as sex offenders should not be treated as "throw aways." People need a chance to win. So many of these ex-offenders are Black, that Black leaders should ensure the system helps such folks position themselves to become contributing citizens again.

This includes voting. Ex-offenders should receive their voting rights as soon as they have done their time. There should be no "ifs" or "buts" about it. We must demand this. Voting moves them to be more responsible across the board. Besides, they have done their hard time. That time was the real punishment. These extra burdens imposed have grown over time. 100 years ago people did not have to go through such a battle just to have their citizenship rights restored after serving their sentences. These are mostly segregation and Southern Strategy tactics aimed at keeping the unfortunate down.

Shame on the civil rights leaders in the felony disenfranchisement states, states that remove felon's voting rights altogether. We must advocate or agitate for them—whatever it takes to get the job done. They are the last and the least who cannot effectively advocate for themselves. We must be their voices. This is why criminal justice fairness is on the agenda.

REPARATIONS

You may have noticed that reparations is not on the agenda. Perhaps you wondered why I left it off. First, let me say that I want reparations, but I am not willing to invest a lot of time and energy to get them. I see getting reparations as a long shot; I do not like to invest a lot in long shots. I am glad that many in our community are blitzing for reparations; I just want us to give it the right priority. I ask that our best energies be saved for a plan like this one. I prefer to spend the lion's share of our resources on our picking ourselves up. With society barely willing to maintain affirmative action, it seems unlikely to me that it will give Blacks any significant reparations.

Having said this, I do commend the work of NCOBRA and of those jurisdictions that have required contractors to reveal whether they participated in or benefited from slavery. I likewise salute the work of other groups that support the efforts of NCOBRA. I particularly want to mention Yuri Kochiyama and Asian Americans who receive limited reparations for the Japanese internment during World War II. This is good work that promotes the larger interests of our people.

I hear the arguments of Whites like David Horowitz who, in his article "10 Reasons Against Reparations for Blacks," argues that this present generation of Blacks is not entitled to reparations because slavery and segregation injured past generations, and besides Blacks have received welfare. These arguments are an affront to those who believe as I do for, first, an injury uncompensated for in one generation follows the benefits conferred upon the next generation. The present Black generation followed the generation that experienced segregation, and the generation segregated against was not compensated for their injuries. The Black generations that suffered under segregation followed the generations that suffered under slavery—none of which were compensated. On the other hand, Whites and the country benefited from lower labor expenses on our exports and domestic goods. Finally, it is an embarrassment to propose that welfare, a program that provides subsistence assistance to the poor and mainly goes to poor Whites, is reparations for Blacks. Thankfully, Horowitz is nearly alone in this view.

Horowitz has a team of Blacks who assist him in advocating against reparations and affirmative action. Black mouthpieces like Shelby Steele (not the supportive Claud Steele, his brother), Clarence Thomas, Ward Connerly, Walter Williams, and Star Jones are more vociferous than are non-Blacks at waylaying programs that help Blacks. Curiously and hypocritically, some of them have benefited from affirmative action on their way to lambasting it. They burn the bridge they needed and walked across, in the face of those like them who yet need to cross. How could they do it?

With the establishment hardpressed to grant affirmative action, let alone reparations, and with a hardened corp of Black conservatives around them making their arguments vociferously for them, it will be very difficult if not impossible to recover meaningful reparations. We have wised up to the game and gone after progressive White advocates for us like Tim Wise, who powerfully presents the pro-affirmative action position. Yet, I still feel that should we get anything, it may not be enough to really matter. In fact, I wonder whether we sound pitiful, as if we are begging for reparations. I am reminded that not all money is good money. I do not like to beg. Perhaps we want to be like the Lakota Nation that has received its hundred plus million dollar judgment for the violation of the Fort Laramie Treaty, but has not taken the money. Their reason has to do with sovereignty; ours could be for pride.

I could go either way, though. If offered the compensatory resources, I will take them. Yet, I would not invest the lion's share of our assets in order to get such resources. I just want us to keep our eye on the big prize. No one can long take away nor claim credit for what we do for ourselves. Get reparations if you can; give your best efforts, though, to me in this great effort to save ourselves. This is why reparations are not on the agenda.

MAKING DISCRIMINATORS MOVE ON THIS PLAN

It irks me when I am in meetings in which Blacks give evidence of discrimination, and then do not know what to ask for adamantly. I have been in such meetings when Blacks asked for large sums and then settled for little to nothing. I have been in other meetings when we did not ask for anything specific and only got expressions of regret.

I am of the tribe that calculates a realistic damage accounting and then asks for this in a lump sum. If we do not get it, then it is back to points made earlier about a schedule of things that we will do to press our claim. I am of the belief though that we must be realistic in terms of what can be received. Sometimes even governments are cash starved, or are beset by constituencies that make lump sum payments political suicide for the officials that award them to Blacks. In such situations, I believe in asking for future contracts. Here we must have business savvy and ask for sufficient amounts. What do I mean?

Well, we must ask for amounts that are comparable to the damages we have sustained, and the fact that we are being paid in the future. So if those we are confident are discriminating against us cannot pay lump sums, then they can at least award us future contracts in an amount that pays a comparable amount in lost profits plus a premium. Get lump sums if you can; get contracts if you cannot.

This allows us to get the money, increase business goodwill, enhance bonding capacity, and generally grow our businesses. It is up to us to work these contracts in further ways that promote this plan, just as raised in the chapters on Economics: we have to hire Black workers and subcontractors, and use Black suppliers as we have historically. In this way, the money will circulate more times through the community.

Our political leaders have to be as astute as our economic leaders in achieving such settlements. Everyone has to be working from the same page. This includes the Black press doing investigative work, Black educators doing research, and Black politicians doing oversight so that the business and societal soil are turned over much more to uncover evidence of discrimination.

Incidentally, this is not to say that those who can prove discrimination should give their settlements over to the community. No, the contracts should go to the contractors damaged; the work should go to the workers denied. Moreover, if such contractors or workers can prove their cases, then they should pursue their remedies in the appropriate legal venues. The matters settled with community assistance should be those where a lawsuit is too expensive for the parties or the evidence is not readily available.

STOPPING THE SOUTHERN STRATEGY

Political leaders are needed to help the rest of Black America with a major strategy that has secretly, stealthily worked against us. Here we leave discussion of the outside of the community agenda in order to discuss what we need in order to put our political house in order. First, we need to figure out the nature of the political attack against us. Let me put this in its larger perspective: What is showing starkly is that America has manipulated Blacks through three systems. They are these: slavery, segregation, and the "Southern Strategy." Incidentally, it has helped Blacks with two systems: Reconstruction and racial preferences (affirmative action). The manipulative systems have been hard and long; the help, mild and short.

In the past, our political approaches targeted the heart of slavery and segregation. Our approach these days is not targeted at the Southern Strategy. We are ignorant of it, confused about it, or dismissive of it—all of which has hurt us. We must change this. If we are going to be politically empowered, then we must know about, understand, and respect how the Southern Strategy has hurt us. As we do, we must work to change it. So, I introduce to some, and present to others, a system that is undermining Black America whether you know it or not: the Southern Strategy.

During the 2000 Republican National Convention the Republicans clearly divulged that they would stop doing something the average scholar was not sure they had ever begun. The Bush campaign said that they were disavowing the "Southern Strategy." The Southern Strategy is a plan to get southern Whites to join Strom Thurmond in leaving the Democrats and joining the Republican Party, in return for Thurmond's guiding southern Whites into the leadership in the Republican Party. Once in leadership, the southern officials could influence policy in a Jim Crow way so long as it did not look Jim Crow on its face.

Here is how the Southern Strategy came to be. Since the beginning, racist Whites had a home in the Democrat Party, not the Republican Party. During the Roosevelt and Truman administrations, the Democrat Party began to civilize the language of the party in its official documents, making a break from its long racist past. It even added the words "civil rights" to its platform in 1948. The Democrats were hoping to bring the party into the post-Hitler era, broaden the party's national appeal, all without losing its southern support. The South had long been the Democrat's base. The policies of Franklin Roosevelt and Harry Truman had softened Black support for the Republicans, who were not doing anything for them anyway beyond token appointments. For the first 100 years of its existence, the Republican Party had African Americans as part of its reliable base because of Abraham Lincoln. But as fate would have it, John F. Kennedy called Coretta S. King around October of 1960 to convey his concern about the incarceration of her husband, the Rev. Dr. Martin Luther King, Jr. The news fanned through the Black press like wildfire. It led to Blacks doing the unthinkable: they began to vote Democrat. It was a boon for the Republican Party and an albatross around the necks of the Democrats. The Republicans saw their opportunity.

From 1932 to 1964, the Republicans lost the presidency 6 out of 8 times. No one needed to tell them that they had to fundamentally change their electoral approach. The largest block of votes they continually wrote off was in the South. Becoming president means winning 270 of the 438 possible Electoral College votes. The core southern states (North Carolina, South Carolina, Georgia, Tennessee, Mississippi, Alabama, Arkansas, and Louisiana) comprise about 80 votes, almost one third of the number needed to win. If Texas and Florida join the core South, then the number rises to over 130, almost half of the winning margin. The Democratic Party gained Blacks nationally, but lost Whites in the South. One of the plans the Republicans hatched in 1968 (if not 1964) was the Southern Strategy.

The strategy required watchwords, symbolic actions, and a person behind the curtain to lead Southern Democrats to the Republican Party. It was all carefully nuanced and secret, this strategy. But it had its watchwords: 'federalism' instead of the longstanding "states' rights" language, "personal responsibility" rather than "get in your place," and later "freedom" rather than "White rule."

Additionally, there were regular acts to continue signaling that the strategy was in place. In other words, Republicans made symbolic overtures heavily laden with southern appeal: visiting Confederate sites, supporting the Daughters of the American Revolution, or spurning Jesse Jackson. This was necessary in order to show the average southerner that it was better to listen to Thurmond and join the Republicans then to heed Alabama Governor George Wallace who was trying to form a third party or follow Robert Byrd who stayed a Democrat.

Then there was the person behind the curtain. While the ideas behind the plan may have come from conservative thinker Kevin Phillips, the hard work of accomplishing the plan required a southerner with Confederate appeal and political gravitas: that man was former-Democrat-turned-Republican Strom Thurmond. Thurmond opposed racial mixing, racial equality, and had grown to loathe the party of his heritage for not being staunchly against these things. Thurmond was a military man with long southern roots. He was in perhaps the most southern of southern states—South Carolina, the state whose residents were the first to fire on union troops. Thurmond also was a recognized politician of bold language and actions. When Thurmond saw that his Democratic Party was going to vote in favor of putting the words "civil rights" in the 1948 platform, Thurmond bolted from that year's party campaign, formed his own organization, and ran a protest presidential campaign calling his party the "Dixiecrats." He won over 30 Electoral College votes; neither the Green nor the Libertarian Parties have won 1 Electoral College vote. Thurmond officially became a Republican in 1964. Why did Thurmond join in 1964?

Southerners had a type of alliance for about 100 years with Rocky Mountain states members of Congress. Members from the Rockies needed help from the national government in order to establish viable new states: they needed federal troops to protect them from the Native Americans; they needed recognition of their land claims to perfect their property rights; and they needed government-supported infrastructure projects—railroads, waterworks and the like—to support town establishment. With so few votes they had to build a coalition. Similarly, the southerners needed help as well. Although their numbers were larger than the Rocky Mountain states, the southerners did not have sufficient votes on their own to get the northerners to leave them alone so that they could be free to re-establish their Civil War torn way of life. It just so happened that an alliance formed. On a number of occasions in the Congress, the Southern members voted those in the Rocky Mountain states the governmental assistance they needed, and the Rocky Mountain state members, in turn, voted to keep the national government out of the racist business of the South. It is interesting that up to the writing of this book, the base of the Republicans is the South and the Rocky Mountain states.

It is interesting that Thurmond joined the Republican Party in 1964. For this was the year the Republicans selected a man from the southern Rockies for president: Senator Barry Goldwater. Goldwater was a friend and colleague of Thurmond's. He was also from the right region. It was such an odious thing for a southerner to join the party of Lincoln that many elements had to converge in order for southerner like Thurmond to make the party leap. This was especially difficult given that Dwight D. Eisenhower had signed the Civil Rights Act of 1957 and signaled that he would enforce *Brown v. Board of Education,* if necessary. Still Thurmond joined the party. The necessary elements had come together. What they wanted was the South while holding on to their other gains. How they would get it was through the Southern Strategy and its three parts: the language, symbolism, and a conductor.

Richard Nixon successfully ran, in part, a three-pronged Southern Strategy campaign in 1968. He was assisted by then racist Alabama governor George Wallace running as an independent, something that cut more against the Democrats than the Republicans. The strategy worked like a charm. In order to win in 1972, Nixon had to have a Southern Strategy presidency upon which to campaign. He did, and he won. The strategy now had a formidable record. Then came Watergate, a Republican setback.

In 1980, Reagan was smart; he employed a plan that had a track record. As part of his overall plan, Reagan found the Southern Strategy and used it to a 'T.' He put southerners on the inside of his campaign staff. He launched his campaign in the South; in Philadelphia, Mississippi, the place where the three civil rights workers were killed. He visited Bob Jones University, known for its policy against interracial relationships. That brought symbolism. And somewhere behind the scenes, Thurmond was working over time. Thurmond was rewarded handsomely: he became the number two Republican in the Senate; then he ascended to minority leader. When the Republicans won the majority in the Senate in 1995, Strom Thurmond became the President Pro Temporary of the Senate. It is the highest regular office in the Senate and the fourth person in the line of presidential succession.

The behind-the-scenes conductor of the Southern Strategy had arrived. He was a power-wielder in the upper house of Congress. He had brought the majority of southerners in national office to the Republican Party. He had moved the party to focus on the South. Clemson University has an institute in honor of Strom Thurmond. As of this writing, on the site Thurmond is recognized as one of the "architects of the Southern Strategy." And that he is.

Blacks never figured out what was going on, although many knew that something was afoot. We had no surveillance. We did not turn to Black conservatives who may have known. We could not crack the code. We were too confident in our new-found gains. We were too superficial in our approach to politics. It is now clear, looking back on it, that Blacks were pawns in a game bigger than they, being played by pieces more capable than they. At just the point that Blacks had gained a modicum of political power, a strategy was hatched to neutralize that power; and it worked like a pharaoh's amulet. The leaders' and scholars' inability to out the ruse cost the mass of Black people dearly at the moment of our liberation, at the border of our promised land. I, and those like me, failed the people. Interestingly, the Democrats were struggling in the game as well.

I said the strategy was carefully crafted and quietly executed. It was hard to see, but no less hard on its targets. If slavery was simply and blatant, and if segregation was more complex and downplayed, the Southern Strategy was utterly complex and covert. I can remember my Dad describing the ploys southern Whites used to take Black land as selling us the "trick bag": the bag that was not as deep on the inside as it looked by all appearances on the outside. As more southerners moved into positions of power, it became clear that the Southern Strategy has turned out to be the mother of all trick bags. The rhetoric of the plan promised freedom for all who were personally responsible under the watchful eye of a humbled federal government. It delivered governmental program cutting, increased blue collar immigration, blue collar wage decreases, union busting, stricter criminal laws, beefed up policing; all of which led to higher Black male unemployment, the end of the decrease in Black poverty, slower Black upward mobility, a decrease in Black marital rates, and a higher percentage of Blacks incarcerated. It was not Jim Crow in name, but it was Jim Crow in effect.

I missed it too. I saw such measures as anti-civil rights but not as a continuation of the Southern Strategy. There was simply too little information on the strategy, and it was still too hard to clarify. Although the plan had been in place since 1968, I taught college students throughout the 1990s about slavery and segregation. I said nothing of the Southern Strategy. I had no significant or reliable information on it.

So back in 2000 Bush was confessing, sort of repenting for a public sin to an unsuspecting people. With more ethnic diversity on stage than in the convention center, the Bush campaign signaled that they were breaking from the secret racial playbook that the Republicans operated from over the last three decades. They had Colin Powell on stage pledged to help them, making their repentance seem even more sincere. But did the Republicans change; did they repent? I took Bush at his word.

I admit it; they fooled me again. Since 2000 and Bush's admission, I had seen the Southern Strategy as something the Republicans were finally admitting to because they had disavowed it. I remained in this ignorance even after then Majority Leader Trent Lott recognized Strom Thurmond at Thurmond's 100th birthday party in terms that broke the code of the strategy. In a moment of rare public candor, Lott said, "If the country had listened to you in 48, we would not have had all the trouble we had." Bush and the Republicans removed Lott, and then appointed a very conservative judge to the Federal circuit; they put a wreath on King's tomb and then submitted a brief against affirmative action. The pattern of Attwater's coaching of Reagan and Rove with Bush in the primaries became vivid: give African Americans something symbolic while taking away something substantial.

Then came the 2006 election. During it, the Republicans ran a couple of race-baiting ads in close elections. Just when Harold Ford was turning the corner in Tennessee's Senate race, they ran an ad at the end of which a blonde woman came on and asked Ford to "call her." This still triggers anti-miscegenation (inter-racial relationships) sentiment. Ford lost by a couple of points. Then the Republicans picked Trent Lott again as their number two person in the Senate. Articles began to appear to the effect that the Republicans need to return to the Reagan strategy in order to counterbalance the Democratic landslide. I did not need to see or read any more. I know now that the only place for Republicans to go is to what has worked for them, and what they know well. They are going, at least partly, back to the Southern Strategy. In fact, I really believe Bush never left it. One could argue, furthermore, that Bill Clinton and the Democratic Leadership Conference did a soft form of the Southern Strategy during Clinton's years as president.

It is all secret, nuanced, and carefully crafted. Unless writers, scholars, and activists explain and out this strategy, we will see more of the same. This is a closeted racist strategy. There are no two ways about it. History will reveal it as such. I, however, do not have time to wait for history to iron out the wrinkles and to parse out the double-speak. I will be dead by the time everything is outed generations later. I want to be part of this generation leading a movement to unmask and destroy this system, as we did to the other two. We have been hoodwinked; why continue to be? The Southern Strategy was hatched as a political tactic for the benefit of a party and at the expense of a people; now it is time for Black political leaders to lead Black people, and the entire civil rights community, to expose this system for what it is, and the party that used it to benefit themselves.[2]

So, we have to stop the Southern Strategy. It is incumbent on us to do to it what our forbears did to slavery and segregation. Their job was harder because they were smaller, with less, and without much of a history of victory. Our job is easier by virtue of being larger, with more, and we have their shining example to inspire us onward. We are on the precipice of something great. First, though, we have to handle our political business: we have to break up something that has bound us. Are you ready?

SOURCES OF BLACK LEADERSHIP AND ITS SUCCESSION

We must develop a way to have leadership continuity despite the fact that leaders will come and go. This requires succession and leadership development. Developing new leaders is a priority that involves programming and resources.

So I ask, "Where will the leaders come from to keep us moving forward on our comprehensive plan?" These leaders will have to come mainly from established Black associations, somewhat from governmental organizations, and occasionally from youth groups. First, established Black associations provide the community leaders who have been tested and have demonstrated a measure of leadership. It helps the leadership of our community that these leaders have not had to be reliant on interests outside of the Black community. It is also of assistance to us that they have served in the very associations that are needed to knit us together. Obviously our associations are not quite a government, but they can help us govern ourselves.

We have to be honest, realistic, and fair about this: much if not most of the leadership will come from the pastors whether we like it or not. We cannot go around them; we have to come through them. For they influence the people more than anyone else. Moreover, their skills are such that they are going to impel or impede the movement, given their oratorical gifts. The churches will be largely needed in the implementation, which means again having to deal with their pastors. And why should they not be influential: they are tasked with promoting the kind of moral suasion that makes a people fit for self-determination and with speaking the kind of truth to power that forces even superpower governments to listen. Surely, our leaders will mostly be on loan from established Black associations. Of these folks, few are better position to offer leadership than the pastors, or their qualified designees.

The next place from which we can get leaders are from the ranks of those who have led entities in the larger community. Former public officials, business executives, directors of non-profit organizations, and officers in the military all can have superior management ability. They, along with the associational leaders, are the most experienced leaders the Black community has. The challenge with these folks may have more to do with their commitment to serve Black interests exclusively. For some to do this it may mean that they may never be able to lead in the larger community again. It is a test of one's love for the community to be able to serve to this degree.

Finally, comes the group of emerging younger people who do not have an associational title. There is a lot to be said for experience, and generally speaking, we will need to rely on those individuals who have proven they can collaboratively direct people in the people's best interest. Still, we have to provide a healthy place for the younger generation and for emerging talent. It is in the mix of the older and the younger leading together that we best serve all of the people. Although King was an associational leader at the time, we must remember that he was younger than 26 when Montgomery called on him to lead the Bus Boycott. That is pretty young.

We will need to spot students and adults who want to serve the people from these areas. They need classes on serving the people. The reading list for these classes merges with the reading necessary to help launch this effort from the beginning. Recall that I said earlier that before calling the leaders together we first need to launch reading groups to prepare the air for community development. The emerging leadership as well as the reading groups to prepare our people for action should both select from the following works:

LEADERSHIP DEVELOPMENT READING

Martin Luther King's *Where Do We Go from Here?*
Claud Anderson's *Powernomics*
Tavis Smiley's *The Covenant*
Dr. Khalid Abdullah Al-Mansour's *Betrayal by Any Other Name*
William Julius Wilson's *The Bridge Over the Racial Divide*
Tony Brown's *Black Lies, White Lies*
Carl Livingston's, *Shoestrings and Bootstraps*
Amy Garvey's *Marcus Garvey*
Oba T'Shaka's *Great Black Leaders*

The leaders to be should master the above readings. In addition to doing the book work, they should do the leg work. They need to shadow those doing the work so that they can learn firsthand. They need tokens to encourage them to continue serving the community. Some will need grants and scholarships in order to get the proper degrees with which to better serve. They should be encouraged to work outside of development for a time so that they can get their financial legs underneath them, as well as gain life experience. They may need job assistance so that they are not struggling to make it while giving their life for the people. Such is a recipe for indiscretion and graft. We owe new leaders more than that.

NAACP AND BLACK ATTORNEYS

The legal beagles are crucial to Black political advancement. We need them to help us enforce our plan outside of our community and to help protect our interests when we are being discriminated against or harassed. Sometimes we will need to bring suit, or at least a brief signaling that we might sue, to give to those in power. The NAACP can help uniquely with this effort. Besides, if those outside of our community are held to supporting the plan, then surely every group that purports to exist to help the Black community must support the plan as well. This especially includes traditional groups that have a lot of goodwill in the larger community as a result of their heritage and their dual membership of Blacks and non-Blacks together. I am speaking of groups like the NAACP and the Urban League.

During the best of times, the NAACP has brought suits that have done what its name represents: advanced Black people. This tradition must be made new. It need not work alone. Every major city has a Black bar association that should assist. In Seattle, that group is called the Loren Miller Bar Association, named after a person who devoted his time to serving the legal interests of Blacks. Communities must raise more funds for their local NAACP so that its attorneys can regularly bring claims of the aggrieved against those wrongfully causing them grief, rather than turning most of them away. Supplemental community resources should come in the form of help from the local Black bar association. With the local Black bar assisting, the NAACP should bring some of these matters to trial and appeal, if necessary, to serve Black interests legally.

I need to state something here that may first seem a little shocking: neither the NAACP nor the Urban League should lead the effort to bring the Black renaissance. This is especially so at the state and national levels. I am sure that many of those reading this will be taken aback by this statement. Am I against the NAACP or the Urban League? Do I not understand their unique and indispensable contributions to African American progress?

Well, I am not against either organization. In fact, I have been a member of the local NAACP. I have supported Urban League events, and I will continue to do so. My point here has nothing to do with animus against these fine organizations. Instead, I am clarifying from the beginning that the leadership has to be Black led. Only organizations that are led and funded by Blacks should be in the leadership inner circle of the movement to bring a renaissance to Black America, in every area.

Both the NAACP and the Urban League are stellar organizations that bring Blacks and non-Blacks together in ways to support Black interests. Neither is presently or historically exclusively Black, especially at the national level. For its part, the NAACP, the oldest of the two, was the brainchild of Blacks and mainly Jewish Americans who were appalled at the lynchings of Blacks and the system of segregation against them. The Whites in the organization were not as exercised as the Blacks were about Black poverty, but they were generally against it too.

Likewise, the Urban League was an organization of Blacks and non-Blacks determined to improve the economic and social plight of minorities, especially Blacks. These two groups are thus helpful bridge associations.

Yet, neither the Urban League nor the NAACP were big supporters of Martin Luther King. Certain leaders in the NAACP claim that the NAACP did more than Martin Luther King to end segregation. Some even deign to say King did nothing that directly ended segregation; while every case that the NAACP brought tolled the death knell for the Jim Crow beast. They seem to downplay the importance of the civil rights movement, the Civil Rights Acts, and how the former caused the latter. In fact, after the *Brown v. Board of Education* case, one has to labor to find another case that the NAACP brought that made a significant difference, and *Brown* was in 1954.

Certain establishment groups maintain a presence on the NAACP board, and especially in the Urban League. This gives them a look of diversity and it gives these groups needed, needed funds. When either the NAACP or the Urban League are moving to make change on a grand scale it can upset establishment interests. These interests may threaten to withhold funds, or actually do so. Moreover, certain establishment individuals who are on the board of either of these groups, or are in other positions of influence, may threaten to or actually resign. As we saw in the matter with Ben Chavez, as soon as what is perceived as a misstep occurs, say being too strident in what they want to do for the community or linking with associations seen as too militant, then the institutional money leaves the organization. These become ways in which interests outside of our community try to influence what happens inside of our community.

It is going to be hard enough trying to lead our large and opinionated people without outside influence. If we add to the equation trying to develop a plan or to carry out a plan to the satisfaction of those outside our community as well, then it is likely we will not end up doing anything to improve greatly our people's condition. This is the main reason why I want my people to know that we have to have the assistance of these premier organizations, but we will complicate everything we are trying to do if we make them the umbrella group.

Besides, we have had both of these great organizations in place, and since 1968, the year of the death of Martin Luther King, both of them have brought hundreds of millions of dollars of value into the Black communities of this country to their credit. However, over the past forty or more years neither of these organizations have brought the renaissance that Blacks need. This is not an indictment; it is just a fact. We must understand the purpose of organizations and keep them in the center of it.

Well, since this plan calls for local planning and action, why not use the local NAACP or Urban League as the base, or as the main leaders? Although the local branches are often almost entirely all Black, the national organization oversees and can supersede the local branches. Therein lies the rub. Also, some of the local branches are not Black organizations; they are wonderfully integrated ethnically.

So then does this mean that I am proposing that only Blacks can help Blacks? No. Some non-Blacks who are Black in culture and connection can and should be on the umbrella committee. For the most part, though, this comprehensive leadership committee must look like the people for which it exists to sacrifice. Still, I recognize that certain non-Blacks, including Whites, have done legions more to help Blacks than the average Black, and that certain Blacks have hurt the interests of Blacks in general—such as Clarence Thomas. Yes, I understand this.

Some may ask whether I am a racist? No, I am not a racist. I thoroughly understand that non-Blacks have helped make the difference in our advancement and that a host of Blacks have crippled our interests. Yet, we are not talking about an average association. This is the, *the* organization that will lead the local renaissance of Black people. The leadership of this organization has to be singular in its aim to do just that. It has to have exclusive allegiance to the people it deigns to develop.

Let all of our other associations and organizations be open and inclusive. However, demand that this one umbrella leadership be made up exclusively of those whose hearts are invested singularly in the development of Black people. Whatever safeguards we put in place, the umbrella group will still have outside interests. For it will be infiltrated, surveiled, and greatly pressured from outside. Yet we must do everything we can to help it be unshakable in its effective service of our people. Non-Blacks will be represented at the leadership meetings anyway, for there will always be those African Americans who will look as though they are representing the interests of their own people, but who in reality are just conduits for those outside of the community to use to do whatever they want. These folks will be reporting everything, will be voting like others want, and doing what they can to prosper themselves at the expense of their own people. Non-Blacks will be up front and center in the innermost circle through them—and that's enough.

Besides, if we need others to come in to help us direct how we will pick ourselves up by our bootstraps, then maybe we are not yet ready to be so picked up. Finally, all those who will clamor that this is separatist, discriminatory, or racist, go look at the other groups like Jewish, Vietnamese, and Cuban Americans. Go find their master plans they used to make major progress, particularly early on. Go see who was at these most sensitive and crucial meetings. I am willing to bet it was solely people who looked like them at the innermost level.

And guess what? Our motives will be so pure and our aims so fair that it will not matter. So it really does not matter whether non-Blacks are there in person or in Black face, if you know what I mean. This is the benefit of being right from the beginning. On the other hand, at the meetings of other groups that have put plans together, part of which included exploiting and using us, real Blacks were not even allowed in. This is the challenge of the development of what France Fanon called the "wretched of the earth."

FLETCHER – JACKSON

We need a standard to which to hold those Blacks in government. I have just the thing: First, Arthur Fletcher was an excellent public official, and he was a Republican. He served Richard Millhouse Nixon as Assistant Secretary of Labor. He was the architect and the builder of the Philadelphia Plan that launched the most lucrative part of affirmative action: government set-asides. He was known as an expert on the Civil Rights Acts of 1964 and 1968 and counseled those who would listen to pursue Title V with the same resolve with which we championed Title VII. Arthur Fletcher may have done more for African Americans than any other African American public official. His contribution was not in talk; it was in action.

Second, Maynard Jackson was the former mayor of Atlanta, and a Democrat. He finally steered federal and state funds to Atlanta and built a first-class airport with them. But he did much more than this for African Americans. Jackson made sure that African Americans received their fair share of the contracts and jobs. The impact of the airport project did more than beautify and enhance the infrastructure of greater Atlanta. It was a boon for Black Atlanta, as well as the rest of Atlanta. Securing for Blacks their fair share meant that not millions, but hundreds of millions of dollars in time would circulate into Black households. This is using one's position to make a positive difference.

These two gentleman—one a Republican, and the other a Democrat—must serve as the model for all Black public servants. Fletcher-Jackson leadership is the kind that brings net improvement to the community. It helps a community achieve its 10% real growth. It is about outcomes, ladies and gentlemen. What legacy is one leaving his or her people? I say, "Make sure each official is held to the Fletcher-Jackson test."

Inside and outside of the community, leaders must do better, much better, to support the interests of their Black members. Serving as a leader should mainly be about sacrificing for the community. It should not be about dictatorship, self-serving, or inaction. Let me say, though, that the leaders who serve the people should receive respect and honor.

We have had a host of leaders whose service has been suspect in the critical hour of testing. They were like Colin Powell and Condoleeza Rice doing press conferences on behalf of the Bush Administration as to why the administration would not be joining the Durban Conference on the global discrimination against indigenous and minority peoples, as they shielded a President who for years refused to meet with the leaders of the NAACP. Powell deserves credit for twice standing up in favor of affirmative action in Republican conventions. Still, given his inability to stop the Bush Administrations whittling of affirmative action and his spokesperson role for the administration not participating in the Durban conference on international racism, Powell's legacy under Bush is one that is on balance against his people. Powell and Rice were like Ohio Secretary of State Ken Blackwell who, it is reputed, was complicit in the efforts of the Ohio leadership to dilute the Black vote in the 2004 presidential election. For his part, Clarence Thomas benefited from affirmative action at Yale Law School but worked at the bequest of the Reagan administration to log-jam the discrimination cases while at the Equal Employment Opportunity Commission. Although these are examples of Blacks serving Republican administrations which, admittedly, Blacks have less influence in, certain Blacks serving Democratic administrations have at times been as bad. I submit that these leaders do not pass the Fletcher-Jackson test.

DEMOCRAT AND REPUBLICAN PARTIES

Politics is about parties. Political leaders have to help the rest of Black America understand this. As boring as they may seem, parties run countries everywhere, as they are the groups that put people into power and then work to keep them there. In fact, every government is really not so much its documents facing you, but a party in power holding the reigns. Sometimes the party in power goes by the documents, and sometimes they do what they want to do. The Republican and Democrat parties run the U.S. and put people into the greatest power in the world. Until the mid-year elections in 2006, it had mainly been the Republicans running the U.S. from 1980. So, our plan has to deal with the parties. In neither of these parties do things look that favorable for Blacks.

In fact, I am convinced that the Democrat Party has failed African Americans, whereas the Republican Party long ago abandoned us. As a result, I join those who advocate for African Americans not to continue to give the Democrat Party 90% of our vote; vote for the Green and Independent Parties until either Democrats come around or the Republicans come back to us. This needs to be a major part of our political approach. Let me explain.

For our longer period of voting as a people, Blacks voted against the Democrat Party, the party of the slavers. Having issued the Emancipation Proclamation, outfitted Black troops to fight in the Civil War, and met with Frederick Douglass three times, Lincoln captured the African American heart; his party became their party. Time would show, however, that what was thought to be regard for African Americans who were largely in the South was really the desire for revenge against White southerners. When the desire for revenge abated, the regard for Blacks proved non-existent. (except for the "Radical Republicans").

Starting in 1877, Republicans made their peace with segregation, would not push through anti-lynching laws, and only placed a few Blacks in token positions, such as Frederick Douglass as ambassador to Haiti and Ralph Bunche as part of the U.S. delegation to the United Nations (and that was probably upon the prompting of Eleanor Roosevelt).

After winning, Ronald Wilson Reagan brought his people into office, removed a bevy of non-Whites from positions of power, log-jammed the civil rights cases, slashed inner-city program funding, proscribed Black contracting (by relaxing the monitoring of affirmative action set asides), and generally signaled to America that a new anti-union, anti-affirmative action, anti-environmentalist, anti-welfare, anti-feminist sheriff was in town.

Half the country was not voting—the half that is very progressive; the half that voted was moderate, but leaning conservative; Republicans had captured them; Democrats were just waking up to the fact. Since 1980, the party of Abraham Lincoln has been the most successful at winning elections in America, winning by turning against Lincoln's values and the people the Civil War was mainly about. The party of Lincoln had thrown Blacks overboard and had in the process gained many more new passengers in their ship.

The Democrats would not win the presidency from 1964 through 1992 unless there was some kind of national calamity (i.e., JFK assassination or Watergate). Southern and Rocky Mountain Democrats led others in the party in figuring this out and forming within the Democrat Party the Democrat Leadership Council (DLC). The DLC advocated the Democrats distancing themselves from the National Organization of Women, unions, environmentalists, and Black groups without losing their vote. Like former lovers that agreed to simply be good friends, the Democrats needed space from their most loyal groups. The aim was to show southerners and White males that this party was not beholden to these four groups, and had moved closer to the "center." In time, William Jefferson (Bill) Clinton became a leader in this effort.

Bill Clinton won the presidency in 1992. In his campaign, Clinton picked Jackson's campaign manager as his own, but kept Jackson away. Clinton went after Sister Souljah and had his campaign explain that he was a new kind of Democrat. Clinton explained the need to reform welfare. All of this was before he got in office. It was becoming clear that the DLC and Clinton had learned from the Republicans and their Southern Strategy. Given that the Southern Strategy is in the evil pantheon of slavery and segregation, this means that the Democrats were flirting with a closeted racist strategy. The Republicans mastered it, and the Democrats were learning from them.

Alas, after a healthy dose of Ronald Wilson Reagan and George Herbert Walker Bush, Blacks saw Clinton as the best they could do. Clinton at least brought much more diversity to positions of power, promoted civil rights enforcement, and spoke in favor of affirmative action. He selected the first Black Secretary of the Treasury and of Agriculture. He likewise picked a number of Black judges. With more of an interest in diversity in a rising economy, the Black middle class grew a bit, and Black homeownership grew a lot. Some were so smitten with him they dubbed him the "first Black President." However, we need to evaluate things more dispassionately.

Let the facts be conveyed to a candid world: When Clinton got into office, welfare was reformed to remove most longstanding recipients from the roles; this hit Blacks the hardest. Police presence in "at risk" communities was expanded as a dragnet in "high crime" areas; this struck Blacks the meanest. Criminal laws were toughened to impose tough sentences on offenders; this hurt Blacks the most. While about a third of Blacks made great gains, the larger two-thirds languished. All of this made it clear that the Democrats had truly distanced themselves from groups like Blacks despite the positions given Blacks and the good faith attempts to preserve affirmative action, which continued its slow demise. Perhaps this was the best we could do, but it was hardly the kind of record to celebrate as good, or as "Black." I am hoping that Blacks wake up to the fact that it was an attempt to move the Democrat Party a couple of degrees towards the Southern Strategy, a strategy the Republicans have moved every degree towards.

What happened at the national level was repeated at the state level. The sum of the story is that federal politics have been tough to and on Blacks since their fabled desegragation. Most of the Black poor experienced no improvement in their lot since 1970. The Black prison rate has almost tripled, as has the Black murder rate. Washington, D.C., still has no voting representative in either house of the Congress, a chocolate city the size of Seattle being treated like foreigners. The Republicans say they are for democracy, but giving democracy to the District would add votes to the Democrats, so they refuse to do it. Curiously, the Democrats do not advocate for the District either, despite the fact that it will help their numbers in the Congress.

Blacks have the highest rate of contraction of HIV. Given all that we are facing and that fact that we are the Democrats' most reliable voting block, one would think that the Democrats would devise a plan of development for Blacks like it would tackle any national emergency. For this loyalty, we should be at the top of their agenda. Instead, we get from the Democrats what the Republicans gave us when they made their peace with Southerners after the Reconstruction: token Black appointments, an attempt to hold on to the programs in place, allowing local leaders to pretty much do what they want to Blacks, and no new national strategies. Could it be that all of this reveals how much the Democrats are still flirting with the Southern Strategy?

Can you see now that one party abandoned Blacks and the other failed us? As a result, Blacks have lost ground relative to most every other groups in this country. Now, Blacks are positioned in one of those unenviable places: the Republicans do not really want us as, and the Democrats do not know what to do with us. Hence, most of us do not know what to do or where to go politically.

Well, I know where we should go. We should make our case to every party, and not be too tied to any party. We should venture over to the Democrats first, but to any party next if the Democrats will not fairly include us in policymaking and resource distribution. We can afford to listen to any party tell us that they want to do more but that doing so would hurt them in presidential elections.[3]

Thus, the Democrats have failed us. Consequently, Blacks need to present their agenda and meet with any party that is viable both at the local and the national levels. We have to be this sophisticated and this engaged in our own political empowerment. With our vote and our pennies, we must strongly support those who support us, and strongly sanction those who sanction us. Thus, our outside of the community plan, and particularly our meetings with candidates around our agenda, must reach Democrats, Republicans, and third parties.

BLACK REPUBLICANS AND DEMOCRATS: CONCERN ABOUT THE NEW CONSERVATIVES

I am not against Black conservatism as a matter of conscious and ideology. I am against those who are really not doing anything to pick-up our community as they are doing to take away the programs that were aimed at picking us up. Clarence Thomas, Shelby Steele (not the supportive Claud Steele, his brother), Ward Connerly (a Black who was being paid to say what Bush wanted on education), Walter Williams, Star Jones have done much, much more to take away programs that would help us. They have done desperately, desperately little to build us up.

It is for this reason that I support Booker T. Washington. It could successfully be argued that he was a Black conservative. Yet, he built Tuskegee and launched other initiatives that helped Blacks in major ways. I think he set us back a bit by directing Blacks away from law, politics, and the like. Still, the goodness of his motives were proven by his fruit, fruit that trained a generation in ways that helped them gain a foothold in society.

Black liberals (or Progressives) are those who believe that a larger government is needed to provide programs that businesses will not, or cannot, provide their workers.

There are capitalist and socialist solutions to problems. Each has its benefits and detriments. Each can fit the bill, and it is really a mixture of both that is what governments around the world are settling on as the most workable choice. It seems to me that the real answer to what ails us is not even ideology; it is heart. If people's hearts are right and they are committed to solving the problem, almost any idea will work. Conservatives can solve our problems. In fact, my ideas are very capitalistic specifically because we are in a capitalist country. It could be argued that in this regard I am conservative.

So my issue with Black conservatives comes down to their commitment to better the Black community. Blacks should have seen that commitment in three different ways. First, Black conservative should be involved in large-scale private initiatives to rebuild the Black community. This is what Booker T. Washington and Arthur Fletcher were doing. While engaged in such work, they should have steered corporate money into the Black community, the very corporations that their connections have gained them favor with.

Second, Black conservatives should have helped Blacks with a comprehensive plan that was capitalist in its core, like this one. Then they should have explained with models how Blacks could build themselves by their own initiatives, with Black conservative assistance. Such grand endeavors do not happen at a distance, or in an arm's length way; Blacks need to see that those who are giving them advice are willing to get involved in the trenches with them. Lastly, Black conservatives should have discovered the Southern Strategy and revealed it to Black America. This is the very strategy hatched by those in the party in which Black conservatives are.

Hence, my problem with conservatives like Clarence Thomas and the rest is not so much their ideology as it is their hearts. Their hearts seem to be more in "getting over" than in helping their people "get over." These folks cannot pass the Fletcher – Jackson test of leadership. These people do not have the people's interests at heart. As a result, I have a problem with Black conservatives, but not so much with conservatism. I could never do what I see them doing. Anyone doing this must be outed. Moreover, we must let those who use them as cover know in no uncertain terms that employing these folks is really anti-diversity, and we take this personally.

Incidentally, I have problem with Black progressives, as well, who do not serve the interests of the people. Speak to Black officials who do not serve Black interests. We have to demand more of Black conservatives and progressives. We have to hold them both accountable. We have to oppose them if they do not support what we are about. They may stay in position, but it should be clear that they do not represent the interests of those behind the plan.

On the other hand, we have to be reasonable. We must know that they need to represent their entire constituency. This means, especially in a city of Seattle's demographic, that they must mostly represent non-Blacks. The problem has been that our politicians have not given us our fair share of representation. They further have not acted as if the Black community is their heart and soul, such that they have an underlying determination to fix our problems from their great mental faculties, social abilities, and positional amenities.

Well it is a new day now. The old way is over. It is time for accountability and delivery for all people, particularly Blacks delivering for Blacks. About some things we have to be certain: this is one.

COALITION BUILDING

When one is in the minority, one has to link with others in order to have more influence. After preparing an agenda, we will have to devise an effective strategy to deliver on it. This requires coalition building.

With a tad less than 14% of the population, African Americans are in the minority in the U.S. As a result, we must link with Latino, Asian, and Native Americans in order to have decisive influence in the U.S. Of course, this depends on what the facts are on the ground. In some place, African Americans are at or near the majority. In such places, they may act more alone. In places like Washington state, Blacks have to coalesce even more. Harvard Professor William Julius Wilson has made these points as poignantly as anyone else of late.

Dr. Wilson has explained the importance of both economics, self-investment, and ethnic group coalitions in his book *The Bridge Over the Racial Divide* (1999). Viewing the problem, Dr. Wilson concluded that the smaller size of the Black community, the great needs in the community for wise capital investment, and the lack of Black capital to meet the needs all posed too great a investment challenge for Blacks to solve themselves. He advises that Black Americans have to work with other ethnic minorities, conferring on an agenda, and moving out on initiatives to fulfill it.

Wilson's work is a lucid, clear-headed work that rightly emphasizes economics. He also is right about the need for linkages. I think that his logical and concise work is too slanted towards what society needs to do for groups like African Americans. Given that he is one of the foremost economists, I feel that his work should offer more ideas about how to build our own businesses from our own income. I suspect that the problem to him is so massive that he feels money we would invest in ourselves would be too little. Another idea of Wilson's that I take issue with is his willingness to jettison affirmative action where there is hostility to it, and instead replacing it with "affirmative opportunity." George H. Bush used similar language in the 2000 campaign to mask his anti-affirmative action, pro-Southern Strategy policies that he carried out when in office.

FOR A RENAISSANCE, NOT REVOLUTION

We need leadership, but how far do we go with developing such political structures? Do we need to pick a Black community government and mayor? No. Doing so would be treasonous, especially in this country, leading the society and the government to react strongly against every positive thing we are doing and to crush every negative thing ruthlessly. I can understand those who lament the fact that we do not have power over our own place, because such power would give us true self-determination.

For Black Americans have no real unified political structures. It is part and parcel of our minority status nationally and locally. We usually do not have the benefit of a government that can unify us and from which we can develop policy. In such a situation, wise and committed leadership is indispensable, and Blacks have not consistently had this, as has been mentioned.

In our largest city in which we are the majority, Washington D.C., Congress has the ultimate control. There Blacks are treated worse than any citizens in the U.S. and only slightly better than the U.S. treats the citizens of Puerto Rico on Puerto Rico.[4] There are a number of majority Black towns and cities (smaller than D.C.) now that are special cases because they do present Blacks with political structures from which they can effect policy.

Still, it would be counter-productive to do anything that looks like the formation of our own government. This is about prosperity, not sovereignty. This is a renaissance, not a revolution. We do not have to have a flag, although we have the colors of our liberation (black, red, and green). We do not have to have a Black national anthem, although we have what James Weldon Johnson called the Black national hymn ("Lift Every Voice and Sing"). Why? We are not trying to lead an insurrection or some kind of violent revolution. We are trying to prosper in this land as African Americans, and we are determined to do so.

The government and certain Black leaders shut down everything positive and negative Garvey was doing. We would run into what the Black Panthers ran into when they decided to brandish guns like they were commandeering ideas. The government and certain Black leaders closed every positive and negative thing the Panthers were doing. No, we do not need a separate government or mayor. We have our sovereign countries on the Motherland: Nigeria, South Africa, Ethiopia, and the like. We have our sovereign countries in the West: Jamaica, Bahamas, Haiti, and others.

Why is it necessary to say this? I want this movement to prevail and not to be misdirected from within or undermined from without. The U.S. government will not allow Whites to break from it; it is definitely not going to allow Blacks to do so. Because of its militancy and the employing of weapons, the FBI made the Black Panther Party in 1969 the #1 threat to the internal security of the U.S.—not the Soviet or Chinese spies, but a group of Black citizens. Now 40 years later, I know of people who want to be part of a Black movement to make a place, say the state of Georgia or Mississippi, the base for Black America, a separate country.

These are the thoughts of more than a few fringe groups. I know that writers, even scholars, are writing on a future Black revolutionary separatist movement. That is the fear of the *Turner Diaries*. That is the fear of Chittum's *Civil War II: Coming Break-Up of America and What You Should Do About It*. But this fear is not only in the writings of extremists and Aryan Nations types. It is also making its way into the most acclaimed of scholarly material. Chittum says that the group that is most likely to be the spark are African Americans who may start the rhetoric in the northern cities, but will take the action that matters in what he calls the "black belt": Mississippi, Alabama, and a portion of Tennessee. He warns Whites to watch out in these areas.

The above picture depicts what is called the "Black Belt nation thesis." The ideas are most originally attributed to the Commnunist Party movement's adoption of such a possible strategy in 1928, and to one Sol Auerbach who wrote under the pen name James S. Allen:

> *This basic contradiction can only be solved in the course of an agrarian revolution in the Black Belt when the Negro farm tenants and poor farmers will dislodge the white landowning class and take possession of the land and the farm stock and tools. With these basic weapons in their hands, they will be able to set up their own government and obtain full liberation.* (Auerbach, Negro Liberation 24)

Some former Black Panthers and others formed the Black Liberation Army. Its years were 1971 – 1981. *(Logo shown at right.)* Any such efforts only misdirect us and lead us into direct confrontation with the government.[5]

I know that the FBI (or its precursor, the OSS) monitored the Black community from before the days of Ida B. Wells through the days of Martin Luther King up to the days of the Black Panther Party. (OSS agents paid Ms. Wells a visit after her civil rights activities around 1920; FBI agents bugged King for years while he was on the road.) I suspect that their surveillance will only be enhanced, and that Homeland Security is doing something similar. What is the point of saying this, to cause Blacks angst? No. It is to get us to give up all illusions about revolutionary separatism. It is not going to happen. Let's not even be associated with such ideas.

We cannot do what we want to do at the expense of the country or even the exclusion of the country. No, our motives have to be pure. What we do has to be for the excellence of the country. It comes with being a minority: our motives have to be pure and our ends, in the end, have to be for the good of all. The wisdom and magic of both the anti-slavery and the civil rights movements are that they were for the good of all. Both movements made the country better (although many saw the opposite as the case at the time). Both movements fueled other proper liberation movements. Both movements are part of the ennobling story of what makes America great.

Our example must be Jewish Americans (and the same could be said for Indian [from India], and perhaps even Cuban, Americans). Jewish Americans are not trying to form a separate sovereign state for themselves in the U.S. Jews regularly distance themselves from such ideas whenever they are raised, ideas from those Buchanan mentioned concerning a Jewish cabal around George Bush, to more extravagant global ideas of takeover going back to the Protocols of Zion. They distance themselves from such and focus on their development in ways that promote the greater good.

We want to obtain our empowerment in ways that promote the country's advancement. The modus operandi of Jews in a foreign land was laid down in Jeremiah's letter to the captives in Iraq – Iran (Babylon – Persia):

> *This is what the Lord Almighty, the God of Israel, says to all those I carried into exile from Jerusalem into Babylon: "Build houses and settle down; plant gardens and eat what they produce. Marry and have sons and daughters; find wives for your sons and give your daughters in marriage, so that they too may have sons and daughters. Increase in number there; do not decrease. Also, seek the peace and prosperity of the city to which I have carried you into exile. Pray to the Lord for it, because if it prospers, you too will prosper. ...I know the plans I have for you," declares the Lord, "plans to prosper you and not to harm you, plans to give you hope and a future."* (JEREMIAH 29:4-7, 11 [EMPHASIS ADDED])

This was then, and is now, the key for them. This plan incorporates these ideas and becomes key for us.

DON'T MISS THIS POLITICAL MOMENT

All told, over the last 30 years, the Black leadership missed the opportunity to bring hundreds of millions of dollars into communities like Seattle all across this country.[6] The leaders just did not rise to the occasion to accomplish the task. The rest of the people did not pick up the ball where the leaders dropped it. I know that it would not have been easy to do this, and I know that doing this would have cost Black folks something. On the other hand, what it would have done for our people would have more than made up for the personal loss. This is what leadership is about. Incidentally, during the era of Sound Transit, I bear some of the blame as well, as I am one of the local leaders in this community. As pastor and community developer John Perkins teaches, a leader takes responsibility and moves resources toward problems. We must follow the lead of Fletcher and Jackson.

We cannot afford to miss this moment in the development of our people and, through us, the advancement of all people. We have to stop electing leaders who do not rise to this level pushing powerfully a plan like this. The people will have to take matters into their own hands.

NEW COMMUNITIES, NEW DIASPORA, NEW WORLD

I have discussed at length our practical goal of achieving 10% annual growth. What we are endeavoring to achieve, however, is much more impressive than this modest goal. We must endeavor to see African Americans rise to such a place in the U.S. that they are the conscience of this country and the defenders of Africans in the diaspora. We must help the Motherland and those in the diaspora too. We are called to do so. W.E.B. DuBois called us to do it. Marcus Garvey called us to do it. Malcolm X called us to do it. Shirley Chisholm called us to do it. Poets like Gil Scott Heron, Lauren Hill, and Common call us to do it.

So the leadership that superintends the policies has to help the people fulfill our grand *purpose*, a purpose others will not understand, a purpose that many of our people may not get. Blacks in the U.S. can still play the role of conscience to this country given what we have suffered and how we have persevered. For differing reasons, both the countries of our birth and of our origin need for us to play these divergent roles. In very real ways we are for new communities, a new diaspora, and a new world.

Our movements have made this country better. Our leaders like Douglass and Truth, King and Hamer have served as prophets of public moral character. Furthermore, the civil rights movement became a big tent large enough to assist all kinds of people languishing at the bottom of American society. All one has to do is go back and re-visit the language of laws like the Civil Rights Acts of 1964, 1968, and 1991, as well as the Voting Rights Act of 1965. There one finds language along these lines: these acts outlaw discrimination for race, ethnicity, creed, color, national origin, and sex. Sometimes disability and sexual orientation are added to companion laws. This is as broad as broad can be. The Black vein of the civil rights movement, at least in the 1950s and 60s, contributed to similar civil rights movements among women, Latinos/as, and Native Americans. This gives us the goodwill necessary to play our prophetic role in this country.

Then there is our contribution to Africana. We in the U.S. do have a resume with regard to helping Blacks beyond our borders. Black Americans are well on our way to playing the role of defender given the following:

- African Americans joined the pan-African movement around the turn of the 1900s.
- Blacks protested western colonialism or imperialism of African peoples.
- African Americans supported Jamaican Marcus Garvey to the point that his organization in about 1925 was the largest African American association with $5 million members.
- Black support of Ethiopia in its struggle with Italy included some Black Americans who left the U.S. to join the battle in the place then known as Abyssinia.
- Malcolm X, linking with African leaders in consultation with African leaders, was moving to bring a case against U.S. racism and imperialism in the United Nations.
- Certain civil rights leaders from Richard Allen, Paul Cuffe, and W.E.B. DuBois, to Vernon Johns, Martin Luther King, and Andrew Young had an African consciousness.
- The work of groups like NAACP, the Congressional Black Caucus even more, Black student unions in universities around the country more still, Americans in the the pan-African movement a century ago furthermore, and TransAfrica more than any other group led to U.S. concern about the Italian takeover of Ethiopia, sanctions on South Africa, the release of Nelson Mandela, and the return of Aristide to power in Haiti.

I earlier quoted Marcus Garvey about the importance of the U.S. to African descent peoples everywhere. While Afro-Brazilians and Jamaicans may beg to differ, Afro-Americans remain the most import enclave of Africans outside of the Motherland. We are still needed to help Africa. There can be no doubt that Africa needs the help. Someone needs to step up to help her in her early spring of continued need.

If our politics are right, then our people will have a renaissance. African Americans must work both in the Black community and in the larger community to get leaders to represent Black interests in a responsible and fair way. This is how we act to raise ourselves politically: how we order, provide for, and protect Black America. This is how we position ourselves to play a powerful role in this country, in the Black diaspora, and in the Motherland. This is how our leaders guide us to fully pick ourselves up by our own bootstraps, to fairly secure our share of community resources, and to fulfill our high purpose in the world.

SOCIETY: BALANCED PERSONS, HEALTHY RELATIONSHIPS, RESPECTED ELDERS

Because we have forgotten our ancestors our children no longer give us honor. Because we have lost the path our ancestors cleared, kneeling in perilous undergrowth, our children cannot find their way.
Because we have banished the God of our ancestors, our children cannot pray. Because the long wails of our ancestors have faded beyond our hearing, our children cannot hear us crying.
Because we have abandoned our wisdom of mothering and fathering, our befuddled children give birth to children they neither want nor understand.
Because we have forgotten how to love, the adversary is within our gates, and holds us up to the mirror of the world, shouting, "Regard the loveless;"
Therefore, we pledge to bind ourselves again to one another;
To embrace our lowliest,
To keep company with our loneliest,
To educate our illiterate,
To feed our starving,
To clothe our ragged,
To do all good things, knowing that we are more than keepers of our brothers and sisters. We are our brothers and sisters.
In honor of those who toiled and implored God with golden tongues, and in gratitude to the same God who brought us out of hopeless desolation,
We make this pledge.

(Maya Angelou, Black Family Pledge)

Maya Angelou is not only our poet-laureate, she is our prophet, pointing the way to our redemption after a candid analysis of our condition. She admonishes us to assess what has happened to our children and to pledge to embrace, to educate, and to "do all good things" for our siblings and their children in honor of our ancestors who taught us better than we are doing. What we do for children and families concerns things social. The social area brings us back to our families and every relationship that nourishes us, or that would do so if we would but let it. It is time for us to pledge to find our social selves again, and our leaders in this area can help us with this.

Although it will not be easy, the social leaders could—like the political leaders—lead the movement for a Black renaissance, if they had to, by themselves. The counselors, therapists, guardians, advocates, and the myriad service providers have a unique advantage that comes from working so closely with individuals in need and their families: they gain a clear understanding of what is going on with, works for, and does not work for those in our community. Their challenge is that the real problem—the causal link—might be a few steps away from what it is that they first assess.

To be more specific, what first appears as a violence or drug problem may, upon closer inspection, be a parent or family problem, that upon even closer analysis reveals itself to be a poverty or education problem. Once the knot is unraveled, social leaders gain uncanny insight into the community condition. They can provide indispensable assessment. They can then raise their collective voices to deal with the problem, forging solutions. So this is a call to the social leaders to prepare, plan, and proceed with a plan to help Black America starting right where you are.

Yet, it is no easy thing to go from individual problems to community-wide answers. It is difficult to go from individual problems to understand what ails the community. It is hard to see the forest when standing before one cedar tree after another.

No important thing that needs to be done for African Americans can be done alone. What ails us can only be solved by us collectively, in groups, in associations. This requires healthier relationships. We must renew our relationships and thus restore our villages. We need to do so until the lion's share of our households are headed by healthy married couples in extended families that raise well beloved children and that help to take care of their seniors and those with special needs. The members of these balanced extended families need to be involved in at least one religious and one other non-religious associations, associations that are connected to one another. The fabric of the Black village has to be mended so that we can have true community.

I do not consider myself competent to advise what should be done in this area. I look to social leaders to develop a real social plan. In fact, I will need leaders to propose a plan in the next four sections: social, medical, educational, and artistic. What follows are some ideas as food for thought.

We must renew our relationships and thus restore our villages. We need to do so until the lion's share of our households are headed by healthy married couples in extended families that raise well beloved children and that help to take care of their seniors and those with special needs.

PLAN DEVELOPMENT AND EXECUTION

It is time to move on a social plan. The social area has to do with promoting healthy relationships and caring for those who cannot physically care for themselves. In order to greatly improve our relationships, the following steps should seem as self-evident as they are indispensable:

DEVELOPING AND IMPLEMENTING THE SOCIAL PLAN

- Launch plan study groups and best practices analysis.
- Call social professionals together.
- Confer on an overall plan.
- Call social professionals together in areas
- Adopt specialized plans.
- Isolate the major initiatives we will do for ourselves.
- Clarify the help we need from outside the community.
- Agree on a social area plan.
- Determine how to measure the success.
- Present the plan to the overall plan leaders.
- Execute the plan
- Quality control how the plan is proceeding

We need not say much about these above steps, except that we should do them. I must elaborate though on a few points. First, this is one of those areas that is beyond my expertise, so my comments are few and measured here. Second, hopefully the discussions that lead toward plan development will begin with serious study. This means uncovering and keenly analyzing what is working around the country, even the world. It also means looking at whole groups in order to weigh whole ethnic approaches to promoting healthier, balanced relationships.

Third, I hope to see clear measures put in place. This is one of those areas in which it may not be easy to evaluate success. On the other hand, there are still those traditional indexes: marriage rate, divorce rate, level of homelessness, estimates of drug use, and so on. These are good places to start. It is time for social leaders to come together in order to heal our relationships.

WHO SHOULD BE AT THE TABLE

If we are going to promote healthy relationships and care for those who cannot physically care for themselves then we will need to convene all of the social area providers. The relationship arena concerns loneliness, dating, shacking, marriage, civil unions, parenting, and divorce. All of these counselors and providers need to be at the table. Caring for the needy entails services to adolescents, addicts, alcoholics, the disabled, the disruptive, the de-institutionalized, and the aged. All of these counselors and providers must be in the plan conference. For a more exhaustive list, see the following:

Relationship & Marriage counselors & resource providers

Separation & Divorce counselors & resource providers

Mental disorder & depression counselors & resource providers

Grief and traumatic stress counselors & resource providers

Authoritative influence stress & abuse counselors & resource providers

Sexual orientation counselors & resource providers

Substance abuse counselors & resource providers

Physical Abuse counselors & resource providers

Crisis & suicide counselors & resource providers

Compulsive behavior counselors & resource providers

Emotion management counselors & resource providers

Disability counselors & resource providers

Food assistance counseling & resource providers

Shelter assistance counseling & resource providers

Parental counseling & resource providers

Child protective counseling & resource providers

Senior support counseling & resource providers

Parole and probation counseling & resource providers

Vocational counseling & resource providers

Debt counselors & resource providers

Immigrant counseling & resource providers

Social scientists & public officials

Call these leaders across the board together. They can lead us out of our social jungle. Tying their area plan to an overall plan, they can lead us to a renaissance.

BLACK MALE – FEMALE RELATIONS

Quite often the black woman is affluent, with two cars and a condominium but without a man who can satisfy, while the brother is broke with too many women. When we let the revolutionary initiative slip through out fingers after the Sixties, the brother got lost in the cracks. You used to could go through the black community and see a lot of working men and a lot of pretty women. Now you see a lot of working women and a lot of pretty men. (NATHAN AND JULIA HARE, THE ENDANGERED BLACK FAMILY)

There's a war going on, a war of harsh words and animosity. Within this overall war is the explosive battle of the so-called "strong black woman" and the not so successful black man, the kind of man she's too often forced to settle for, or have nobody at all. But finding all too quickly, in too many cases, the loneliness she hadn't quite reckoned on, plus the social stigma of being alone or without a man, many sisters can't understand why, even when they lower their requirements in a man, they have picked up another problem. The sister with SBWS [successful Black woman syndrome] leaves no perk uncovered, expense accounts she pads to boost her reimbursements and cruises. She still has to learn to live with the reality that the higher she climbs, the more she personally achieves, the greater her chances of suffering acute consequences of what sociologist William Wilson called the dwindling marriageable black male pool. She may quickly discover that too many of our upper middle class brothers are inclined to exploit their scarcity; as if they were messiahs sent here to service the over-abundant supply of strong black women. (JULIA HARE, HOW TO FIND AND KEEP A BMW [BLACK MAN WORKING]).

These two quotes of Julia Hare and her husband say it all. We have a serious and gathering problem in our community. Relations between men and women generally are, as is said about countries, characterized by cooperation and conflict. Relations between Black men and women are even more conflicted than other ethnicities. It is the result of generational pain, as well as this generation's poverty and imprisonment. These maladies make for a situation in which both boys and girls grow up with negative associations of manhood owing to fatherlessness; many boys are pipelined to prison; of those not imprisoned, too many have difficulty offering financial support due to joblessness; of those left, they either lack the skills to maintain a healthy relationship, or else they want to play given the fact that there may be three to four eligible women for every eligible man.

Joblessness and poverty were the focus of earlier chapters. Here we focus on negative associations, relational skill-building, and reversing the need to play the field. Black health professionals need to devise programming to address such issues, and it should be a condition of employment that those who can benefit from such programming must attend. This will fix the maladies plaguing Black male – female relations. This will make relationships healthier.

Healthier relationships should mean that they last longer. More of them should flow into marriages. More marriages should work better and longer. This will provide children strong, more balanced mentorship. It will also provide the children more resources: two providing from within the home are better than one doing so, or even one from within the home and the other from outside.

Perhaps we will arrive at the place at which the lion's share of our households are headed by healthy married couples in extended families. Such families will do better with the children and in assisting their own seniors and those with special needs. The members of these balanced extended families need to be involved in at least one religious and one other non-religious associations, associations that are connected to one another. This is how we mend the fabric of the Black village so that we can have truer community.

MARRIAGE AND FAMILIES

Of all of these items, marriage and family counseling and resources are crucial. Marriage is the foundation of society. It is the first institution most religions speak of God creating. This is definitely the case with Christianity, Judaism and Islam. It can be said that as marriage goes, so goes society. We need to learn and re-learn how to live together. We particularly need this in ways that speak to differences in gender but fairness in roles. We need teaching that focuses on the way people believe, behave, and belong. We have to do this in ways that are not sexist, androgynous, or homophobic. Men and women, and Black men and Black women are far too distrustful and combative, perhaps more so than any other ethnic group. This is a clear and present danger to the fabric of Black society.

A good place to start is with the book *Men Are from Mars, Women Are from Venus*. A number of social scholars see this work as too heterogeneous and simplistic. They feel that men and women are alike in fundamental ways, and that many of the differences are pronounced through how we are socialized. They feel that playing up the similarities as opposed to the differences may work better and bring society closer together in the long run in less sexist ways. Others feel that the book is just too simplistic in its discussions about men needing caves and women needing non-answer laden listening.

Well, I have been married for decades, and I have read the book. I find it helpful. I am not naïve about gender: men and women share more in common than they are different. However, we are different enough that parsing out the distinctions as this book does is very helpful to those in relationships. Neither am I alone in this view.

The book has been a best seller because it makes sense to millions. So I still recommend it, until I find something better. Another place are the gender studies, particular those on the behavior effects of testosterone and estrogen. The Gottman Institute and the books of John Gottman and Julie Schwartz Gottman, husband and wife, are superb places of information as well as training. Whatever we recommend for further studies, we have to make sure that it provides solutions to what causes marriages to suffer, and does so in practical ways.

For, when marriages suffer, single parents—usually mothers—are left to raise the children. Without the other partner in the home, it is especially tough to raise children well. Boys particularly become impossible for many mothers to discipline. Too many of these young people make poor choices about their homework, school, gangs and the like. These single parents, heroes to whatever degree they are holding their families together, need more community assistance from a relevant plan.

THE PLAGUE OF BLACK ON BLACK VIOLENCE

Better jobs will improve another scourge in the Black community the problem of violence we perpetrate against ourselves. The majority of non-violent crimes against property and person are Black on Black. The minor thefts, defacing of property, the disturbing the peace usually happens between Blacks. Black people sell more drugs to other Black people. Moreover, the violent crimes are Black on Black to an even higher degree. Black people rape, burglarize, and murder Black people. We must do something to solve our self-harassment. Our social professionals are the people for the job.

We need classes that address selfish, toxic behavior that moves our people to see preying on one another as a means to make money. We must require dependency programs and anger management sessions for those so needy. We have to make them part of their employment and contracting plans to ensure that they attend.

THE PROBLEM OF SUBSTANCE ABUSE

Drug use remains at epidemic levels in and around a hood near each of us. A number of different communities make money off of shipping such product to or near ghettos. The resulting problems shatter careers and wrecks families. Substance abuse is a major social ill.

We have to deal with dependency and co-dependency, and it will constitute a major initiative. There are simply not enough expert, intensive, in and out-patient programs without waiting lists for those who need substance abuse counseling. Providing such programs includes finding resources to provide such facilities for people who largely have no insurance or income to pay. It will mean a major commitment of community and societal funds.

In the meantime, clinicians, counselors, and therapists sympathetic to the Black community will need to volunteer as much as possible; others hopefully will make the scholarly case for the need to devote more governmental and charitable dollars to the point of this need.

THE PROBLEM OF FATHERLESSNESS

Girls and boys need mothers and fathers. Mothers are there for their children even in the Black community. However, too many of our children suffer for want of fathers materially engaged in rearing them. When fathers are missing, little children lose an added sense of security; boys fail to see the model of a male as protector. When fathers are gone, little children lose an added degree of support; boys miss the example of a male as provider. When fathers are absent, little children lose the everyday lesson of a long term, committed relationship; boys are growing up devoid of the normalcy of a man loving the same woman like a holy paramour, hanging in romance through the ups and downs of life.

As with all of the other maladies above, good paying jobs are a major part of the solution. However, we need specific seminars, classes, and programs as well to ensure that children and young adults are taught about why and how to father. Moreover, we must require that participation in such instruction is necessary to remain in good standing at the workplace.

OUR EMBATTLED SENIORS

Becoming a senior should be a badge of honor. Their mere survival means that they have done some things right. Theirs is the generation in possession of more of the country's wealth. They are the harbingers of most of the practical wisdom of society. Mostly, precipitously but sometimes overnight, they lose the ability to take care of themselves. Having taken care of so many others, families and society gain the right to return the favor. A good family, a good society invests in and takes care of its seniors.

Our families and society are not doing enough to take care of our seniors. In our youth-oriented culture, "throw away" society, too often seniors are ignored or warehoused away. We allow too many elders to languish with insufficient resources as their fixed incomes pale in the face of rising costs of living. Even those with decent retirements find that they may have medical care but they lack dental care, as corporate retirement plans and Medi-care exempt such coverage. Some are facing these eventualities after raising not just their children, but their children's children. It is not just wrong; it is a crime. Who will speak for them?

Then there is the subject of visitation. Too often we mean to get by and see our elders, but we fail to do so. I have not done a good job of seeing my own grandmother when she was in the nursing home one city removed from me. Thank goodness my grandmother's children have regularly seen her, for her grandchildren have been only periodic in walking by her way. When we do visit, our brief time is spent asking some of the silliest questions or barely listening. We could do so much more to share with our seniors whose minds our sound.

We could help them for more than ethical and spiritual reasons. We could do so out of sheer selfishness: we are all trying to live long enough to become a senior some day. What we do for them now we do for ourselves later. How shortsighted and suicidal is our thinking.

Our seniors deserve a period of worry-free, doting rest as they move into the dusk of their lives. We need to visit them, to listen to them, to make sure that they have all that they need, and to make their surroundings as honorable and beautiful as possible.

We also need to provide them ways in which to give back for as long as they are capable. Some seniors in their seventies still have so much to offer their families and society. They can volunteer at the place they retired from. They can serve social service agencies in critical ways. They can write down the histories and processes that would help us do what we need to better.

I will never forget being in the Oklahoma Intercollegiate Legislature, sitting in the Oklahoma State Capital as a delegate from Oral Roberts University, and hearing of a mock bill presented by a woman whose last name was Kirk: YET—Youth and Elderly Together. Her bill was a program for marshalling the great talents and remaining energy of our seniors through coordinated volunteering throughout society, especially where their services were needed most. It was catchy, simple, but ingenious.

People in the various social areas need the necessities of life, parenting, mentoring, counseling, friendship, and education. When a people are poor, then they are prey to pathologies. They developed substance abuse and behavior problems. Their family life suffers and they lose the ability to manage their own lives.

As more people fall into these problems, the social safety net is taxed, at times beyond the breaking point. People are under-served or disserved. Deviance and abnormalities become policing matters by default. This criminalizes the problem as the police are not sociological professionals. As more people are incarcerated, the problem gets worse. Too often society's answer is just more police and prisons. So, Blacks must develop sociological answers to their problem and to put these ideas into practice. It will require bringing sociology professionals together. It mandates more resources devoted to solving these problems.

It should become the goal—if not the norm—that Black couples enjoy loving relationships, and raise their children in healthy families. They should reside in communities that are holistic villages, catering to the elderly and serving the disabled. At every age level, Blacks should be in associations of their choice that provide them recreation, fun, and community service. These are social concerns, concerns that have an indispensable place in a development plan.

EVERY BLACK PERSON IN ASSOCIATIONS

I have already explained why associations are foundational to connecting the Black community. They are crucial as the base for the development plan. That more Blacks are not associated in churches and sororities says something about how much we are struggling socially. We must fix this. I propose a new rule: every Black person should be in one religious association and two non-religious ones.

Minorities of every stripe need their groups for power and community. The majority can afford to be more individualistic because it will have its way through the democratic process. Minorities that do not collectively act will get nothing resembling their share of the power, property, and prestige in the larger community. So associating is paramount to political and social survival.

In these groups, the members must make their needs clearly known. They must do something like voting, polling, and agenda setting. This is how taxation with representation occurs. This is how duty is imposed on the dues organizations require, be that organization the church, the club, or the company.

Blacks need organizations and businesses that care about their members' or employees' total well being. We need organizations that will address our needs that are ill-served.

Westerners, including Seattleites, need to hear this especially. In the West, African Americans imbibed the individualism and isolation of those who settled this region (or who took it from the Native Americans). When Blacks came out here, they arrived to find that, naturally, the institutions they had known were not out here. There were no large Black churches, established fraternal associations, or business strips. So they founded such institutions themselves, but they were an infantile form of the institutions they had left. Moreover, attendance itself comes with a cost of time if nothing else; not having to attend the meetings folks had grown up in was a type of freedom. The West is known as the most unchurched region of the country. Plus, attending was against the tenor (the zeitgeist) of the times. So because the familiar institutions were infantile, because of a sense of being personally free, and because belonging was not what it seemed others were doing, Black associating waned. This is but one example of its individualism.

Something like this happened to many who left the familiarity of the South, and moved to crowded enclave areas on the East coast. First of all, the environment was new, and that created isolation in the midst of population. Moreover, some did not want to immediately go to church or join other familiar institutions. With the new territory, they wanted new options. They had new styles to try and partying to do. With the poverty and over-crowding as it was, crime was a problem. Distrust abounded. All of this led to further disconnection. So, it was not only the West that experienced this kind of phenomenon. It may have more pronounced in the West, but it is apparent wherever peoples have migrated.

TOO FEW BENEFITS FOR OUR SOCIAL PROVIDERS

The salaries and benefits of those who serve in the social area are too meager. Something must be done to provide them better wages, and to help them into the kind of capitalistic investments that will gain for them a retirement that bespeaks the value of what they do for society. Blacks should help lead a movement to do this for social professionals.

HEALTH:
PREVENTIVE, PROFESSIONAL, AND HOLISTIC HEALTH CARE

Health disparities is a term that describes a disproportionate burden of disease, disability, and death among a particular population or group. Racial and ethnic minorities make up roughly one-fifth (18 percent) of Washington State's population. Yet their disease burden is significantly higher. For some ethnic groups, the incidence of a particular disease may be five times the rate for Caucasian residents. The infant mortality rate for African American and American Indians/Alaskan Natives in Washington, for example, is twice what it is for Caucasians.

(Board of Health Policy Goals, Washington State Department of Health, 2006)

Most of the serious health conditions affecting African Americans – cancer, hypertension, strokes, diabetes, STDs, arteriosclerosis—are caused by diet, lack of exercise, irresponsible behavior, high stress, smoking, inadequate rest, lack of annual examinations. If Blacks would just improve these things we could dramatically improve our overall health and put a lot of medical professionals out of business.

(Dr. Ben Carson, speech at University of Washington, 2005)

Black Americans are, as Washington State Dr. Maxine Hayes often warns, "sick and in need of medical intervention." As the Board of Health Policy Goals states, we are disproportionately diseased, disabled, and dying. Dr. Ben Carson, the premier brain surgeon in the country, explains that most of what ails us can be addressed by us. So, the Black community needs two things in particular: it needs its medical professionals to direct us to wholeness, and it needs a plan that includes health preservation.

The Black community cries for its medical professionals to unify around a medical plan, and then to allow that same synergy to result in the formation of a comprehensive plan for a Black renaissance. This is a call to doctors, dentists, nurses, anesthesiologists, psychiatrists, chiropractors, optometrists, naturopaths, herbalists, masseuses, therapists, medical professors, and medical officials to do more than inform the community of the problems in your area: craft solutions and then connect them to the economic and other areas that render people devoid of resources and power to help themselves.

Medically, African Americans need a plan. The aim of all of this must be to decrease infant mortality and disease, while simultaneously increasing pre-natal care, quality of life, and life expectancy. Medical professionals can and must help us with this. With their help, we must improve the way we eat, exercise, and rest under the guidance of caring health professionals for our healing. The medical plan must address preventative care, primary care, specialty care, and alternative care. We have to do so until the quality and quantity of Black health is as good or better than that of Whites in America.

This is a call to doctors, dentists, nurses, anesthesiologists, psychiatrists, chiropractors, optometrists, naturopaths, herbalists, masseuses, therapists, medical professors, and medical officials to do more than inform the community of the problems in your area: craft solutions and then connect them to the economic and other areas that render people devoid of resources and power to help themselves.

PLAN DEVELOPMENT AND EXECUTION

It is time to move on a medical plan. The medical area has to do with enhancing overall health, and controlling disease. In order to greatly enhance our health and effectively fight disease, the following steps should seem as self-evident as they are indispensable:

DEVELOPING AND IMPLEMENTING THE MEDICAL PLAN

- Launch plan study groups and best practices analysis.
- Call medical professionals to meet regularly.
- Confer on an overall plan.
- Call medical professionals together in sub-areas (i.e., generalists, specialists, nurses, and alternative practitioners).
- Adopt specialized plans.
- Isolate the major initiatives we will do for ourselves.
- Clarify the help we need from outside the community.

- Agree on a medical plan.
- Determine how to measure the success.
- Present the plan to the overall plan leaders.
- Execute the plan.
- Quality control how the plan is proceeding.

MEDICAL PROFESSIONALS NEEDED

Medical professionals span a broad range: doctors, dentists, nurses, anesthesiologists, psychiatrists, chiropractors, optometrists, naturopaths, herbalists, masseuses, therapists, medical professors, and medical officials. Perhaps the medical officials will call the community together given the move of conservatives for local and private initiatives. In fact, the government has even combined with religious institutions in its service, under the moniker of "faith-based initiatives."

However, this is mainly a bootstrap plan. We cannot wait for the government to lead the community to where it has to go; we cannot wait on any other entity to do this for us, for that matter. We may get a shoestring, or we may not. We have to do for ourselves. So non-governmental medical professionals that have a great love for our community are needed now to call the community together. Someone needs to coordinate the various entities that are separately producing and presenting reports on the medical condition of the community in certain areas. Some persons or groups need to connect these reports into a "state of the medical union" report in every locale.

Hopefully, the doctors will take the lead in this. However, it may be that they are too busy or self-serving. In that event, others will have to step forward. In fact, the nurses could do this by themselves. They provide a lot of the health care anyway—way more than people know; sometimes they even have to tell doctors how to do what they do. Whoever will do it must do it. When they get together, they will have to devise a plan that addresses issues such as those following.

PREVENTIVE CARE

Preventive care is the patient doing the following things for him or herself: eating a well-balanced diet, exercising, lowering stress, resting, self-testing, and engaging in safe behavior. Primary care involves a family physician that conducts annual check-ups, regular examinations, and basic in-office procedures. Specialty care is the examinations, diagnoses, surgeries, and other procedures a specialist performs. Alternative care involves naturopathic, chiropractic, massage, and far eastern health care.

People generally need a lot of preventive and primary care and some specialty and alternative care as the primary care physicians approves. In fact, of all of these items, Blacks need preventive care the most. Remember the Dr. Ben Carson quote that led this chapter. He says that all Americans would greatly promote their general health by implementing basic preventive care measures. He knows what he is talking about—he teaches doctors. We need a plan that addresses what we can do to help ourselves, from how we eat to how we sleep.

Our diet needs changing, we need regular medical check-ups, we must exercise more, we have to lower our stress, we need rest, and we must forego unhealthy habits. There are no two ways about it. Our efforts have to target diabetes, hypertension, cancer, and sexually transmitted diseases both fatal like HIV and those that are debilitating like Chlamydia or herpes. We must enforce the plan in our homes and in our associations.

Let me be blunt: it is high time that we stop the behaviors that are killing us. Nobody makes us put the kinds of food in our mouths that we do (unless we are poor, as has been shown by recent works); no one makes us eat the amounts we eat; no one orders us to smoke; no one prevents us from exercising; no one bars us from getting check-ups (here I am speaking only to those with health insurance); no one forces us to live exploding in anger from one scene to the next—these things we do to ourselves. We have to become fed up with anything that is self-destructive, from drive-by shootings to over-eating.

Do not forget: every day that we take off our lives we do so at the very time that we are wiser, wealthier, and freer generally speaking. In other words, our bad habits compromise our purpose in ways that hurt ourselves, families, and community. Enough is enough. Even if we do not receive the help we need from outside of our community to resource our well-being, we have enough to do for ourselves that can move us as a people from sickness to health. Even here we have bootstraps.

So we have to better celebrate our discontinuing bad behavior. Certainly, we could move this celebration right into Development Week. We can do this by a walk, a run and an award. A "Shoestrings Walk" might be the Saturday before the week begins. A "Bootstraps Run" could be the Saturday morning of Development Week. An award for the person medical professionals have determined has improved his or her overall health the most can be given out at the banquet Saturday evening. Perhaps we should give an award as well to the association that does the most to provide for its own members preventive care.

PRIMARY CARE

To provide this for an entire community, we will have to study affordable health care, HMOs, community clinics, mobile examinations, and especially more doctors and hospitals to serve the under-served. The plan has to bring more doctors to Black patients. We need resources to make this happen, and an appeal to civic duty to fill in the gap where the resources run short.

Concerned Blacks need more community medical services and more health care coverage. The community medical services can be in the form of community clinics, in physicians providing free or reduced medical services, and in preventive care information available to schools and Black associations.

We are forced to lobby governments to establish more clinics, but if they will not, then we have to build our own clinics ourselves. Likewise, we have no choice but to move on our own physicians, and others who are willing, to provide Blacks with affordable care. Lastly, we need information disseminated to our people of various ages so that we are armed with what we need to know to preserve our own well-being. This includes mobile testing units that leaders are the first to make use of so that it becomes second nature to be a self-monitoring community. We will base such units on the site of certain of our associations.

Blacks need more health care coverage so that we can make use of the very good health care system that is geared to the upper middle and upper classes. I do not care who provides the health care—whether it is the government or the businesses, or even non-profit agencies—the people need coverage. No American should be uncovered medically. We have to convene Black medical professionals to confer on these items and to suggest what should be done about them.

SPECIALTY CARE

Blacks do not receive the specialty care that Whites and communities like Jewish Americans receive. In fact, the specialty care received is towards the bottom of the ethnic (stratification) scale. Like others, Blacks need the services of those doctors who specialize in one or a few organs or bodily systems. More general physicians need to refer Blacks to specialists. Specialists need to advocate for this happening. The same specialists must move to help find the resources for this care, the most expensive part of health care.

ALTERNATIVE CARE

Chiropractors, naturopaths, herbalists, acupuncturists, hypnotists, medicine men, and the like can provide the care of choice for certain patients. Moreover, traditional health care can at times be too drugs and surgery focused. Holistic health care has to be the watchword. I would even put prayer in this category. Too me we should combine certain of these remedies. If Jesus, the Great Physician, who operated through prayer could say, "They that are sick need a physician," then physicians can in turn say, "They who are sick can be helped by prayer." We can be additive in our approach rather than exclusive.

THE PROBLEM OF HIV / AIDS

As we address our categorical health needs from preventive to alternative care, we have to focus on certain issues as well. One such issue has to do with HIV and AIDS. While the larger community is seeing the incidence of infection and death level off in the U.S., the rate of Black infection and acquiring immune deficiency is increasing. It is increasing most with Black women. It is the saddest thing.

It seems clear that Black men are the dominant cause for the infection rate of Black women. Many of these men are having sex with multiple partners even if they are married. A large percentage are having bi-sexual sex, living life on the "down low." A preacher said it best when he preached a sermon entitled, "The Down Low is Low Down."

Others contract the virus in prison through voluntary or involuntary sex. They come out of the "joint" free in the world but bound to the virus unknowingly. They begin spreading the virus in short order. All of this is a prescription for an ethnic epidemic, and that is exactly what we have. Some estimate that in Washington, D.C., as many one out of four Black males between 20 and 40 are infected! It is an estimate because Blacks are not getting tested at all, or as often as they should. In fact, this is the second line of defense against the disease. The first is safe sex or abstinence.

I gave my son a condom when I gave him the birds and bees speech, and I am a pastor. The speech and condom were not about condoning sex. Quite to the contrary, I gave him every argument I knew of for not having sex until marriage. However, I wanted him to know that there is no excuse for having unprotected sex, and that I would judge him favorably for having a condom in his wallet. That is a good thing. I am sympathetic to those who say that this encourages sexual behavior. However, we have tried ignorance or pushing abstinence only and we see where that has gotten us. It is time for us to be more holistic so that are young adults are better able to grow into healthier adults.

After safe sex, the most important thing we must do is test every one early and often. We have to determine who is infected. We should test every person going into jail and leaving it. Every person should be tested before having sex [I am serious]. We have to know who is infected. An HIV test should be part of every annual medical examination. Annual associations should have mobile testing units that their members are urged to make use of.

Once we inform those infected, we have to encourage the infected person to fully inform their partners before engaging in any sexual activity. The penalties have to be severe for those who do not do so. There are no two ways about it. Every home must be the purveyor of this information; every association has to be a house for these kinds of seminars.

It is time to get our arms around this virus so that we can turn the tide on it in the African diaspora. From the Motherland to the Caribbean to Brazil and the U.S., people of African descent are suffering at alarming rates with HIV and AIDS. Due to it alone, whole countries' populations are declining, and a generation of foster children are growing up parentless. It is as if the drug were a modern day slave master, or an ardent segregationist, so racist have been the impacts of this micro taskmaster. Africans everywhere need us to best HIV here.

DIABETES

Because of eating problems and lack of proper exercising, diabetes has come to be worse in the Black community than almost any other ethnic community in the U.S. Blacks are experiencing sugar and glucose difficulties. They have to go on medications to do for them what their gall bladders and other organs used to do well. They are having circulation problems. They are having foot and hand swelling, numbness, and deadness. They are losing limbs. They are losing the desire and ability to live. It is time to get back to preventive care in a big way.

HEART DISEASE

Preventive care problems and genetics are causing Black Americans to suffer high incidence of artery hardening and plaque build up in the capillaries and veins of the heart. When the walls clog or tear, it leads to a blockage in the heart that kills heart cells and can lead to heart stoppage. If a tear is the trigger, the blockage can occur in as little as 15 seconds, if you can believe it. Whether a tear or plaque build-up, often the blockage leads to death.

Those experiencing such conditions describe, if they are lucky, a shortness of breath or a pain in the arm. If the person is unfortunate, they experience a feeling of getting hit by a bat or else they feel as if they are instantly choking. I suspect that this explanation has gotten your attention. It has mine. It is time for us to work a plan for our total renaissance.

STROKES

A heart attack is the blockage of a vessel in the heart; a stroke is the blockage of a vessel in the brain. No wonder some have called the obstruction of plaque or the tear in the vessel wall in the brain a "brain attack." Symptoms can be as mild as slight movement impairment, memory loss, or a headache; they can be as severe as a splitting headache, complete memory loss, paralysis, and loss of consciousness. In either case, death can occur, sometimes within minutes. Don't you think we ought to decrease the incidence of such austere conditions?

CANCER

It was in the 1960s that medical professionals began to clarify cancer's causes and risks. It became clear then that the single most changeable factor leading to cancer, especially lung and throat cancer, is exposure to cigarette smoke. Well before HIV/AIDS became the looming epidemic, cancer was the great fear. So many resources went into medical care and prevention that there have been great gains.

However, we know now that minimizing second-hand smoke as well as direct sun exposure prevents various cancers. Unprotected sun exposure has made skin cancer about as deadly as lung cancer. It is likewise important to investigate carcinogens in one's environment. Certain communities suffer cancer's effects due to radiation or other contaminants in drinking water, soil, or the air.

The leading threat now from genetic causes is breast cancer. It strikes both women and men. Self examinations and annual general examinations are crucial. Questionable masses should be imaged; direct your doctor to order x-rays or MRIs if you feel the situation warrants.

SEXUALLY TRANSMITTED DISEASES (STDS)

STDs affect something like one out of every three sexually active Americans. Some of these diseases—like syphilis and crabs—are curable, although there is concern about drug resistant bacteria or about symptom-free incubation that can lead to sterility. Others are incurable so far, such as herpes or HIV. The best remedy for all STDs is safe sex or abstinence. This means more than condoms. Beware, some have gotten STDs of the throat, and it is technically possible to mix bodily fluids through French kissing where both persons have bleeding such as of the gums.

ASTHMA

One of the curious outbreaks has been the elevated levels of Blacks contracting asthma. It is affecting infants and adults. Those with asthma long for the ability to consistently breath fully and easily. Slight asthma conditions compromise the respiratory performance enough to make recovery from strenuous activity longer, but not enough to prevent slight asthmatics from playing sports and maintaining a normal life. Some have no idea that they even have asthma.

Those who experience asthma attacks or chronic acute asthma know what it is like to feel like the lungs are closing and one is unable to catch one's breath. They know what it is like to have to an oxygen device for assistance. Acute asthmatics must reduce their physical activity starkly. Some are warned against getting excited, laughing too hard, or exposure to anything but the freshest air. Those experiencing a full on attack begin to hyperventilate, take on an oxygen-deprived coloration, quiver, and then lose consciousness. Death is not uncommon. Asthma is not a good thing.

The culprits appear to be contaminants in the environment in addition to genetics. It is paramount that we check every aspect of the environment. Poverty is part of the environmental conditions in that the poor live in dustier, dirtier places replete with paint chips, rodent droppings, freeway belts, and polluting industrial plants. Their concrete environments are devoid of the oxygen-producing flora that makes for fresher air. Dealing with the conditions that raise the incidence of asthma has to be part of the plan.

WHEN WE WILL KNOW THAT WE HAVE ARRIVED

The aim of all of this must be to decrease infant mortality and disease, while simultaneously increasing pre-natal care, quality of life, and life expectancy. We must improve the way we eat, exercise, and rest under the guidance of caring health professionals for our healing. The medical plan must address preventive care, primary care, specialty care, and alternative care. We have to do so until the quality and quantity of Black health is as good or better than that of Whites in America.

It is time for medical professionals to help Black America with community medical plans. Then they have to take the next step: be the catalysts to bring leaders across the board together to agree on a comprehensive plan for a Black renaissance. Why not? There is nothing healthier than community health.

A TETHER OF LIFE

Loads have to be secured when in transit for the protection of the load and of life in the vicinity. Straps are good for this purpose. If you do not know what I am talking about, just ask any mover or hauler, whether it be a shipper, railroader, or trucker. That person will speak of the function of a good strap. The straps work very well for holding the item tightly. In fact, securing a load is often called "strapping it down."

Albeit, one need not consider large loads and protecting some other life in order to learn this lesson. For every day the average person secures a very personal load by strapping it down. We do so in our cars through the simple means of a seat belt. The belt is not a shoestring. No, a string could not do the job. A string cannot well protect life or a load.

NASA knows about this. At times they send an astronaut out of the spaceship into space. They do not tie that person to a string. No, they use something substantial for this purpose. What they use may not be called a strap, but you can be sure that it is closer to a strap than to a string.

This work we have to do is an endeavor demanding a lot of resources. When we are commanding such resources we will need to use something with holding power, something that will protect life and load, something that can secure a person traversing the challenge of developmental space. A shoestring might be sufficient in a pinch, but a strap is what we really need. Only a strap is something used to tether a life to. We need such a tether to promote our health and wellness. We need a strap in order to enhance our education. Strings may add to life but it is really straps that save lives.

EDUCATION:
INVOLVED PARENTS, SUPPORTED CHILDREN, AND AFROCENTRIC TEACHING

When you control a man's thinking you do not have to worry about his actions. You do not have to tell him not to stand here or go yonder. He will find his "proper place" and will stay in it. You do not need to send him to the back door. He will go without being told. In fact, if there is no back door, he will cut one for his special benefit. His education makes it necessary.

(Dr. Carter G. Woodson, The Miseducation of the Negro)

When you learn your history you learn your greatness.

(Unknown)

An idea is irrepressible, and it is irresistible when its time has irretrievably come.

(Carl Livingston, Jr.)

Knowledge and the world of ideas can work for a people or against it. Dr. Woodson's quote above is a classic, and it captures how ideas have been used against Blacks: as Woodson makes clear, Blacks have been taught in ways that disempower us, and we have so internalized our disempowerment that we teach our children to disempower themselves. It is a type of Willie Lynch situation: although the letter is probably not true (something we have to accept until we find the original written in seventeenth century English), the ideas of internalized division and self-hatred are something we know all too much about. Black Americans must break out of this module and then teach ourselves about ourselves. In fact, if Dr. Leonard Jeffreys of City University of New York's Black Studies Program fame is right, we may need to begin teaching ourselves about ourselves in order to fully break out. So this is a call to our educational professionals.

As we learn our greatness, we position ourselves to make knowledge work for us in an irresistibly powerful renaissance. It is the educational professionals who will lead us in this learning. They must teach us how to excel at investing in our own and our children's education in order to maximize our potential. They must show us how to do so to the point that Black student college and vocational graduation rates are as good or better than those of Whites. Moreover, they especially have to explain to us how Africa is the cradle of humanity and cradle of civilization.

Those who are spiritually in tune teachers will show us that African Americans are the Joseph people who will assist Africans in their rise back to empowerment and leadership in the world. As the progenitors of civilization, we helped to invent societies of diversified jobs, belief in divinity, writing, and mathematics. We have no patience or room for Blacks being uneducated, or under-educated. The time for knowing and understanding is now. Thus, it is beyond time for educational professionals to help lead the way.

It is the educational professionals who will lead us in this learning. They must teach us how to excel at investing in our own and our children's education in order to maximize our potential. They must show us how to do so to the point that Black student college and vocational graduation rates are as good or better than those of Whites. Moreover, they especially have to explain to us how Africa is the cradle of humanity and cradle of civilization.

PLAN DEVELOPMENT

Educationally, African Americans need a plan without a doubt. This plan will have to do with pre-school, academic, and vocational education. Pre-school education is everything from pre-natal up to kindergarten schooling. Academic education is primary, secondary, college and graduate instruction. Primary and secondary schooling these days include public, private, charter, home schooling. Collegiate education is public or private. Vocational schooling entails blue and white-collar certificated and licensure programs from construction work to cosmetology. Here I would like to include the military, although it is not really vocational education. It begins by calling the leaders together.

DEVELOPING AND IMPLEMENTING THE EDUCATIONAL PLAN

- Launch plan study groups and best practices analysis.
- Call educational professionals together.
- Confer on an overall plan.
- Call educational professionals together in sub-areas (elementary, middle, and high school; vocational school, college, and university).
- Adopt specialized plans.
- Isolate the major initiatives we will do for ourselves.
- Clarify the help we need from outside the community.
- Agree on a educational area plan.
- Determine how to measure the success.
- Present the plan to the overall plan leaders.
- Execute the plan.
- Quality control how the plan is proceeding.

The steps needed are no different from the ones covered in the other sections. The difference is that in this area and health, the government much of the plan involves assisting the sizeable work of the various governmental districts and agencies. In this case, governments fund school districts doing most of the heavy lifting. However, most of these schools are practically failing our children. Moreover, states provide universities that too many of our people lack the resources for, or are ill-prepared for. So remediation from kindergarten to college is paramount. Added resources are needed, as is teaching our selves of who African people are.

EDUCATIONAL LEADERS

To whom is this call directed? The educational professionals are the following: principals, professors, teachers, counselors, writers, speakers, and commentators—all those who are instrumental in providing formalized instruction. This is to them. What follows are certain of the more specific things that they need to help us do.

IMPROVING PUBLIC EDUCATION

We have to be clear about the fact that Blacks need public education as it is in place now in their own neighborhood, and is by far the largest commitment to education in the country. The public education resources dwarf any other in the U.S. Moreover, in many communities, most all African Americans have by far are public schools. So, the primary part of the plan has to be making public education work for all, particularly African American students.

Some public officials have the same commitment at least in terms of insightful rhetoric. What follows is a quote by the Governor of Washington state.

> *We have lots of studies about what's wrong with our education system. We need to accept responsibility, be bold, find solutions and move forward to make education a centerpiece of our economic development.* CHRISTINE GREGOIRE

Note that she links education and economic development. Simply in terms of language this is important, and something we can work with. We have to get people to say the right things and then work hard to hold them accountable to what things they say. Much of the points addressed below concern how to make public schools work better for African American students.

FAMILY INVOLVEMENT TO ASSIST WITH PARENTAL INVOLVEMENT

Studies affirm the greatest factor for student success, after competent faculty and sufficient facilities, is parental involvement. Our children simply do not have enough parental support from ensuring homework is done at a high quality, to enforcing proper classroom behavior, to intervening to protect our kids from disrespectful staff, to helping schools get the resources they need to do the job they have to do. In other communities, their parents do this more effectively.

So our extended family members will have to help out. Grandparents, aunts and uncles, or second cousins will need to help share some of this load. If a family member is retired, then perhaps they will have the energy to play a substitute role. Perhaps they can make the classroom visit that the parent cannot, or will not make. Maybe they can attend a PTSA meeting at the beginning of the year and at the mid-year point. From what we are learning in the Asian American community, the oldest child can do a bit more in some of these things—especially helping with homework.

While I am on this subject, I need to offer a compliment along with a criticism. Our parents have been very effective at increasing Black child graduation rates. From 1940 to 1980, Black high school graduations went from less than 50% to more than 70%. This doubling is a major success. Our parents were the primary reason for this change—fighting for civil rights and demanding that children take advantage of every gain that was so hard won.

On the other hand, our parents must put more pressure on children to perform well. We do it, but we have to do better. Sometimes it will mean special help for the oldest child's academic success and then urging the oldest child to help the others. Other times this will mean parents or others in their world educating themselves so that they can help their children learn at home. At the end of the day it means raising expectations so that children know that 'A' potential means we want to see 'A' results. We demand that our children do their best. We see in the Asian American, Jewish American, and Ethiopian American communities that this can cause children some measure of added stress. That is a concern. On the other hand, their results are spectacular, and worthy of duplicating. We need to obtain their results while minimizing the stress they induce in their children.

ADOPT A SCHOOL

Blacks are going to have to do what we can to provide the schools where their children struggle a fairer share of the resources. For, the larger society has a vested interest in ensuring at least some inequality in order to preserve a continued larger share for their own children. So Black communities have to commit to a public school in the neighborhood. Neighbors within a block or three either direction should adopt a school. Associations in the neighborhood, whose members are from a school's neighborhood, or who simply want to, should adopt a school. Churches especially should adopt a school.

Adoption should mean watching out so as to protect a school from threats, including vandals. It should mean doing a project at least once a year to beautify the school. It should mean helping with a drive to raise money to improve the school's resources. It could mean participating in a plan for the school's major improvement. Some can help a school garner the kind of resources that will make it a magnet school, and provide the school a mega-grant for capital improvement. If nothing else, an annual campaign to pick up trash and landscape will promote the kind of love of the school that will engender more love in the school; for love is contagious. Tony Brown reminds us that we can find the resources to do this work.

If the Talented Tenth—the elite of Black society— has $16 billion to spend on annual meetings of Black organizations each year, we certainly have enough money to save the boy or girl who may discover the cure for some mysterious disease. (Tony Brown, Black Lies, White Lies, 2)

Some associations will be able to share their resources with the school. Sometimes the resources will be members who are good at math or science and are willing to give out their phone number for those teachers or parents who could use the help. Other times it may mean letting a school use a computer lab, a stage, or a parking lot. Adoption means many things, all of which translate into community care for an institution caring for our kids.

REMEDIAL PROGRAMMING

Black children in the U.S. are the lowest performing of all groups SAT, IQ and WASL tested, and have been so since such tests were devised. We have a problem. In a system that purports to be a meritocracy, in which education is the primary way of upward mobility, this is a wall preventing our advancement. It is totally unacceptable. It augurs for remediation for school aged young people to a massive degree.

The first thing we must do is expose the paltry remedial programming in the schools. Some of these programs are so bad that they simply baby-sit the students as they fall further and further behind. Others have more to do with drugging the students with mood altering medication merely to make the child docile—nearly comatose—as other students excel beyond them. It is a travesty. As these kids fall further behind starting mainly in the second grade, social engineers calculate the number of prisons they will need to build to house these children when they become young adults. Real and across the board remediation is needed immediately.

We need to pour resources into the re-education of our people. They need to master the 'three Rs': reading, writing, and arithmetic. In school at study hall or in school-provided remediation classes, or after school in on or off-site classes, programs with a track record are needed to help our students falling behind catch up. This is crucial.

Incidentally, West African students in the 1990s were some of the very highest performing college students in Western Europe. Moreover, anecdotal evidence suggests that

Ethiopian and Eritrean American students perform not at the bottom but towards the middle on SAT and Assessment of Student Learning tests. What does this suggest? It suggests that it is not nature that causes African Americans to score lower but nurture.

What we do should engender fun and excitement in order to get around learning being boring. We have to have contests and games for our children that require them to learn deeply. They need audio/visual materials for such learners. We need kinetic activity for those who learn through movement; and so on.

PRIVATE SCHOOLING

Where public schools are failing, private schooling is an option for some Black families. Private schools generally are a full level above public schools in student academic preparation. On the other hand, they are expensive. Few Black families can afford the fees. Then there is the question of supply: there are just not enough seats for all of the Black students whose parents seek their entry even if they could find the resources for tuition and other fees. So private schools are for the foreseeable future a limited option for the Black community educational plan.

CHARTER SCHOOLS

Charter schools also provide Black parents an option where schools are sub-standard. Albeit, this option is even more limited than is private schools. The charter school movement is starting to take off, yet there are fewer charter schools than private schools, although they are a type of private schooling. Some Blacks can afford to establish their own private or charter schools. Most could not begin to do so. This is at best a partial remedy.

HOME SCHOOLING

There are Black parents who are part of the home school movement. It takes fewer resources to home school a few children than to establish a charter or other private school. Children who have been home schooled perform well on board examinations like national assessment of student learning tests (in Washington, that test is called the WASL). Still, most parents are working too hard for too little, and frankly, know too little to home school their children effectively. Home schooling, like charter and other private schools, remains a limited option in our overall educational plan for Black America. Most of our attention has to be in making public schools work for our children and assisting this through as much remediation assistance we can muster. This, likewise, is at best a partial remedy.

VOCATIONAL SCHOOL, MILITARY, UNIVERSITY

We must encourage our young adults who can to attend the university. Those who cannot must go to community college. They will need tuition, books, and boarding money. Others must go to vocational school. This may seem like a shocker, but I support our young people joining the military. For those who have diminished opportunities, this can be "a great place to start."

Lastly, we must lobby government to change anti-educational laws like those that deny federal funding to students with a felony. What sinister group established this? How did we allow this to happen? This hurts our adults proportionately more than any other.

TEACHING OUR HISTORY: AFRICA, THE HEART OF PANGEA

Now for the more fun part of this chapter: our educational professionals need to guide all of those interested, especially our students, into understanding the unique place of Africa, and the unique contribution of African people. The truth is not as it has been sold. The real truth will not be told right unless we do it our selves. The truth of the matter is that Africa is not one of many places from which humans began, or minor to the development of civilization. No the truth is much more delicious.

It begins with the physical world, the world of geography. Africa the land mass was at the center of the combination of most all, if not all, of the continents of the world. Many millions of years ago, the continents began to drift apart. They are on plates, and these plates are drifting (plate tectonics). The last I checked, this larger land mass was called pangea. The continents, including Africa, seem to be on plates that have them moving away from Africa generally.

The advantage for Africa is that it has apparently remained straddling the equator. It has not been frozen in glaciations. Instead, it was the place animals and, in time, people could go to in order to be protected from the cold. This has made the African geologic record rich in fossils and material that has helped humanity discover the past chain of life.

When it comes to geography, it is also important to engage the world in a discussion of maps. What do I mean? Africa has historically been portrayed on maps much smaller than it is, and the northern hemisphere is depicted as much larger. This is true. The map I am referring to is the Mercatur Projection. Believe it or not, it puts the equator 2/3rd of the way down on the page instead of in the middle of the page, and amplifies North America and Northern Europe. Africa, as a result, and South America are reduced accordingly.

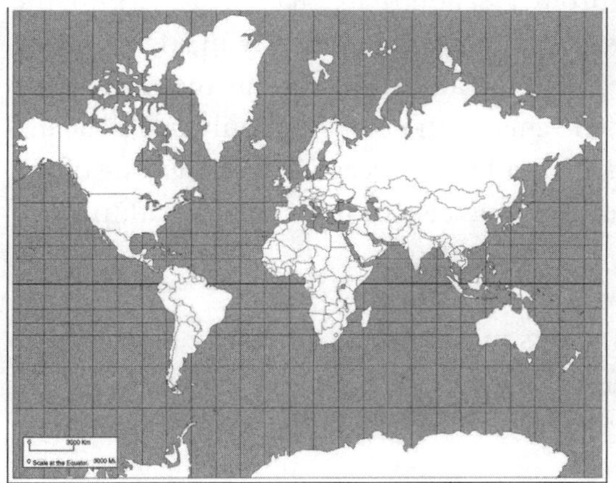

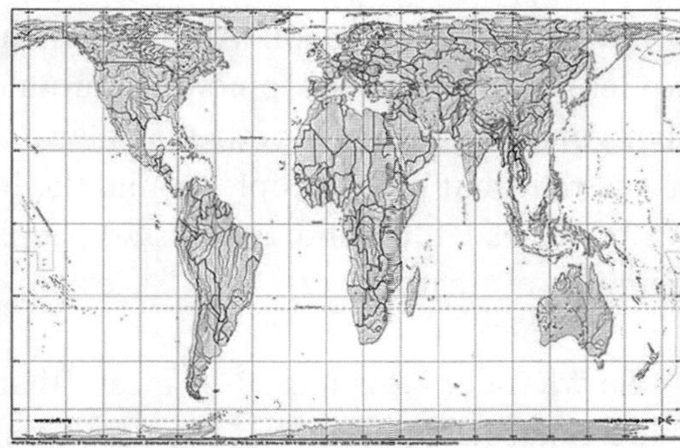

Mercatur Projection *(left)* and Peter's Projection

A better map is the Peter's Projection. When one sees Africa, the continent on the plate that has moved the least, one sees that Africa is a huge place. It is larger than every continent other than Eurasia. This should help a person understand that a continent so large has to be rich resources. For, Africa is not a poor place. Quite to the contrary, it is rich in natural resources from diamonds and gold, to oil and uranium. Fortunes have been made from its soil and shores; fortunes continue to be made. Yet, too little has been done to share those resources with the people whose ancestors have long inhabited such rich geography. Africa is not poor.

TEACHING OUR HISTORY: AFRICA, THE CRADLE OF HUMANITY

Africa is also the place from which human life has dawned. Scientist used to believe that human life formed independently in a number of different places, Africa being merely one. The 'Out of Africa' theory competed with this idea, arguing that all of human life came from Africa alone. Further scientific finds, including two important DNA tests, proved that all of humanity had to come from a common mother and father.

In other words, the idea of a genetic Adam and Eve seems to be confirmed. That couple was from no other continent than the continent of Africa. So this means that every person originally hailed from Africa. Thus, we are all African in ancestry.

It further means that darker skin is very likely closer to the original pigmentation than is lighter skin. This was confirmed both by genetic and now linguistic studies. Genetic studies demonstrate that there are about five branches of humanity from Homo Sapien Sapien, and possibly a contribution from Neanderthals that made it into the Homo Sapien genetic pool. All five branches of humanity are presently in Africa. Only two left. One left Africa somewhere around 35,000 bc and ended up in Australia as the Aboriginal people. Some of that people's marker remains in people not only in Africa and in Australia, but in the people around the Indian and Pacific Oceans. Another one of the five branches left around 10,000 and peopled everyone else in the entire world, including much of Africa.

So what does this mean? It means that there is more genetic similarity between the lightest person in Iceland and someone in Africa, than there is among people in Africa. It means that each of us come from African parents. Find the lightest person around and let them know that they are originally from African people whose skin color was much darker, and that they are more similar to someone from Africa than many Africans are to each other. It means that the Adam and Eve figures within our religion of whatever type was African. It means that slavery, colonialism, segregation, and imperialism happened to the people who were most like our original parents, starting from the place from whence all of our parents came. It means that when we called Africans the ethnic group closest to the monkeys and thus the least human, we were saying something ugly about our own forbears and our selves.

TEACHING OUR HISTORY: AFRICA, THE CRADLE OF CIVILIZATION

The most forward thinking scholars now clearly admit to the fact that plate tectonics occurs, there is drift mostly away from Africa; and they concede that humans originated in Africa, and that the 'Out of Africa' theory has won the day. However, they are staunch about arguing that civilization really developed with the Greeks. Today they will afford Mesopatamia, the region around modern day Iraq, as having contributed a little to the

Greeks, along with the Phoenicians who lived around modern day Israel and Lebanon. Still, the most open minded scholars doing the cutting edge work are slow to recognize the contributions to civilization of the Nile people, especially those in ancient Egypt.

However, Martin Bernal, Cheikh Anta Diop, and others have provided a long board and fulcrum for overturning this error as well. Cheikh Anta Diop did melanin studies on Egyptian mummies in France as well as work on African societies at the University of Senegal. His work led him to present at a United Nations Educational Scientific and Cultural Organization (UNESCO). At the conference he argued that the Egyptian pharaohs were 'Africoid' and not 'Caucasoid'. Around this time he wrote a major book on the contribution of Africans to civilization entitled *Civilization or Barbarism.* His work was largely ignored. However, owing to his being a chemist and physicist, his research had the rigor that later scholars could use.

Then came Martin Bernal. Martin Bernal is a Jewish American professor of Linguistics and Eastern Civilization who recently retired from Cornell University. He has written four major, major works on how the Egyptians greatly influenced Greek culture entitled *Black Athena: Volume I* (1987), *Black Athena: Volume II* (1991), *Black Athena Writes Back* (2001), and *Black Athena: Volume III* (2006). 15 scholars across disciplines challenged and refuted Black Athena in a work entitled *Black Athena Revisited* (1995). Once Bernal responded to this in 2001, the respect and momentum returned to him. Then when Bernal published volume 3 in 2006, he won more acclaim and regard for his earth shaking position about the Greeks and the Egyptians.

So what does all of this mean? It means that the strongest argument to date is that the very civilization traditionally taught has having launched civilization, the Greeks, were largely influenced by the Egyptians. To be more specific, it is becoming clear that the Egyptians were the first to develop writing, larger societies with diversification of labor. The Egyptians were among the first of the larger political societies. It appears that the Egyptians were the first monotheists. All of these are crucial markers of civilization.

All of this should stand to reason given that Africa is the cradle of civilization. Count Volney may have said it best around 1800 when in the *Ruins of Empires* he stated that civilization probably came from the African people. He said this during a time in which Africans were enslaved in the Americas, and seen as beastial by many Europeans.

Consequently, most all of the major points I was taught in school and college regarding civilization are wrong. Africa was not the place of insignificance civilizationally, a place of darkness. It is most likely a place of primary original civilizational contribution, a place of light. These are points our children must know. They can learn these things basically in primary school, completely in secondary school, and thoroughly in college. We need not wait for shoestring teaching on this from others; this is bootstrap teaching that we need to do for our selves.

In fact, we need to try to take our children to some of these spots so that they can see them for them selves. The best kind of learning is first person learning. A picture is always more descriptive than a word. They must travel to places that will expose them to the world, and particularly the world of where they came from—the motherland. If they cannot go there, they should at least go to Jamaica or the Bahamas.

TEACHING OUR HISTORY: THE WORST IS OVER

As bad as things are, they are not the worst they have been. For all of the African diaspora (African people around the world), the worst was probably 1910. In 1910, the African countries were largely locked in colonialism, with Europeans telling them who their national leaders would be and what their economies would export. In 1910, most of the Blacks in the diaspora were either in Brazil or the U.S. In each country they had just sprung from slavery only to be plagued by a society that still relegated them to the bottom of society. In the U.S. this was by law and austere; in Brazil it was by custom and subtle.

James Loewen has written well on jurisdictions that refused upon threat of violence to allow Blacks to remain after the sun went down in a book entitled *Sundown Towns: A Hidden Dimension of American Racism.* Loewen recounts that there were sundown neighborhoods, towns, cities, and even one state, the state of Oregon. The worst and greatest number of them were not in the north but in the south. Loewen states that the most awful time was around 1910, a time he calls the nadir of racism. Then racist laws returned completely; then the Ku Klux Klan was at its ascendancy; then it was that lynchings were commonplace in the U.S.

100 years later Africa is independent and on the mend. A century later Africans in Brazil and the rest of Latin America are struggling financially but freer politically. Five score years later African Americans in the U.S. are out of slavery and segregation, and slowly discovering how to unlock the subtle control of the Southern Strategy. We are doing better. There is comfort in knowing this.

We must teach our children what Dr. Leonard Jeffreys says, "We are on a victorious path." Our educational leaders can help us with this. We are not on a victorious path to hurt anyone; we are standing in the bright sun in order to help ourselves, and as many others as will listen to our message about the parenthood of Divinity, and the siblinghood of humanity.

ARTS:
SUPPORTING OUR ARTISTS, MESSAGE, THEATRE, AND MUSEUMS

We must never forget that art is not a form of propaganda;
it is a form of truth.
(JOHN F. KENNEDY)

Blacks have traditionally had to operate in a situation
where whites have set themselves up as the custodians of the black experience.
(AUGUST WILSON)

The predicament of our arts would be different if our artists practiced Afrocentricity. Such a development would add even more luster to the power of our creative ethos as we control the dissemination, presentation, and interpretation of our art. For, feeling and time (rhythm) are the key criteria in discussing the aesthetic for black people. The form, feeling, and rhythm must come out of our cultural consciousness or memory. Black people, internationally, can draw upon a collective bank that houses images, symbols, references, and resources based upon history and mythology.
(MOLEFE ASANTE, AFROCENTRICITY)

The artists could lead this whole movement by themselves, such is their creativity and power in the culture. The artistic area is important generally; in the Black community it is impactful beyond measure. Black rappers have the world talking; Black singers have the world crooning; Black jazz artists have the world bopping; Black dancers have the world stepping.

Blacks have influenced the foremost non-Black artists: Kenny G., the leading Jazz artist, was trained by Blacks in Washington; Elvis Presley, called the "king," borrowed from Black singing and dancing styles; the Beatles admit to modeling Black artists, and they are the leading pop group in the history of music. Now Black playwrights, authors, and visual artists are making their marks in the culture. Given that art does more than sell tickets—it informs, inspires, and entertains—Black artists are in the unique position of being able to challenge and transmit ideas.

The question is "what ideas will they transmit?" "what ideas will they challenge?" Will they continue to transmit the ideas of those outside of their community, as August Wilson above chides against. Or will they move toward the transmitting of ideas that are distinct to them? Will they be controlled by those outside of their community, leading them to be purveyors of that which is foreign to them, a type of propaganda; or will they be conveyors of that which is authentic to them, the truth of their own experience. This is what Molefe Asante teaches.

Artists can challenge perceptions, change minds, champion causes. Black artists must do so. For, there are perceptions that definitely need challenging, minds that terribly need changing, and causes that utterly need championing. Accordingly, we must encourage artists to inform Blacks of who we are, where we came from, where we are going, and how to get there. We want more than art that is as good as another group. We want art that moves us to accomplish our 10% growth and to do the other parts of this plan. We want art that moves our people to see that Africa is the cradle of humanity and cradle of civilization. We want art that causes Black Americans to understand that they must serve Blacks in the Motherland and in the diaspora. It is time for artists to step up to the highest level. So this is a call to all artists sympathetic to the Black community's condition. This is a call for the artistic leaders to rise to come together in order to save a people.

The artists could lead this whole movement by themselves, such is their creativity and power in the culture. The artistic area is important generally; in the Black community it is impactful beyond measure. Black rappers have the world talking; Black singers have the world crooning; Black jazz artists have the world bopping; Black dancers have the world stepping.

DEVELOPMENT OF A PLAN

It is time to move on an artistic plan. In order to better portray who we are, what we have been through, how we got over, who helped us do it, and where we are going, the following steps should seem as self-evident as they are indispensable:

DEVELOPING AND IMPLEMENTING THE ARTISTIC PLAN

- Launch plan study groups and best practices analysis.
- Call artistic professionals together.
- Confer on an overall plan.
- Call artists together in areas.
- Adopt specialized plans.
- Isolate the major initiatives we will do for ourselves.
- Clarify the help we need from outside the community.
- Agree on a artistic area plan.
- Determine how to measure the success.
- Present the plan to the overall plan leaders.
- Execute the plan.
- Quality control how the plan is proceeding.

We need not say much about these above steps, except that we should do them. I must elaborate though on a few points. First, this is another one of those areas that is beyond my expertise, so my comments are again few and measured here. Second, hopefully we will study the best of what is being done around the nation, and world and incorporate the best practices.

ARTISTIC PROFESSIONALS

Who are the artists that should respond? They are those who work in the following categories: the dramatic (i.e., plays), literary (i.e., novels, poems), musical, kinesthetic (i.e., dance), athletic, oratorical (i.e., rap, spoken word), and visual (i.e., paintings, sculptures) categories. From the dramatic arts we need producers, playwrights, directors, actors, set designers, apparel designers, choreographers, cinematographers, and stagehands to come together.

From the literary arts we need writers, publishers, editors, and publicists to convene. From the musical arts we need singers, rappers, spoken word artists, producers, arrangers, writers, musicians, disk jockeys to join together. Representing the kinesthetic arts we urge dancers of all forms including marshal artists to come together. As well we appeal to all athletes, coaches, doctors, trainers, owners, agents, scouts, cheerleaders to participate. From the oratorical arts we ask speakers, poets, debaters, and rappers of all sorts to make the meeting. From the visual arts we need to see painters, potters, glass blowers, sculptors, woodworkers, and architects. We need all of the artists to participate and to be part of the answer.

ARTISTS MUST EMPHASIZE THE IMPORTANCE OF ECONOMICS

One of the top five exports of the U.S. is entertainment. In fact, it may be in the top three. In other words, the U.S. is making big money from our music, MTV, movies and the like. Moreover, artists plying their trade want to make a living from what they do—a good living, hopefully. All of this is thoroughly economic activity.

In the Black community art is certainly about money. This is a primary way in which careers are launched and fortunes made. Given the economic nature of the creative expression, perhaps artists can help our community see the primacy of economics to our rise. If our artists were to depict, portray, or express this, it will help our people to get it.

Artists can do more than inform. The arts are a major area for exporting, which holds the specter of bringing millions into our community from outside of it. The more affirming our arts, the greater the likelihood that they will guarantee our rise. The more affirming our arts, the more likely it will appeal to more people in more places. The more affirming our arts, the wealthier and healthier we will be.

For we are such a creative people that art uncontainably springs from our soul in ways that resonate in the world. Rap music rose from the doldrums of the ghetto. Clothing styles surfaced from prison garb. Genres like the blues alighted from depressing conditions. Art explodes from our reality and makes its way across the globe. It is stunning.

Artists should help the community focus on getting the 10% return that we must have in order to really see net growth. It will require that we have an ownership mentality. Sports figures like Magic Johnson can help us with this. Of all of the artists, it is especially the rappers that seem to get the point of ownership and supporting Black professionals.

ART CIVILITY: ENDING THE VIOLENCE

With the death of Tupac and Biggie Smalls the country began to learn about the problem of rivalry and violence in the Black community. It is called "beef." Jay Z and Nas almost came to fire on each other. 50 Cents and the Game's crews had an altercation.

This is really only the tip of a nasty iceberg. The real problem that lies under the water line is all of the violence in the music, for the violent lyrics and images encourages threats, intimidation, and the settlement of problems by force by everyday people in the Black community. The younger generation is the most vulnerable to this. Is it any wonder that Black on Black murder is the leading cause of death for Black male young adults.

It is time to bring civility to this madness. Black art cannot rise to the high calling of a renaissance plan until we deal with this head-on. We have to solve this problem. The solution requires more than town hall summits and resulting agreements. All of this is necessary. Yet it must be linked to honorable wage jobs for our people, particularly our young adults so that they will have more to live for, so that they are more vested in this life, so that they will have greater reason to listen to words of reason, so that they are more distracted by legal labor, and so that they will be more tired after working an eight-hour day.

CLEANING UP OUR ART

The June 2007 issue of *Ebony* has on the cover these words: "Who are YOU calling _ _ _ _ _." Those underlines could be "nigga," "bitch," "whore" or whatever. All of this followed a conservative television and 'shock jock' radio personality named Don Imus who called African American women on the second place NCAA women's basketball championship team from Rutgers "nappy-headed hoes." He said that they were not nearly as attractive as the women, predominantly Black, from Tennessee the first place team. It caused a national stir, leading to the cancellation of his show on the MSNBC television channel.

Imus' defense was that he was simply repeating an oft used phrase of the rappers. Rev. Al Sharpton called for Imus' firing. Supporters of Imus asked both Sharpton and Rev. Jesse Jackson why they were coming against Imus, but not against the rappers who made a living on such language. It led many Black leaders including Sharpton to initate a campaign to remove the 'N' word from use in all music.

Ebony's magazine edition followed the Imus affair. It raised the question, 'What is wrong with us that we are still marketing such language to ourselves and the world?'

Now I can understand rappers who grew up in the worst ghettos using such language, although this still does not condone it. It is their world and what they live. Given that art is a reflection of one's environment and that art springs from such a context, I do not fault them as I do others. On the other hand, artists who did not grow up like this, or who are not any more living like this really need to be held accountable for what they are doing. Rappers are not the only artists who use such language. They are only the most notorious. We must clean up all of music specifically and African American subculture generally.

Moreover, labels and producers, many of whom are suburban and White, need to stop stereotyping artists to perform such gangsta music and make such portrayals under the excuse that "This is what people want." These same producers and distributors finance all kinds of music that demean women and other groups in society. Surely, we need to clean up all of music and the dominant culture as well. People are going to buy the best of what is available. If such trashy words are less available, there will be less demand for it.

NO MORE BEING CHEAPSKATES

We have to deal with the issue of failing to properly pay our artists. The worst way in which we offend is through pirating. African American youth particularly down- load, burn, or copy way, way too much of our artists' product. This is not only a crime outside of our community, it is robbery within our community. The artists deserve their money, including those who represent and distribute the artist. If the artist has contracts with those people, then that is the artist's team. It all comes back to the artist, whom we are not helping if we receive copies from people who are not paying the artist.

For years I had been an art cheapskate in the sense that I was used to buying certain types of visual art. I bought mass produced copies of the original, paper duplications. I bought the stuff either because I liked the image or because the colors matched things in a room. Then for very selfish and practical reasons I had to reassess.

I realized that there were starving artists sales at which I could have purchased original art at about the same price of my worthless copies. It struck me as well that not all artists charge in the hundreds and thousands for their works. Some who are still in school or have hit hard times sell art for tens of dollars. It dawned on me that I could find works of images I liked or even colors that matched, while at the same time obtaining something that had a small chance of being worth money down the road. I figure that of the ten to twenty pieces of original art I have, one of them is likely to be worth thousands by the time I die. That is a better investment of my money.

These are selfish reasons. It is equally, or more, important that we support the people who make our lives more beautiful, meaningful, and joyful. They deserve an investment in their lives to keep them doing what they do so well. Most of them live low to the ground as they cannot afford the lifestyle that would have them living large. So, no more buying paper art or worthless imitations for me.

I hope that all of us have this attitude about art across the board. No more staying at home and expecting others to patronize our movies, plays, dances, and shows. Let's support our artists better. Here is a good place to recognize those outside of our community who are invaluable to our artists. Many of them support our artists better than we do. As my Stepfather would say, "That's a da gone shame"; but it is the truth. We need every shoestring we can get outside of our community.

Some of us think we patronize the arts, but ask artists and they will tell you that we really do not do so nearly enough. Get a group of artists from a community together, and they will snap a community out of its illusions about supporting Black art. They will tell it how it is, a truth many may not want to hear. We do not support our artists as we should; we are art cheapskates. We need an art 12-step program.

WE NEED TO BRING MORE ART TO OUR COMMUNITIES

We need more art in our surroundings. Every family, every association, and every community should do a project annually to beautify the surroundings of places that are vital to them. Families can do something every year for Big Momma's house, yard, or wardrobe. If Big Momma's environment is in good shape, then go to the next oldest person in the family.

Associations can link together to do something with those in each community. This could begin and end with what is done for a school in the community as stated in the Education chapter, if that is all a community can do at first. However, it is my hope that there will be enough support to do an additional project for an important intersection, corner, or street too. Place flowers there and beautify our spaces. Have a professional bricklayer build a half wall on either side of a corner and pay for something distinctive that celebrates the name of the community. Do something that is architecturally appropriate and professionally well done.

Perhaps we can take it step further still. We can encourage the families and associations to take care of members of theirs whose living spaces are in serious disrepair. This is unhealthy for the minds and bodies of such Black folk; it attracts further disrepair and leads to blight. This is bad for business. Make a ghetto near you come alive with flowers, paint, and green spaces. If they destroy it, wait for a number of years for a group to rise who will protect and maintain the improvements. Then do it again. Do not let a small group of vandals and malcontents keep a neighborhood locked in deterioration. On the other hand, do not fix every year that which no one will step up to maintain.

LEARNING TO LOVE YOURSELF AND THINGS AFRICAN

We have to change our thinking though if we are going to encourage the kind of art that will help us with the renaissance, for we are not supporting afrocentric art well today. Too many of us still do not think that it is of them, or that it is beautiful. It bespeaks the fact that we are still not quite healthy. We have too many artists going out of business or going hungry who are producing art that is African either in its presentation or inspiration. It would be a huge disservice to encourage artists to venture more into an area in which we are doing so little.

We need to address this during Development Week. One way to do so is by encouraging African dress during certain days. I do not believe each day should be only indigenous African dress. Certain days should incorporate African American twists to African dress so as to incorporate the American part of our heritage as well. So, it should be all right to have clothes that are an amalgam of African and American heritage. Of course there should be at least one service at which we encourage everyone to have indigenous African dress.

At the venue we should have African artifacts to lend environmental authenticity to what we are doing in the program to push the plan.

COMMISSIONING AN ARTIST TO PRODUCE FOR THE NEXT DEVELOPMENT WEEK

One of things we can do to promote the place and value of our art is by financing it during Development Week. One way to do this is to have a committee vote on and announce the artist who will produce a work for the next Development Week. At the venue we should showcase the last commissioned work, a work that hopefully will encourage us to see a part of our plan as the artist is inspired to show it.

Molefe Asante stated that our artists were in a "predicament." The predicament has to do with the lack of art that liberates us and the lack of support for such art within our community. We have to do something about our predicament. I am pledged though to doing far more, and the needs of our community require such. We need our artists to help convey the points of our plan to our people until our people get it. We need artists for such a time as this to help deliver on the renaissance that will make our children's lives better. It is time for artists to rise.

SPIRITUAL:
GREAT COMMANDMENT, GOLDEN RULE, GROWING SPIRITUALITY

From the establishment of the first black church in America, throughout slavery and beyond, the church has been the foundation of the black community.
(CHARLES A. TAYLOR, JUNETEENTH: A CELEBRATION OF FREEDOM)

I charge you pastors to stop competing and start completing. Turn your jealousy into love. Because what God is trying to do is too big for your church [to do alone]
(MYLES MUNROE, SERMON, COVENANT CHRISTIAN CENTER INTERNATIONAL, PEORIA, ILLINOIS, TELEVISED AUGUST, 2006)

So we come to the last but far from the least area. Personally, I am persuaded that it is the most important area. Whether other groups know it or not, the spiritual arena is always the most important to the protection and care of any and every people, for the spiritual leaders often have the attention of the greater part of the community. In fact, Black spiritual leaders could superintend Black development by themselves. Of all the spiritual leaders, the Black preachers could by themselves cause and carry the renaissance, if only they would simply unite around such an endeavor. As Charles Taylor stated in the above quote, the church has been the "foundation" of the Black community.

The church must become active again in social action reminiscent of what it did during the heyday of civil rights. It must seek to keep channels of communication open between the Black and White communities. It must take an active stand against injustice that Negroes confront in housing, education, police protection, and in city and state courts. It must exert its influence in the area of economic justice. As guardian of the moral and spiritual life of the community, the church cannot look with indifference upon these glaring evils. We must take the advice of Dr. Myles Munroe and "stop competing and start completing" the major work that is before us. What God is trying to do certainly is so big that there is room for everyone to gloriously be their authentic selves, and for every minister to play an honorable role.

Realistically, it is not simply the church that will lead this. Our people are too varied in their religious affiliation. Those of all faiths need to work together to promote love of God, love for ourselves as a people, the golden rule for those inside and outside of the community, the fulfillment of our higher calling as a people, and execution of a plan like this one. The kind of neighborly love of which I speak is a Good Samaritan to those in need; this is the kind of love that there is just too little of. Also, those of all faiths need to be behind every leadership team, the umbrella leaders as well as those in each area, to ensure that they get this job done, for spiritual leaders—particularly Black Christian leaders—must sacrifice more than any other leaders to see that the common good is advanced.

So this is more than a call, this is a cry for the spiritual leaders to rally. It is time for the spiritual leaders to do what their belief and calling demands of them and pursue as a priority the establishment of a way of being so complete that it can only be likened to the kingdom of God. Spiritually leaders need to get clear about what they believe, and need to get in the habit of meeting regularly to make full use of their ministry.

RELIGIOUS LEADERS

Identifying our religious leaders is rather easy. They are the bishops, superintendents, elders, pastors, priests, prelates, imams, deacons, deaconesses, teachers, professors, evangelists, and missionaries who serve in the various religious denominations in Black America. Christianity, Islam, Buddhism, Africanism, and Theism comprise the main beliefs of African Americans. This call is to their religious leaders, especially to the Black church leaders.

So this is more than a call, this is a cry for the spiritual leaders to rally. It is time for the spiritual leaders to do what their belief and calling demands of them and pursue as a priority the establishment of a way of being so complete that it can only be likened to the kingdom of God.

PREPARING TO LIFT A PEOPLE

1. Confer on the oneness of your faith.
2. Become kingdom minded.
3. Meet within denominations.
4. Meet among denominations.
5. Meet among faiths.
6. Prepare a spiritual plan.
7. Incorporate that plan into the overall plan.

INDISPENSABILITY OF THE BLACK CHURCH

The Black church has been the center of Black life and culture. It was our only outlet in the clutches of slavery. It was our refuge during the terrorism of early centuries in this country. It was our base as we devised the overthrow of segregation. It exists still as the prime meeting place during these confusing days dealing with what appears to be the period of affirmative action, but is actually the era of the Southern Strategy.

Our greatest leaders were reared in and were of the church. Richard Allen and Absalom Jones were preachers. Even slave revoltists Denmark Vessey, Gabriel Prosser, and Nat Turner attended church and claimed to have been called to action by God. Sojourner Truth, Ida B. Wells, and Frederick Douglass attended church. Booker T. Washington was known as a very devout church goer, but not so much Marcus Garvey. A. Phillip Randolph was a church leader, as was Adam Clayton Powell, who was a preacher. The greatest Black American leader of the 20th century, if not all time, Martin Luther King, Jr., was a preacher. His lieutenants, Jesse Jackson, Andrew Young, and Ralph Abernathy, were preachers too. Without Black religious leaders, particularly the Black church, there can be no Black renaissance in America.

Throughout the Black community the Black church has had an historic and a symbolic role. It has been the most convenient and effective house for programming. Its speakers have been the most eloquent spokespersons for the community. There are two laudable exceptions to the eloquence examples: Malcolm X and Louis Farrakhan. These two are among the handful of greatest speakers Africa has produced in America.

It is for this reason that I state unabashedly, that the Black church could by themselves cause and carry the renaissance, if only the churches would simply unite around such an endeavor. Surely, the leaders of the Black church could lead this renaissance alone, such is the power of the church of God in Christ. To do so they have to understand how crucial this work is to the kingdom of God, and God's judgment that begins first with his own people. The Black church must take a leading role for the renaissance of Black America; it had better do so if it wants to remain the leading institution in Black America. The preservation of its leading role may well turn on its ability to unify—the very thing believers are commanded to do.

COMMAND TO ONENESS

Oneness is not a new thing. The ancient command in the various faiths to do the golden rule was an edict to be one. The ancient Nile people had such commands. The Hebrews and the nation of Israel had such a command, and they respect it to this day (Leviticus 19:18, 34). The Christian command to oneness is centered on the golden rule and even more on distinct teaching of Jesus on unity.

It is found in the real Lord's Prayer (as opposed to the 'Prayer Jesus Taught Us to Pray' [Matthew 6]):

> *Neither pray I for these alone, but for them also which shall believe on me through their word; that they may be one; as thou, Father, art in me, and I in thee, that they also may be one in us; that the world may believe that thou has sent me....I in them, and thou in me, that they may be made perfect in one; and that the world may know that thou has sent me, and has loved them, as thou hast loved me.* (JOHN 17:20-21)

Christians have no excuse to remain divided. Here our main leader clearly directs that Christians are to be one with each other as Jesus is with God the Father. This is a thorough and utter oneness. Then he states that two particular things would occur were we to do this: first, the world would know that God sent Jesus; second, Christians would know that God loves them like God loved Jesus. I submit to every candid reader that the primary reason that the world does not believe by now that Jesus is who Christians say he is has most to do with Christian division, and then to do with their own understanding of their faith. Moreover, Christians would experience a greater dimension of the love of God themselves if they would be unified through love.

What is the point of all of this to development? In order for Christians, or any religious leaders, to meet regularly to develop and implement a major plan, it is going to require unity. Unity has been sorely lacking. Knowledge that many great faiths demand unity and that Christianity, does as well, provides a point of reflection and conviction which could be used to facilitate the restoration of this unity.

Based on this, Black denominational leaders are urged to regularly convene *within* denominations to get to know each other better and to discuss the matters addressed herein. Next, all of the Black denominational leaders need to periodically convene *among* denominations in each religion, Christian, Muslim, Buddhist, and so on. It is time to unify within denominations and among religious faiths.

DENOMINATIONAL AND INTER-FAITH MEETINGS

The old adage about not discussing religion and politics has to be abandoned with last night's dishwater. If we are going to thrive as a people, then we are going to have to master both of these subjects. Politics was discussed chapters earlier. With respect to religion, meetings will be had within and among religious groups. We need courageous conversations around Christianity, Islam, Judaism, Buddhism, and other religions that have proven themselves worthy in the marketplace of ideas and that have a moral code that all nations can be built upon. At those meetings, they each should come up with proposals for the subsequent level of meetings.

Of these beliefs, none are more important than Christianity and Islam. The Abrahamic religions share something the others do not have: Abraham as a common patriarch. These are the faiths that remind us of the importance of loving God, of the golden rule, and of something like the Ten Commandments. These are the faiths that are strongest in the Black community. Thus, the plan must primarily deal with these two beliefs. In the South, where over half of all Blacks reside, Christianity reigns supreme; it has been the strongest faith, the longest time.

Even if no other people will, religious leaders must guide their people, and they must speak prophetic truth to power. In the U.S., this means helping this country be as good in the world as it is great, as holy as it is mighty, and as caring as it is controlling.

PRIORITY ONE IS TO SEEK THE KINGDOM OF GOD

We need thoughtful, deep discussions and prayers around the most important of subjects: the kingdom of God. Short of this, I am concerned that we will continue to miss God in an essential way. We need an enhanced view of the subject of the kingdom, the ministry of Jesus, Isaiah 61, the Sermon on the Mount, the Good Samaritan, Matthew 25, and the Great Commission.

We are going to progressively see that the religious leaders of old often guided the social, educational, political, and economic systems of their nation. They did this not by default, but by design; not by guessing, but from expertise in all of these fields; not from a distance, but as advisors even to the monarchs. To play such roles, the spiritual leaders had to be philosopher preachers in the ancient sense of the term. They had to be lovers and learners (philo) of all knowledge (sophy). If Jesus is the way, the truth, and the life, then how is it then that the preachers of his are so ignorant about truth and life?

The thoughtful discussions should turn on works within and outside of Christianity. The works within could be these: John Stott, Lukan Kingdom, Howard Thurman, Martin Luther King, John Wesley, and others on the kingdom. I hope my work on the kingdom may also be weighed. We will need to contrast Rushdoony and dominionism, as well as liberation theology. The works outside should look at the role faiths like Judaism and Kemetic religion had on their societies. Black religious leaders must research what Jews, ancient Egyptians, and early Christians did for their people and the role religion played in the nation. In the process, we will learn how paltry is our service to our people, and thus our witness in the world. Religion today is unsavory salt and dim light compared to what the ancient Jews and Egyptians (Kemites) were in their societies.

Once we ascertain the ministry of Christ and the role of religion to society in history, we will discover what we ought to be living up to. Then we shall understand the concept of the "kingdom of God." Once we figure out what the kingdom is, then we will finally be in position to seek it first.

The priority pursuit of the kingdom of God will keep our hands full for the rest of our lives. If we simply sought the kingdom as we have sought getting a car, a home, a college degree, or a mate, we would be so focused and intentional about God's kingdom that it would require at least a lifetime in order to approach such a priority pursuit. The fact that we have sought things on the list of above—some of us have sought all of them—means that we at least know how to pursue major things, and that we have achieved a measure of success.

However, we seem to throw this knowledge away when it comes to the pursuit of the kingdom of God. I am embarrassed, frankly, when I see the effort of the church concerning the pursuit of the kingdom. It looks very half-hearted at best. How we have searched for natural things judges us, and admittedly, convicts us.

On the other hand, I believe the search that God is ordering us to is more than most of us have shown in our pursuit of cars, homes, and relationships. God is calling us to something that I think requires that we examine the lives of biblical characters all over again, especially the life of Jesus. Through the lives of Abraham, Moses, David, Paul, and particularly Jesus we will find a level of pursuit that dwarfs what we have so far demonstrated.

This search will lead us to pursue the kingdom of God like Einstein and the others in the Manhattan Project sought the nuclear bomb. It will move us to search for the kingdom like Stephen Hawking and other contemporary scientist are searching for the answer to how our universe came to be (the grand unified theory). It will move us to search for the kingdom of God like Jordan sought NBA championships, like Florence Griffith Joyner ('Flo Jo') sought sprint championships, like Muhammad Ali sought the heavyweight championship of the world. It will move us to seek the kingdom of God like Jesus sought to live sinless, sought to preach the gospel, sought to endure the cross, sought to despise the shame, sought to give his life, and sought to rise again. We will finally learn what 'priority' means, and then we will be in position to hear the resurrected Christ call us to go into all the world and make disciples of every nation (the Great Commission).

Truly, we have been too distracted and too easily satisfied. Too many of us have merely wanted a church rather than seeking as a priority the kingdom of God. The church is not the kingdom; we are the inhabitants of the kingdom of God but we are not the kingdom of God. The kingdom is the rule and realm of God in all of its holistic power. The church is the "called out ones," the ecclesia. Jesus commanded that we seek first his kingdom; he said "Upon this rock I will build my church." We get things out of order. No wonder we get in such trouble.

HOW WE FARE UNDER A COMPARATIVE RELIGIOUS ANALYSIS OF COMMUNITY IMPACT

When compared to each of these religious systems, Black Christian leaders particularly come up short and have work to do. In each of these periods, the religious system or leaders mentioned provided more effective leadership than what Black leaders are giving their people now. The Egyptian priests governed the educational system, taught and spoke truth to the pharaohs, and governed righteousness in the land (a concept they called "maat"). Jewish priests manned the temple, and the temple was the center of religious, social, judicial, and educational life. With the loss of the temple, the synagogue played this role in a reduced but still central way. These religious systems were providing the values and principles from which sprang the culture that shaped the institutions that molded generations.

Christians have had spells during which they more thoroughly shaped the culture. The main time that this occurred was during the times of and after Constantine as well as during the civil rights era in the U.S. These times show that comprehensive Christian involvement can be a good thing. The civil rights era settled in doubt in the Black community, if there was any, that the Black church could be important to all of Black life. With respect to the early Christian times, the church helped shape the mores and culture of Rome during the times of Constantine and the institutions of northern Europe.

The problem was not that they were involved, but instead how they were involved. Christian leaders, we have work to do. We should be showing due love for all of Black life. This is Christian. Christ himself was mindful of the peoples' spiritual and medical welfare. Some scholars believe that he spent as much as two-thirds of his time healing. Jesus Christ provided material sustenance for those who followed him, sometimes numbering in the thousands. He commented on the nature of the political representation. He said that he was the way, the truth, and the life, and that he came to give people abundant life. He announced that the proof that the Spirit of the Lord was upon him was that he preached to the poor, set captives free, and healed the sick. He warned that the difference between eternal salvation and eternal damnation could be what one did for the homeless, imprisoned, lonely, and hungry. He went further by saying that he was in the homeless, imprisoned, lonely, and hungry. Without a doubt, Jesus was holistic in approach and his gospel was comprehensive in scope.

Black leaders of the Civil Rights Movement did more for the people politically, socially, and at times economically than current Black leaders are doing. Clearly, they had a more expansive and thorough view of their faith to their culture. They cared more that the people would "prosper, and be in health, even as their souls prospered (3 John 2). They wanted the people to be whole mind, body and spirit.

This is not to say that none of the current pastors are doing anything holistic for the people. No, we have many examples of great work being done here and there. *Black Enterprise* in April of 2006 spotlighted a number of pastors working for the economic development of Blacks in their area. Certain of these pastors are politically involved as well. These are examples of where we need to go. Foremost among these pastors are Floyd Flake and John Perkins.

RELIGIOUS LEADERS MUST EMPHASIZE THE IMPORTANCE OF ECONOMICS

Slowly but surely religious leaders are coming to see that the front of the battle is now economic in nature. We could have gotten there a long time ago by combining the teaching of James with the knowledge of the times. James stated,

> *Pure (true) religion and undefiled before God and the Father is this, To visit the fatherless, and widows in their affliction, and to keep himself unspotted from the world....*
>
> *But ye have despised the poor....What doth it profit, my brethren, though a man say he hath faith, and have not works? Can faith save him? If a brother or sister be naked, and destitute of daily food, and one of you say unto them, Depart in peace, be ye warmed and filled; notwithstanding ye give them not those things which are needful to the body; what doth it profit? Even so faith, if it hath not works, is dead, being alone.* (JAMES 1:27; 2:6,14-17 AMP.)

A number of scholars believe that this James was Jesus' half-brother (they had different Fathers although Mary was only with one man). If we would have understood the political gain (end of segregation) but the economic plight of African Americans, and then combined this with simply the teaching of James, we would have come to see that economics must lead the way.

In fact, some of the most impactful ministries in the country are engaged in economic outreach. Pastor and former congressman Floyd Flake, John Perkins (who now has the distinction of an institute at Seattle Pacific University named in his honor), Harold Calvin

Ray, and Myles Munroe are all examples of economically relevant urban ministries. Ron Sider has a book entitled *Rich Christians in an Age of Hunger* that is in multiple editions. Ray Bakke's, *Gospel as Big as a City*, is also an important read. We would do well to follow the example of preachers like Flake or Perkins, and to read works like Sider's or Bakke's.

PRAYING FOR THE KINGDOM OF GOD

Then we must talk with God. It is disfunctional for spiritual leaders to confer on anything without prayer being at the center of our conferences. We should do more than talk to each other—we have to talk with our God as well. To not do so is sort of an atheistic display of a believing people; this is not only inconsistent, it is hypocritical and an oxymoron.

Prayer is our communication to, with, and from God, and thus it must be afforded a favored place in everything that we do. Yet, prayer breakfasts are but the beginning of the prayer that is needed. Ultimately, we need to do the kind of sustained prayer that looks closer to a prayer vigil certain churches hold around New Year's Eve, or a three-day fast such as many of the Pentecostal churches do on a moment's notice upon a pastor's request. It is the continual and fervent prayer that really makes the difference, as opposed to a light prayer around breakfast.

With knowledge of the kingdom of God, the commitment to seek it as a priority, uniting to discuss our condition, and praying with fervency to seek God's wisdom, we will facilitate the kind of spiritual renewal that involves social responsibility. These two—spiritual renewal and social responsibility—are the powerful legs of a church that transforms the culture.

SPIRITUAL LEADERS MUST MAKE THESE IDEAS REAL

- Being zealous about the Greatest Commandment of divine love.
- Being zealous about the Great Commandment of mutual love.
- Taking care of your own members: charity at home.
- Promoting the High calling on African Americans.
- Sacrificing for the common good.
- Speaking truth to power.
- Superintending a plan like this one.

ZEALOUS ABOUT THE GREATEST COMMANDMENT OF DIVINE LOVE

Many religions teach the centrality of loving God (the goddess, or the gods). Christianity is no different. In the *Husia*, Maulana Karenga revised some of the ancient Egyptian religious texts, incorporating them in one work that he subtitled as "Sacred Wisdom of Ancient Egypt."

> *O' Amen Ra, you shepherd who brings forth the flock in the morning, leading the hungry to green pastures. As the shepherd leads his flock to green meadows, so do you, O' Ra, lead the needy to food. For Ra is indeed a good shepherd, never idle, attending those who lean on Him.*
>
> *O' Ra, I love you and I have filled my heart with you.* (KARENGA, HUSIA 18-19)

So the Egyptians had a concept of the love of God(s) that may be thousands of years older than Abraham. For those surprised about a pastor like me quoting words like these, remember that the Hebrews were in Egypt, according to their history, about as long as Africans have been in North America. It Egyptianized the Hebrews similar to being in America Americanized Africans. They intermarried with the Egyptians and they took on their culture, especially Joseph. This continued all the way through Moses, whose very name was Egyptian. When Malachi said that the "Sun" of Righteousness—not "Son"—would rise with healing in its wings (Malachi 4:2), this was one of the images of Ra, the winged sun disk, the very word associated with the phrase 'the rays of the sun' that we still use today.

Moses taught Israel this concept of the love of God and it is clearly stated in the second great reading of the law before Moses died.

> *Hear, O Israel: The Lord our God is one Lord: And thou shalt love the Lord thy God with all thine heart, and with all thy soul, and with all thy might.* (DEUTERONOMY 6:4,5 KJV)

Jesus repeated this same statement some 700 years or so later and made it the greatest commandment of all.

> *Master, which is the great commandment in the law?*
>
> *Jesus said unto him, Thou shalt love the Lord thy God with all thy heart, and with all thy soul, and with all thy mind. This is the first and great commandment.* (MATTHEW 22:36-38)

If this is the greatest commandment of all, than all of our efforts should move people to love God in this way. Once we determine true Great Commandment, we must commit to it and go. We must live that Christianity, that religion, which demands that we love God with all—all of our heart, all of our soul, and of mind, and all of our strength.

I offer no apologies for putting front and center that Blacks need to love God in order to really have a sustained renaissance. Love the Lord your God with all of your heart, all of your soul, all of your mind, and all of your strength. Chambers said it best: we owe our utmost for his highest. When we get this vision of what we are to be and do, we will no longer be embarrassed about who we are and what we have done; we will be prepared to finally be and do that for which we were destined. As African American religious leaders go after this, it will as yeast transform the rest of Christendom and of religion.

ZEALOUS ABOUT THE GREAT COMMANDMENT OF SELF LOVE

I remember viewing in elementary school about a 15-minute black and white film on proper inter-personal conduct. In the film, the moderator described the universal application of the golden rule. Do unto others as you would have them do unto you. He said that it came from the maxim "love your neighbor as you love yourself." The film displayed across the screen those words and the scripture Matthew 22, as well as other sources. I never forgot it.

This was the latter 1960s, a time during which religion had more of a place in the public schools. Even then, it was more religion in the classroom than I had ever seen. I am glad that I, and those with me, had this experience, for this maxim is extremely importance. Service to others begins with loving others; and loving others is the opposite side of the coin of loving oneself.

Whitney Houston re-made a song that was already famous: the greatest love of all. While it is not the greatest love of all from a Christian perspective, love of self is prior to loving anyone else. In this sense, it is greater than loving others. We have to love ourselves. Spiritual leaders must teach and model this kind of love. We need not do much to encourage this, though; Christian leaders already do this well—maybe too well.

Certainly, charity begins at home; we must first love ourselves. Loving the African American community is a type of self-love; it is taking care of home. If we cannot take care of home, loving well those who share our ethnicity, then how are we going to authentically love others? The scriptures discuss taking care of one's own parents and relatives before taking care of those to whom one is unrelated (1 Timothy 5:4, 8; Mark 7:9-13). Paul said it this way, "I lie not, my conscious bearing witness, that I have unceasing pain in my heart for my people, the Jews" (Romans 9:1). We need believers who live themselves like this.

On the heels of this, though, comes love of others.

ZEALOUS ABOUT THE GREAT COMMANDMENT OF MUTUAL LOVE

The commandment provides that we are to love others as we love ourselves. The golden rule states, "Do unto others as you would have them do to you." If we are going to be a truly spiritual people, if we are going to represent God, if we are going to break the cycle of the discrimination and depravity that has hounded humanity then it will be through learning how to love others as we love ourselves. In fact, it could be argued that every crime and every evil inflicted against another occurred because people failed this command of mutual love.

We cannot be so wrapped up in loving ourselves that we fail to love others. It will affect our ability to be completely human, and it will affect our relationship with God. The scriptures state that we cannot love God whom we do not see and hate our brother whom we do see (1 John 4:20). God is love and every one who loves is born of God and knows God (1 John 4:7, 8). So this is the divine way. There are no two ways about it.

In fact, it will require this kind of thinking in order for Black Americans to love all of Black America. For, as one leaves one's nuclear family to reach the extending family, then the cousins down to the third and fourth degrees one gets farther from him or herself; one gets closer to "others." If all one has is self love, then he or she may not be so motivated to help Blacks far removed from his or her family or community. However, if we are also motivated by mutual love, then our love will extend to those near and far, those familiar and those unfamiliar. This is how we please God and show ourselves to be authentically who we claim to be. This is how we aright the world. We are the people to do it. So, this is a plan for ourselves and to help the world too.

OUT OF EGYPT I CALLED MY SON: UNIQUE USE OF AFRICANS

It is imperative that we learn the biblical roots of our Africanity, or better, where our Africanity is rooted in the Bible. In the education chapter, I discussed Africa in Pangaea as well as Africa's being the cradle of humanity. When the Bible teaches Eden, it and what science teaches about Pangaea can go together. It makes sense to me that one river could have left Africa and now be split between Africa and the Middle East, as if they are on separate continents (Genesis 2). The Bible does state that even if people have not the law they can still see God's divine nature and eternal power in the "heavens," or in nature (Romans 1:20). Nature, and true scientific analysis of it, is a type of small 'b' Bible for the nature and power of God.

No one disputes that the Tigris and Euphrates of old are the very rivers so named today, the compound spine of modern day Iraq. What about the other two rivers? The Ethiopians have long represented that the Gihon River in the Bible is the part of the Nile that goes through their land. Scholars simply do not believe them. They used to believe this idea as the King James Version describes that river as "encompasseth the whole land of Ethiopia." For some reason, many of the scholars have over the last century or so come to believe that Eden was in Turkey or Iraq. The other part of the Nile is that which goes through "Havilah" a place of gold.

Well, as we look back on ancient history, it is clear that the two vast areas of gold are Egypt and West Africa, a shoreline that was named the "gold coast." Egypt is the most logical choice. The Coptic Christians have long explained that they house Havilah's river. Science is not listening to Ethiopians and Egyptians. Of course, they have not listened to them over the last 400 years. However, there is no excuse for African Americans not listening to them.

Thank goodness that the African Bible, F. S. Rhodes' book *Black Characters and References of the Bible*, and the Africa Bible Commentary deal with certain of these ideas in a way that is more honorable toward Africa. We have significant cites now for a biblical position that Africa is the cradle of humanity and the makings of an argument regarding Pangaea.

Combine with this the fact that Bible states some very dignified things about Egypt and Cush (Sudan and Ethiopia). It calls Ethiopians the place

> *which sends envoys by sea*
> *in papyrus boats over the water.*
> *Go, swift messengers,*
> *to a people tall and smooth-skinned,*
> *to a people feared far and wide,*
> *an aggressive nation of strange speech,*
> *whose land is divided by rivers.* (Isaiah 18:1-2)

It calls them seafaring, commercial, tall, good-looking, feared, and aggressive [or conquering]. The Bible calls Egypt a cedar of Lebanon that could only be compared to Assyria, which a few years before was the super power of the world (Ezekiel 31). You were the whale of the seas (Ezekiel 32:2). These are high compliments to their greatness. The Bible calls them among the circumcised, as they were the original circumcising people (Jeremiah 9:25). Circumcision was so important that God was going to kill either Moses or his boy before Moses even made it to the exodus. Yet, when Herodotus asked about the people of the Black sea, he concluded they had to be Egyptian:

> *There can be no doubt that the Colchians [people of the Black Sea] are an Egyptian race. Before I heard any mention of the fact from others, I had remarked it myself. After the though had struck me, I made inquiries on the subject both in Colchis and in Egypt, and I found that the Colchians had a more distinct recollection of the Egyptians than the Egyptians had of them. Still the Egyptians said that they believed the Colchians to be descended from the army of Sesotris [Thutmosis III]. My own conjectures were founded, first, on the fact they were black-skinned and have woolly hair, which certainly amounts to but little, since several other nations are so too; but further and more especially, on the circumstance that the Colchians, the Egyptians, and the Ethiopians, are the only nations who have practiced circumcision from the earliest times. The Phoenicians and the Syrians of Palestine [including the Jews] themselves confess that they learnt the custom of the Egyptians...* (Herodotus, The Histories, trans. by Rawlinson 169)

Able scholars clarify that circumcision was to the Jews, and those of the ancient world I might add, as baptism is to the Christians. This is how significant and serious it is.

I could go on about what the Bible states about the Nile people that makes the case for the fact that God was using them in a unique way. Perhaps the most compelling point is that God sent Abraham away from Iraq and toward Egypt. God placed Joseph in Egypt. Joseph completely Egyptianizes from his name to his clothes, and then he married the Egyptian high priest's daughter! God appeared to Jacob and told him to go to Egypt as God will bless Joseph there. This is God ushering the way for Jacob both to go and to stay in Egypt.

Joseph had two children, half Jewish and half Egyptian, mind you. When Jacob saw the two children after having an encounter with God, Jacob did not upbraid Joseph. Quite to the contrary, he blessed Joseph and his half-Egyptian children; Jacob's blessing is that Joseph's two children would each be a tribe; it would be as if Jacob himself had directly fathered Joseph's half Jewish and half-Egyptian children. The Jews did not leave Egypt for another 430 years.

I could go on about the 10 Commandments and the 39 Negative Confessions, the intermarrying of the Levites and the Egyptians, the parallels between the temple of Israel and Egyptian temples, how Amen gets incorporated in Israel, and the fact that Moses' name and education were all Egyptian; but this is not the proper work for that. Suffice it to say, the Bible has wonderful things to say to indicate that God was at work within the ancient Nile people in a unique way. God commands Isaiah, the greatest prophet, to go three years naked, not for Israel but for Egypt (Isaiah 20). He commanded lamentations for Egypt (Ezekiel 31, 32). What the Bible states, though, is not in Genesis 10 – 12 where it should be because God was fed up with the polytheism of Egypt by the time of Abraham.

No, the high compliments God gave Egypt is in the prophets at the time that God was fed up with the polytheism of Israel and the entire region. When God gets to the end of a dispensation, he is less interested in speaking in honor of the nation(s) that has disappointed him of that dispensation. If you do not believe me, go to the New Testament and look at what it states about the Jews. If all one had was the New Testament, the view of the Jews would be quite skewed and negative. In fact, by the time one gets to Revelation, one finds them being called the "synagogue of Satan." I rest my case.

Black religious scholars, and those sympathetic to the truth, can take this the rest of the way. The point here is that spiritual leaders should be tracking if not leading the instruction of the educational leaders concerning who African people are and where we came from. We are not the people of darkness and ignorance. We are the original people, a people God was dealing with too, and no doubt dealing with first. I bet most religious leaders still do not understand the significance of Jesus having to be born in Bethlehem, raised in Nazareth, but out of Egypt. The scriptures state in Hosea, "Out of Egypt I called my son." Well, if it blessed Bethlehem that Jesus was born there, and blessed Nazareth that he was raised there, why is there no blessing for Egypt? And if no other people in the world will see the importance in this, should not we? What's wrong with us?

CUSH SHALL LIFT HER HANDS: UNIQUE CALL ON AFRICANS

The Bible expresses fantastic things about the future of his work with the Cushitic or "burnt faced" people (the meaning of the term "Ethiopia"). Remember, in the

Bible, Cush is everything lower than Egypt [which means about half of modern day Egypt]. They did not then have the borders we have now. Cush was everything south of Egypt, except for Punt (sometimes "Put"), which was the coastal area probably around Eritrea or Somalia. From the Nile area, all of Africa was populated. Many of them made their way to West Africa, from which the African Americans hailed. Here is what the Bible says:

> *Rebuke the beast among the reeds, the herd of bulls among the calves of the nations. Humbled, may it bring bars of silver. Scatter the nations who delight in war.*
>
> *31 Envoys will come from Egypt; Cush will submit herself to God.* (PSALM 68 [EMPHASIS ADDED])
>
> *18 In that day five cities in Egypt will speak the language of Canaan and swear allegiance to the LORD Almighty. One of them will be called the City of the Sun.*
>
> *19 In that day there will be an altar to the LORD in the heart of Egypt, and a monument to the LORD at its border. 20 It will be a sign and witness to the LORD Almighty in the land of Egypt. When they cry out to the LORD because of their oppressors, he will send them a savior and defender, and he will rescue them. 21 So the LORD will make himself known to the Egyptians, and in that day they will acknowledge the LORD. They will worship with sacrifices and grain offerings; they will make vows to the LORD and keep them. 22 The LORD will strike Egypt with a plague; he will strike them and heal them. They will turn to the LORD, and he will respond to their pleas and heal them.*
>
> *23 In that day there will be a highway from Egypt to Assyria. The Assyrians will go to Egypt and the Egyptians to Assyria. The Egyptians and Assyrians will worship together. 24 In that day Israel will be the third, along with Egypt and Assyria, a blessing on the earth. 25 The LORD Almighty will bless them, saying, "Blessed be Egypt my people, Assyria my handiwork, and Israel my inheritance."* (ISAIAH 19 [EMPHASIS ADDED])

Notice that God states that Egypt will be his people because he will send them a savior. Note that he lists them first in the last part. Order of listing was important in the ancient world. God is saying that he has a special role for the African people to play. Will you play your part?

All of this means much, much more than we have been taught. We are guilty of having been bound by the commentary notes at the bottom or on the side of the Bible instead of having really read the Bible itself. We suffer from having read other commentaries that have been tinged by ignorance or racism. As a result, we have read our forbears and ourselves right out of the blessed book. Our theology is someone else's. How can we ever understand God's unique purpose for our lives? We need to renew our theology so that we can discover our destiny.

DEVELOPMENT AND (CUSHITIC) RENEWAL THEOLOGY

Theology is the spiritual theory of in whom we believe, and why. By extension, it includes the thinking behind the thousands of things we believe beyond the rudiments. So we speak of a theology regarding all of the things on which we can take a position, things on which we must depend.

Our theology has to include the best of the teaching from works like The African Commentary and others. It must position our people in the plan of God as it has unfolded from past to present. Surely, it has to direct us into a type of modern-day healing ministry reminiscent of the healing ministry of Jesus: during his day the people who had shelters and food almost exclusively needed health care—so he was that; where we are the people need shelter, food, and health care—will we be as Jesus was?

While it is liberating theology, this is not liberation theology. While it concerns dominion, it is not dominion theology of Rushdoony. While it centers on Blacks rising as if a nation, it is not black Nationalism theology.

It is closer to what Nehemiah was talking about when as a Jew he said, "Let us go rebuild the walls that we be no longer a reproach among the nations" (Nehemiah 2). It is closer to what Paul as talking about when he said, "I would give myself as a sacrifice in hell if it would mean the life in heaven of my people, the Jews" (Romans 9:1-3). It is Diaspora Cushites coming back to El and coming for the first time to Yah___ [the name observant Jews will not even write]. The Psalmist says in the 68 division that Cush shall lift her hands to God. Isaiah states that there shall be a highway from Egypt to Assyria. Egypt shall be first during that time. We are coming back to God as a people.

Our spiritual development must teach us of the Africanity of the roots of our faith. It has to help us see our place in end time events. As Marcus Garvey foresaw, Blacks in the United States are especially crucial as a bridge, or Joseph, people who will assist all of the other Africans from the vantage point of this great country. In other words, our spiritual plan has to move us to see Africa as the cradle of humanity and cradle of civilization, and African Americans are the Joseph people who will assist Africans in their rise back to empowerment and leadership in the world. In other words, it is time for African Americans to rise to save ourselves and to help save humanity. Remember, God is with the least, and he chooses the foolish to confound the wise; well, we surely are the least society, and at times we have been beyond foolish. It is time now to do some confounding.

Our theology has to be inclusive, or it will become another mis-truth. Thus, it must be a theology that embraces and unifies all of Christianity and that reaches out to the world. As to strategy, the gospel needs to be broader in the East and deeper in the West; as to priority, it may need to go deeper in the West before it can effectively go broader in the East. In order to go deeper it has to embrace a Good Samaritan type of mutual love, and it must peel away from the Bible all of the falsehoods. We have to help Africa, the African Disapora, and we must prod this great superpower toward being a better neighbor in the world.

We must catch up with science and the African consciousness movement of Black studies programs, ghettos, and the prisons or risk irrelevance. Please know that when I make these points in the Black studies programs or in the prisons, I find students who are hungry for the information. Moreover, I can stand toe to toe with the most passionate teacher of faith-based movements like Nation of Islam and 5 Per centers who are gaining ground in our community. I remind Black religious leaders again that if they do not open up to these ideas, then they stand the risk of losing the ability to reach the generation that is upon us. We risk missing the move of God in this generation. We risk continuing King's legacy of teaching humanity, as he said it, about the "Fatherhood of God and the brotherhood of man."

DEVELOPING AND EXECUTING A PLAN

So religious leaders must come together. This time it is not a call—it is a cry. No group of leaders is more vital to the survival of African America and maybe to the entire Black Diaspora. We need spiritual leaders to unify enough to forge a spiritual sub-plan. Whereas as the political area is the purse umbrella covering the areas, the spiritual area is the golf umbrella the covers even the political area. The spiritual area has to ensure that all leaders, even themselves and the crucial political leaders, serve the people with character, competence, and courage.

Religious institutions and their leaders should not be used though—and will not be. We cannot make churches be the welfare office such that it fails its essential purpose to preach the gospel. Neither can it serve others to the detriment of itself in terms of health or business. So the plan will have to promote, as it pulls from, the churches and mosques. It has to add to the membership rolls without taking too much away from the financial coffers. It has to support the religious mission without taking too much of the time of its members. It has to be that good.

WHY THE SPIRITUAL AREA IS LAST ON THE LIST

So you ask, "if this area is of first importance then why is it listed last of the seven areas, and why has the entire book been about economics leading the way?" The reason has to do with the fact that not all of the areas are at the same place; Black spiritual development has long been better than our economic development. As has been explained earlier, the Black church has been the center of Black American culture, and this position has allowed the church to maintain a sense of godliness in the community from one generation to the next. Despite the spiritual deficiencies of which the spiritual leaders are all too aware, this area is still better than the rest. And it is so important.

The spiritual area is the center on which everything hangs. It is utterly important because revelation, righteousness, service, and sacrifice are so important to everything we want to do. In revelation are the larger answers to reality and the reason for why righteousness and service are in some sense rational. Sacrificial service is what is needed for us to do the great work that is before us; and righteousness, the credibility necessary to get others to buy in.

But beyond these items, I have to say that the spiritual area is most import because the spiritual area is about the "Spirit." It is about God. If God is real—and I am confident that he is—then the area that directly concerns God means everything. God is all wise, and his wisdom extends to those who legitimately speak in his name; God is all powerful, and his power flows to those who act in his name; God is all encompassing, and his presence reaches through those who are positioned in his name. Since God is most real, those who represent him are most essential. Of those representing him, none are more vital in the West than the church. In the Black community this is truer still.

HELP YOUR OWN MEMBERS

Even if you do not make disciples of your community, even if you do not even meet to prepare a plan, at least help your own members in a holistic way. Earlier in this work

I stated that the church I am in had only 40 active members when I joined it. Shortly thereafter we instituted a plan to do these four things:

- Add to our monthly benevolence offerings.
- Provide small gifts to our children going back to school.
- Pay at least one elder mother of the church money monthly to help with medical costs (1 TIMOTHY 5).
- Provide up to $1500 annually to someone purchasing a house or condo.

We could do this because I had a full-time job, and the church was willing to invest in this important endeavor. This little bit that we are doing is more than a lot of large churches are doing for their own members. Yet it is so scriptural. We are commanded to demonstrate our love through giving, and for believers, by sharing things in common. There are no two ways about it. Either we are going to live the book, or we need to put it down.

We could have a renaissance even without leaders meeting. If every church would take care of its own members along the lines of this plan, then we would get there. We would have a renaissance. The fact that we have not done this should speak to the reason why a major shake-up is needed in the religious realm.

Given your great position the needs are not too distant from you. Given your vast possessions, the costs should not be too expensive to you. Given your divine connection, the problems should not loom that large to you. Black pastors and bishops have set their aim on the following: mega-churches and mega-salaries. But, what shall it profit you to build a mansion by the water while your people live in ruins by the gutter? What shall it profit you to build a mega-church on a hill when your community languishes with mega-challenges in the 'hood'?

JUDGMENT BEGINNING IN THE HOUSEHOLD OF GOD

Three things should have brought us together without outsiders asking us to do so: the Great Commandments, the Great Commission, and the priority pursuit of the kingdom. No wonder judgment has to begin at the household of God. We have not been faithful witnesses to what we believe. We might as well fall on the rock so that the rock will not fall on us. We start things without finishing them. This is not a good witness. Jesus Christ said to Sardis, I have not found your works complete for this very reason (Revelation 3).

How do a people judge its religious leaders' leadership? One way is the subjective test: do you feel as though you are represented well? Another way is more objective: have the people excelled under the religious leadership, and how does their leadership compare to other religious groups' leadership? With regard to the subjective test, too many feel that the leaders are not serving the people well. This is reflected in more than their absence from church. It is reflected in their presence in mosques and in the bed on Sunday morning. It is reflected in their poetry and polemics in search of leadership. Objectively, the numbers are mixed. In some ways we are growing, and in some ways we are falling behind. The evidence is both subjective and objective.

There has to be one reliable group of leaders who serve for righteousness sake—not for power, prestige, or property. There has to be one group of trustworthy leaders who will take care of rich and poor alike, strong and weak equally, the beautiful and the commoner as one. We must have a group that is so committed to purpose, heritage, and timing that they know no less than God himself will not allow them to disserve or under serve the people. This group behind it all has to be the religious community.

Too many Black pastors think their job is building a church instead of extending God's kingdom. The kingdom of God is the lordship of Christ over every area of life. I reiterate something that cannot be emphasized enough: God said "I" will build my church (Matthew 16); "you" seek first my kingdom (Matthew 6). The kingdom is not only the rule and realm of God demonstrated in holistic power, it is the government of God in the world, against the world, and over the world. The church is the assembly of the covenant community of called out believers. We need more Christian leaders who are concerned about the lordship of Christ over every area of life than about only having full pews in a building housing spirited services and varied programs. Some of these church leaders are the best God has in a locale; if they do not have a vision and burden for God's rule in the entire locale, then who will?

You leaders have the attention of the greater part of the community. You teach that you represent winning values that cannot only turn a life around but can heal the land and make a people the head and not the tail. You, moreover, have faith that cannot only placate pain but can move mountains. On top of all of this, you say that you believe in a God that is omnipresent, omniscient, and omnipotent. So, your God is everywhere your God wants to be, knows everything, and is all powerful.

This puts such believers in a favored position with a God in a position of invincibility. Why then have you not used your favored position, your vast abilities, and your great connection to work a renaissance for your people? Given your great position, the needs of your people are not that distant. Given your great possessions (abilities), their problems are not that costly. Given your divine connection, their problems are not that large. What is the good of having a mansion on a hill when your people live in the gutter? What good is it to build a mega-church, while your community is strapped with mega-challenges.

It is time for the sleeping giant in the Black community to rise. Edmund Burke stated that no man ever made a greater mistake then he who did nothing because he could little. He also wrote that all that is necessary for evil to triumph is that good men do nothing. God said to Abraham that through him all of the peoples of the world would be blessed. Jesus remarked, "You feed them." Later he said, "Go into all of the world and make disciples of every nation." Help your people with big straps, and then use your big hands to help them pick themselves up. You can do it and you must. You were born for such a time as this.

HOW TO GET STARTED

HOW TO GET STARTED: CALLING ALL LEADERS

You cannot lead our people if you do not love our people;
you cannot save our people if you cannot serve our people.
(Cornel West)

If this plan is going to work, it will do so because leaders make the necessary commitment to it for the requisite amount of time, giving the required resources to this endeavor because the need is great. Why should not the leaders do so? For while most of the people are individually weaker, the leaders are personally stronger. The strong must bear the burdens of the weak. We must be our brother's (and our sister's) keeper.

We need real leaders, leaders who are thinkers and workers. Even I at times can be a "show leaders." Black communities in both the African continent, our motherland, and the U.S., our homeland, have had too much of the wrong kinds of leaders serving the people. Watch out for the "show leaders." You know how we do: no show when there is grunt work to do, show out when they cannot get their way, and show up again when the cameras roll.

Black communities in both the African continent, our motherland, and the U.S., our homeland, have had too much of the wrong kinds of leaders serving the people.

LEADERSHIP AT THE COMMUNITY LEVEL

So, at the community level, the organizational leaders, and some grassroots people should come together to devise and deliver on a community plan. Put a plan together that launches the businesses, businesses that will increase the demand for Black and poor labor. Put a plan together that pressures the government to hire Blacks and the poor in greater numbers. At the community level we need to do the following items:

A. RESOLUTION
   1. Renew our faith.
   2. Renew our leadership.
B. VISION
   1. Know who we are, where we are going, and how we are going to get there.
Agree on a plan.
Center it on economics.
C. ACTION
   1. Develop a committed corp.
   2. Rely on two key institutions: churches and families.
Execute the plan.
Amend the plan where necessary.

Call the community leaders together, say, late in the Fall in order to approve one of 1 – 2 proposed plans for primarily economic development (i.e., *Powernomics*, *The Covenant*, or *Shoestrings and Boostraps*). I need your help to mobilize a committed core of leaders and volunteers who will do the work of carrying out this plan. I especially need those who will continue the work for the necessary years. They will be this plan's founders.

And when you come to the community planning meeting, come to serve instead of being served, to pay in instead of getting paid; and let him who would be the greatest, be the servant of all. Organizations whose members and funding are from the community represent the community alone, and so they must speak most for the community primarily. Organizations whose membership or funding comes mostly from the broader community have other legitimate interests they must represents. Such organizations should play a secondary role within the leadership. Also, your greatest economic minds must forge the economic plan; your greatest educational minds, the educational plan; and so on. Our preachers should be the first ones to keep us together, to keep us focused, but to bring our other professionals to the forefront in the areas of their expertise. This is servant leadership.

Leaders need to come together to have a teach-in, then a strategy session, and then a commitment meeting on capitalism and how to lift African Americans in every area. It is time for leaders to come together to study *Powernomics* and this plan. A time should be set for when to act so that the meetings are not just about discussing. We have discussed (and argued) too much. On the other hand, one cannot just launch into a plan as complicated and comprehensive as this without doing the necessary groundwork, and that includes study. So start meeting. Say three months are given to reviewing all of these works; three months to agreeing to one specific strategy that is tailored to these ideas and what is doable in this city; then start mobilizing the people to join the effort.

One set of leaders will not be able to do it all. It is important to have different groups of professionals meeting to work on the other aspects of the plan: health leaders need to meet to work on that component; political leaders, to work on that component; social leaders, for theirs; and the same for educational and artistic leaders. These groups need to propose how to come up with sub-plans to be fit into this plan. They will need to learn this plan, and meld their ideas to it—or to whatever the community leaders specifically devise.

The leaders in the sub-groups need to humble themselves and submit what they want to do to what the larger group agrees on. If what the larger group of leaders wants is too meager or too slow for the sub-group leaders, then the sub-group leaders should change in order to promote the greater good. Sub-group leaders can get into the larger group and change it from within. No more sniping and obstructions, one leader against another. Aren't we sick of this? Haven't we had enough? As long as we are headed in the right direction, we will work out the challenges if we do so from within, united and committed to the common community good. It is time for those who call themselves leaders to come together.

Christian pastors and other religious leaders are the conscience of the community. If anyone has a heart for the entire community and for service in the best interest of the people as opposed to in one's personal interest, it has to be the religious leaders. If the religious leaders have no gumption to continue to call the community together for its own survival and progress then there is no hope for the community. If Black leaders in Seattle have no gumption to continue to call Seattle African America together for their own survival and progress then there is little to no hope for Seattle African Americans. This is what larger compassion and vision are about. It reminds me of the scripture: without a vision the people perish; perish here means that they lose the directional restraint a vision contains and then they begin to act chaotically. Chaos was the enemy in the old show *Get Smart* and it is the enemy of any community in any day.

No plan in the Black community is going to work without the stalwart assistance of pastors and other religious leaders. They hold sway (or their God does through them) on the largest, regularly meeting portion of the Black community. They can rise up or shut down any would-be Black movements. They are the doorkeepers and the way makers. Without them, ye can do nothing. Pastors and religious leaders, please help this movement. I beg you. What can you do?

The pastors and other religious leaders must meet to make sure that the larger group of leaders continues to meet. They need to see that the larger group of leaders is committed to the plan as they continue to meet. They need to see to it that the larger group of leaders is really serving the people and not themselves. The pastors and the religious leaders need to meet regularly and to learn this plan as well as its underpinnings. They must speak truth to power in the event that the larger group of leaders is not doing what it is supposed to do.

It is all right if the Christian pastors and leaders from other religious groups want to add to our comprehensive plan belief in the One God, commitment to the commands (the Greatest Commandment, and the Greater Commandment, and the 10 Commandments), and the need to open and close in prayer. We cannot just use the faith community by getting it to move us together economically while stripping it of its spiritual work. That's not going to work in the long term—nor should it. In fact, openness to their broad values should help the pastors and other religious leaders be more interested in being the conscious of this great work.

On the other hand, pastors and other religious leaders have tried in the past to do too much. Mostly by default—because no one else could do it—but at times intentionally—because they thought they knew it all—pastors have tried to lead the spiritual, economic, political, and social development of the community. They have tried to prescribe the theme and the details for every area of Black development. Well, if the truth be told, pastors and other religious leaders are able masters at things spiritual but honorable amateurs at things that are economic and social. The results speak for themselves: pastors have not solved the nagging non-spiritual problems as the sole leaders . . . not in any community. I do not mean this as criticism; I mean it as insight.

Not to worry: this is why we have economic, political, and social leaders in our community who have mastery in these areas. We have in our community business owners and bankers, politicians and lobbyists, counselors and therapists as well as educators in each of these areas. Use them. Pastors need to push these leaders out there to provide the details, while being there to weigh in on the themes and particularly the underlying values and aims that are so vital to any endeavor. Be glad that there is a larger group of leaders—of which you are a part—as well as other sub-groups of leaders all working together to push the community forward. Be the drive behind this genius. It is good for us all.

This is what I believe the Jewish priests did for Israel, when they were acting right. In the temple they spoke truth to political and economic power and yet gave these leaders place to serve the larger community. In each tribe they did the same, just at the local level. They were the conscience of the people. What did they remind them to do? They reminded them to keep to the law, to be faithful to God, to work together, and not to exploit one another. In fact, they themselves worked as well as living off of the offerings. They were relevant to the community.

Perhaps an even better example is Egyptian (or Kemetic) priests. They did all that the Israeli priests did and more. They oversaw the educational and scientific institutions. They, along with the Pharaoh, ensured that everyone from the smallest to the greatest lived maat. Maat was their way of saying righteousness, balance, order, and goodness. Maybe this is what Jesus was referring to when he said that he was the way, the truth, and the life. Jesus is the Jewish prophet respected by Christian and Muslim alike, through in greater and lesser ways. This is a call to all leaders. It is time to save the community, for the hour is ripe for the prosperity of our people.

The leaders also have to be committed to an uneven rise. Some will go up before others. Many will rise eventually in a big way. Many will just go up a little. But if we hold together, the entire community will rise. The question is, though, will we have leaders so committed to the community that they will sacrifice for it; that they will get satisfaction out of seeing the community rise even if they have to give money to the cause without receiving money from it. God give us such leaders.

THREE SPECIAL ABILITIES OF THE LEADERSHIP

One of the greatest abilities these leaders can display is useable research: providing the people the best of information so that the people can make highly informed choices. Another ability is choice: giving the people two to three well developed choices along with open information on who called the meeting, who benefits, and how the two to three choices were arrived at. A third ability is shared leadership: the best leaders know that they do not know everything, nor can they lead well in every area; great leaders promote leaders with particular expertise in particular areas and make room for them to use their particular expertise.

In other words, the leaders over the entire plan should call together separate meetings of economic, social, political, artistic, medical, spiritual, and educational leaders who will determine what should be done in their areas. The overall leaders should trust the findings and recommendations of the leaders in these separate areas. When there is a problem with Blacks not receiving construction contracts or jobs, the leaders of the plan should encourage the contractors, tradespersons, and design professionals to take the lead in advocating for contracts or jobs. The rest of the community, especially the plan leaders, should back our construction area leaders and force the larger community to listen to them, even if it means we may have to confront leaders or protest publicly.

The last ability leaders must display has to do with writing: Blacks have been too oral in a Europeanized world that is more written; the environment in which we must thrive demands written strategy. We have to have written agenda, written proposals, and written minutes. We must agree to a written plan. We must make full use of the Black press and should write letters to the editor in the non-Black press. We have to write press releases, articles, and books. It is what our circumstances demand. This is how this world works. Like the Sons of Issachar, we must understand the times. It is why I have written this book.

To lead in this way, our leaders will have to be more effective, on one hand, and more humble, on the other. If they have the community's interest at heart, then they will do this without personality wars and without personally benefiting.

When a people's political leaders are not regularly in communication, and gathering to solve problems, then that people is in trouble. They will struggle with protection, order and provision, and continue to do so until their leaders provide policy and policing in appropriate ways for their polity. This is what politics concerns, hence the development plan must address this.

BLACK DOLLAR DAYS MOVEMENT

African Americans need to engage a plan, the center of which involves supporting their own businesses in a sustained way as part of a thrust, an effort seeking to get all involved. Call it what you want, this is really at the heart of what Black Dollar Days is about. We will need all the models we can find. Black Dollar Days is one such model.

Now, I am not, nor have I ever been, on the board of Black Dollar Days—not in Seattle, not in another city, not anywhere. I am not an officer or contractor involved in this effort. I have no vested financial interest in pushing this idea. I am not the originator of the concept, nor someone who has added to it significantly such that I have a social interest in seeing it advanced.

I did speak at a Black Dollar Days event, as I forthrightly stated in the forward. I probably received a small honorarium (a *very* small one). So why am I so much in favor of starting with dedicating a period for sustained community support of Black businesses? Every road has led to the re-direction of Black dollars into Black hands as the catalyst for a renaissance. The conclusion became inescapable. We need to recognize those who are former. My ideas are later; Black Dollar Days is former.

Black communities have not supported its Black Dollar Days Task Force effort well. Maybe five percent of the African American community changes its habits, or sustains its already supportive habits, during the month of February as a result of Black Dollar Days. The sad thing as that too few leaders support this effort. They are too little interested in learning about what the community needs.

Others have personal issues. They may have an issue with those advancing this effort. Others are just jealous. They did not come up with it, and they do not want to support those who did. It complicates things further for certain leaders that a man who does not have long roots in Seattle came up with the idea.

On the other hand, those who are pushing Black Dollar Days here must know their audience. Leaders seeking to get things done must not get ahead or behind the people. We have to take the people as we find them. We have to love and lead them from where they are, not from where we want them to be.

Those who have launched this effort must love and forgive the leaders who are cool to this indispensable initiative. They must keep trying to get through to them. They must get to know them on a personal level. They have to go out of their way to be persevering, big, and supportive of these leaders' ideas that are beneficial. The importance of the Black Dollar Days effort is worth this kind of coddling, some would say "sucking up." Why? Because of the greater good. Jesus said, "Suffer it to be so."

Somebody has to be big so that the community will not remain small. Some folk have to stretch themselves so that the community might heal itself. Some have to be inconvenienced in order that the community may be comforted.

Find the Black Dollar Days Movement in your community, join them, and exponentially expand the program they are already engaging. Help them with the Black business directories. Support the "Buy Black" month. Help them with their other initiatives.

Here is the outline of the rest of the things to proceed on.

ADOPTING THE PLAN

I. Adopt Rules
II. Select Chair, Vice, Secretary, Treasurer
III. Establish Rules of Order
IV. Establish a Code of Conduct
V. Start Collecting Our Coins and Bills
VI. Set Timetable for Completing Work
VII. Agree on Committee Criteria
VIII. Select Committee Members
IX. Get and Review Info on State of Black Community
  A. See Washington State African American Affairs Com'n
  B. See Mayor's Office
X. Compare and Contrast to Whites and Other Ethnic Sub-communities
  A. See Mayor's Office
XI. Establish Committees For Review Strengths and Weaknesses of Plans
  A. Shoestrings and Bootstraps Committee
  B. Powernomics Committee
  C. The Covenant Committee
  D. Non-Economic Plans Committee (mainly Educational, Medical, Political and Social)
XII. Propose Criteria for Committees
  A. Comprehensiveness (does it include all levels and areas)
    i. Levels
      a. Micro (household and associations)
      b. Macro (community and government)
    ii. Areas
      a. Social, Educational, Political, Economic
      b. Medical, Spiritual, Artistic
  B. Effectiveness (will it bring a Black Renaissance)

C. Practicality (can it be done with the resources at hand)

XIII. Have Thorough Committee Presentations to the Larger Group
- A. In Writing
- B. With Visuals
- C. With Findings, Conclusions and Recommendations

XIV. Adopt a Plan
- A. Votes
- B. Findings
- C. Conclusions and Recommendations to be Disseminated
- D. Groundwork for Convening Preparation Group
  - i. Determination of Who Cannot Stay
  - ii. Determination of Who Should Stay
  - iii. Determination of Announcement to Invite People to Join

PREPARATION AND YEAR ONE IMPLEMENTATION

I. Preparation

II. Keep Collecting Coins and Bills

III. Keep Non-Economic Sub-Committees Working Towards Recommendations

IV. Establish Committees
- A. Micro
- B. Macro

V. Disseminate Plan

VI. Copy Plan
- A. Utilize the Black Press

VII. Teach the Plan
- A. Get Implementation Group in Place

VIII. Implementation

IX. Continue Collecting Offerings for the Budget and Development Fund
- A. Micro
  - i. Household
  - ii. Associational
- B. Macro
  - i. Community
  - ii. Government

- C. Enforcement
  - i. Soft
  - ii. Hard

X. Oversight Committees

- A. Household
- B. Associations
- C. Community
- D. Government
- E. Politics
- F. Economics
- G. Social
- H. Medical
- I. Spiritual
- J. Educational
- K. Artistic

YEARS TWO - FOUR

I. Meet to assess the plan.
II. Make revisions.
III. Open up the leadership further.
IV. Remove people who could not finish, and do so in honorable ways.

APPENDIX

DEVELOPMENT THEORIES

The creation of a single Caribbean economy also calls for the putting in place of a new Regional Development Fund whose resources are to be applied predominately to financing programmes to spur the social and economic upliftment of the lesser developed members of the community.
OWEN SEYMOUR ARTHUR

In Africa today, we recognize that trade and investment, and not aid, are pillars of development.
PAUL KAGAME

Whether in the Caribbean or in Africa, development is about economics, and more specifically, about helping lesser developed communities with funding. This holds true for sub-communities in the U.S. that need development. If in the U.S., the government will not do this, then we have to do it for ourselves. Yet, we should learn from the best of the ideas in the world on development.

We need a plan that involves two types of development plans that governments have used transitioning from colonialism: *import substitution industrialization* and *export led industrialization*. Please do not let these terms discourage you. They are the two main development strategies that Southern (developing) nations considered when transitioning from colonialism to independence. Simply put, we need to spend more within our community on businesses owned by people from our community. Then we need to promote businesses within our community by investing in our businesses so as to prepare them to compete in the larger community.

We should start the import substitution commercialization (instead of industrialization) with something simple like a beauty supply company or gas station and then go to a grocery store and related businesses. We should invest in the exporting of those businesses that have proven viable and have some appeal outside of the community like Catfish Corner, Ezell's, and other such businesses. We can use this one until we get a better one.

The two main economic concepts behind the plan are import substitution commercialization and export led commercialization. These ideas are my adaptations of the two main Southern (or Third World) development strategies that anyone can find in the average Political Economy text. These two development strategies are called import substitution industrialization (ISI), and export led industrialization (ELI).

ISI is when a people replace goods made or services provided by foreigners with goods made or services provided by its own people. ELI is a people helping its own businesses get into exporting goods or services to foreigners by identifying its own businesses most likely to be make the jump into the global economy, and giving them long-term loans and technical assistance to help them jump in successfully.

> *[A]n economic development strategy should strike a realistic balance "between the state and the market so as to stimulate a positive and dynamic interaction between them." [cite omitted] Whereas ISI policies emphasize state intervention and give too little consideration to market signals, orthodox liberal approaches disregard the fact that late industrializers often require an active role for the state. Governments in East and Southeast Asia were particularly adept at using market interactions to their advantage, and this enabled them to register some striking economic gains, even during the 1980s foreign debt crises. However, the East and Southeast Asians have also too often substituted "political whim . . . for proper risk assessment for commercial activities," and their failure to provide sufficient banking regulations was a major factor contributing to their 1990s financial crises."* (COHN, GLOBAL POLITICAL ECONOMY: THEORY & PRACTICE, 2ND ED. 407)

This is a long and indirect way of referring to ISI and ELI. Both of these plans use the four factors of development that famous Economist Paul Samuelson referred to.

> *The key to development lies in 4 fundament factors: human resources, natural resources, capital formation, and technology.* (PAUL A. SAMUELSON [NOBEL LAUREATE] AND PROF WILLIAM NORDHAUS, ECONOMICS 14TH ED.)

Import Substitution industrialization has been used mainly on this side of the world.

Policies of import substitution have often been popular in Latin America. The policy most frequently used toward this end has been to build high tariff walls around manufacturing industries so that local firms can produce and sell goods that would otherwise be imported. For example, Brazil has placed high tariffs on automobiles to encourage firms to assemble autos at home rather than import much less expensive cars from North America or Japan. (Id.)

But we also need export led commercialization.

A successful economic development strategy must focus on improving the skills of the area's workforce, reducing the cost of doing business and making available the resources business needs to compete and thrive in today's global economy. (ROD BLAGOJEVICH)

JAPAN'S LEADERS PROVIDED THE MITI DEVELOPMENT PLAN

For example, the Japanese devised a plan in the 1950s to first become competitive in the toy market, then with small consumer electricals like radios, then larger consumer electricals like refrigerators, then small cars, mid-sized cars, and large cars. Next they delivered on the plan. They started with the easier markets first. They put money up for long term investment and technical assistance in businesses in these areas. They incubated the businesses within the country and then launched them to compete in the world. Each under-represented group needs to do something similar.

The average Black American is in a situation of low demand for their labor. Low demand for their labor means employers hire them last, if at all. It means they fire them first when they need to fire someone. These are the dynamics behind why we are the last hired and the first fired. We can add real numbers to this dilemma. Author Timothy Bates stated it best:

Even those white employers whose firms are physically located in inner-city minority communities hire a work force that is predominantly white; roughly a third of all such firms employ no minorities whatsoever. By contrast, 96 percent of black-owned firms operating in urban minority neighborhoods employ a labor force that is largely minority. Even outside minority neighborhoods, in areas where most white-owned businesses have no minority workers at all, black firms rely on these workers heavily. (BATES, BANKING ON BLACK ENTERPRISE 3)

Thus, one third of the White businesses in Black areas, right under our noses, have no minority employees as shown in a study from the late 1980s. Alternatively, 96 percent of Black businesses have a majority minority workforce. Many, if not most, of these workers will be Black. This is the key for increasing the demand for Black laborers: help the businesses that hire them.

For those thinking that affirmative action is the key—that getting White businesses to hire blacks at least in federal employment is the answer—think more deeply. Affirmative action helps a lot where it is in place. On the other hand, it does not apply to private employers unless they are contracting with the federal government and only on those contracts. Even then it only applies beyond $50,000 (and this may be increased to $250,000) and may not apply if the employer has fewer than 50 employees (and this may be increased). This cuts out small businesses, the engine of growth. Affirmative action, thusly, is a limited remedy. Economist David Birch's research publicized widely that in the 1980s 88 percent of all net new jobs nationwide were created from businesses with 20 or fewer workers (Birch, 1987 p. 16). More reputable studies have placed the small business percentage at closer to 51 to 56 percent. Still, however one cuts it, a majority of jobs are from small businesses, the very businesses that affirmative action does not reach. These are also the very businesses that, if owned by whites, one third of which are likely to have no Black employees at all.

> *To be black in America is to know that you remain last in line for so basic a requisite as the means of supporting yourself and your family. More than that, you have much less choice among jobs than workers who are white.* (Hacker, Two Nations: Black and White, Separate, Hostile, Unequal, 110)

This is compounded by the fact that black businesses are not experiencing the kind of multiplier of the black dollar that other ethnic groups receive from people of their same ethnicity. A low multiplier means that when we make a dollar we spend it on things we do not make, or bank it in places that we do not own. Our community is a leaking sieve. It is 'quick in, quick out' when green dollars are in Black hands. We are a coin bag with silver-dollar size holes in it. Money pours out as fast as it pours in. We cannot directly blame non-Blacks for this; this, sadly, we do to ourselves. But it is primarily a leadership problem.

> *Most important for members of the ghetto community, if business success increases in their area the resulting economic development will tend to reverse the drain of resources that exacerbates their poverty. Profitable operations build up additional capital and reinvestment, greater ownership of businesses by local residents strength-*

> *ens the flow of income within (rather than leakage out of) the ghetto, and capable business people are retained in the community where their enterprises create income and jobs.* (BATES, BANKING ON BLACK ENTERPRISE XXII)

I thank Bates for his help: business success reverses that which causes poverty. This is how we create jobs for our workers and contracts for our businesses. Like it or not, the answer to the problem has the word "capitalism" all over it.

ECONOMETRIC MODEL

We need an econometric model. *Webster's Encyclopedic Unabridged Dictionary* defines econometrics thusly, "the application of statistical and mathematical techniques in solving problems as well as in testing and demonstrating theories." Such a model quantitatively predicts what will happen over a period of time, say 10 years, of staying the course of this plan. This is what we need in order to be patient in the outset years in which the gains are large in percentage but small relative to the need.

An economic metric model contains definitions, assumptions, parameters, findings, conclusions, and recommendations. I submit this proposed model in hopes that Economics professors will take this the next step and devise a complete econometric model that the people can use in each community in which a plan like this one is employed. This proposal starts with findings and then goes into definitions, assumptions, parameters, conclusions and recommendations.

FINDINGS

The macroeconomic findings are as follows. In 7.2 years we should rise to \$1,284,890,000 nationally. In 15 years we would be at \$2,569,780,000.

Black communities across this country need to meet 10% goals. The overall goal is a 10% increase in Black community gross product annually. In order to facilitate this, Black communities need a 10% increase annually in Black business profitability and a simultaneous 10% increase in non-Black (governmental and firms) direct investment in Black communities. If possible, Blacks should shoot for a 20 – 30% increase in Black business profitability in the short run. The aim is to shepherd these increased economic gains all the way to the employment level. In other words, Black communities need alternatively 10% annual decreases in Black unemployment and, even better, a 10% increase in Black employment.

DEFINITIONS

Microeconomic: The household or firm level of economics.

Macroeconomic: The local, state, national, or international level of economics.

Banking Rule of 72: The banking rule of 72 says that anything growing at 10% doubles every 7.2 years.

Target rate: The interest rate that this plan aims to meet or exceed. It is 10%.

10, 10, and 10 Plan: 10% increase in personal investment, 10% increase in black community investment. 10% increase in holistic development.

GNP: This is the acronym for gross national product. It is the total of what the firms and individuals (and governments, and quasi-governmental entities) produced in a year.

Black GNP: What Black-owned firms and individuals produced in a year.

Black GNP per capita: multiplying the total Black GNP by the population size.

ASSUMPTIONS

- Seattle's population size is 47,541. 47,541 is the lower Seattle number, a number that does not take into account first generation Africans.
- Black Enterprise and the National Black Chamber of Commerce report that the Black community GNP is $500 million as of this writing.
- The Greater Seattle African American community has $642,445,303.5 in gross annual income. This figure is derived by taking the Black Enterprise annual income estimate of $500 billion, dividing it by 37 million equals $13,513.51. These numbers should be on the lower end as Seattle and the Puget Sound region probably makes more on average than Blacks do nationally.

PARAMETERS

The purpose is to double Black productivity every 7.2 years. Black Seattle's GNP is $642,445,303.5.

CONCLUSIONS

What should this number mean? The doubling of and then doubling again of Black productivity should translate into $1,284,890,000 and then $2,569,780,000 in new wealth pouring into Black businesses, money Blacks generated themselves by using the principles of economics in their favor. This will allow Black businesses to better survive and to thrive. It will afford them the ability to increase inventories, purchase necessary equipment, and to upgrade their services. It should also assist their paying off burdensome start-up loans, start-up investors, or high-cost creditors. This profitability should mean more money with which to buy from Black contractors or suppliers and for the hiring of Black employees. What does this mean for the community?

Take the Seattle area, for instance. Blacks businesses probably employ about 2% of the total Black workforce. So if there are 20,000 Black workers in the Seattle area then Blacks employ 400. Black unemployment is estimated to be around 15% or 3000. If Black employment increased 10% across the board that would mean that 2,000 more jobs were available. One way to achieve this number is by increasing by 25% Black business employment of Black workers (100 new jobs), and then making up the difference through an increase in the hiring of Blacks by non-Black employers (the other 1900 positions; in a county in which over 500,000 people are working, this is more doable than it may appear).

The contribution of Black employers to solving the Black unemployment problem starts small and over time becomes great. It requires continued 10% increases n Black business profitability and resultant hiring. In 7.2 years Black business employment opportunities could conceivably double. That would mean that they would go in Seattle from providing 400 jobs to 800. In 15 years the number would double again to 1600, and then begin to approach 10% of the total number of Black employment, given a Black employment population that remained at around 20,000. Multiply 600 new jobs by $15,000, the likely average pay to those workers, then you can see the power of the wealth returned to the Black family. This is $9 million dollars that Black people created for themselves.

China has grown between 8 – 9 % on average every year since 1982. If China can do it, so can Seattle African America. Japan grew at about 8% from 1962 to 1975. If Japan can do it, so can Seattle African America. Jewish Americans had a meteoritic rise in this country from the 1900 through 1990. If Jewish America can do it, then so can Seattle African America. Vietnamese Americans are rising fast now in the U.S., with Ethiopian Americans just a decade or two behind. If they can do it, then so can Seattle African America.

Japan did this from clear comprehensive plans starting in the 1950s from their Ministry of International Trade and Industry. China is doing it as its Communist Party leadership works in league with its department of commerce. Jewish, Vietnamese, and Ethiopian Americans are doing it through family and associational plans in an atmosphere of cooperation which their family elders and their religious institutions facilitate.

RECOMMENDATIONS

We can develop individually and communally if we work together from a plan targeted for our development. We are not limited to 10% growth: we can exceed 10%, but let us not decrease it. Thus, all of these groups have developed and are developing from different plans like the one herein. This is how Blacks have to do it. It is time to develop a clear, comprehensive plan.

CASE STUDIES: JEWISH, VIETNAMESE AND ETHIOPIAN AMERICANS

The realization of a sustainable economic development strategy for Maine's Native American communities has always been a priority and a critical element of my administration's overall economic development strategy.
(John Baldacci)

JEWISH AMERICANS: ASSOCIATIONAL APPROACH

The Personal – Associational approach emphasizes the association most but gives great weight to the family. This is largely the way in which Jewish Americans have found success in this distant land in their global sojourn.

A PHENOMENAL RISE

How well are Jewish Americans doing? They are doing extraordinarily well and this is what makes them the ideal group to study first.

> *So well nurtured were the opportunities offered them that Jews today represent the prototypical American ethnic success story. In only two generations, Jewish Americans collectively accomplished a truly phenomenal upward mobility that makes them a compulsory case for the analysis of American ethnic relations.* (Martin Marger, *Race & Ethnic Relations* 2d. 219)

Let's put their success in an economic income snapshot.

The median family income of Jewish Americans in the early 1970s was $12,630, more than $2,000 higher than the median for all U.S. families (Massarik and Chenkin,

1973; U.S. Census Bureau, 1973). By 1986, 77 percent of Jewish American households earned more than $20,000 compared to 61 percent of American households in general (Cohen, 1987; U.S. Census Bureau, 1988). By 1990, the median Jewish American household income was $39,000, 34 percent higher than for the society as a whole (Kosmin et al., 1991; NJPS, 2003). ..[M]edian household income of Jewish Americans in 2001 was $12,000 higher than the median for the total population. (Marger, *Race & Ethnic Relations* 2d. 225)

Along with the disproportionately higher incomes, Jews are more highly concentrated in higher-status occupations, especially the professions, business ownership, and managerial positions. Moreover, they have high, if not the highest, educational achievement. (See Murray & Hernstein, *The Bell Curve*) How did it happen? To discover the answer, it is important to first understand what it was like when they arrived over time in this country.

> *This is what the Lord Almighty, the God of Israel, says to all those I carried into exile from Jerusalem into Babylon: "Build houses and settle down; plant gardens and eat what they produce. Marry and have sons and daughters; find wives for your sons and give your daughters in marriage, so that they too may have sons and daughters. Increase in number there; do not decrease.* ***Also, seek the peace and prosperity of the city to which I have carried you into exile. Pray to the Lord for it, because if it prospers, you too will prosper.*** *...I know the plans I have for you", declares the Lord, "plans to prosper you and not to harm you, plans to give you hope and a future."*
> (Jeremiah 29:4-7, 11 [emphasis added])

SPANISH, GERMAN AND EASTERN EUROPEAN JEWISH IMMIGRATION

> *A second and more sizable Jewish immigration to the United States was made up of German Jews who came with the great wave of other German immigrants during the 1840s and 1850s. These Jews were socially and economically several notches below the earlier Sephardic Jews, who by that time were relatively prosperous and respected. Although most were merchants, their trade was at a level considerably less significant than that of their Sephardic predecessors. Many, in fact, were peddlers who moved westward with the country's expansion. Indeed, at the middle of the nineteenth century, most of America's 20,000 itinerant traders were German Jews* (Lipset and Raab, 1995 qtd. in Martin Marger, Race & Ethnic Relations 2d. 221)

Where they [German Jews] settled, they commonly established clothing and dry goods or general stores, the vestiges of which are seen today throughout the United States (Brockman, 2001; Pressley, 1999). A few developed into large national chains. Many familiar department store names, including Macy's, Bloomingdale's, Saks Fifth Avenue, and Neiman-Marcus, stem from German Jewish founding families. (*Id.*)

> *By the turn of the century, German Jews were so thoroughly assimilated that they had lost much sense of ethnic identity. Only their religious affiliation distinguished them from other Americans* (HERBERG, 1960 QTD. IN MARTIN MARGER, RACE & ETHNIC RELATIONS 2D. 221)

The great bulk of immigrating Jews came between 1880s and 1920s. However, they hailed not so much from Germany or Spain, but from eastern Europe. These 2 million or so came escaping repression, and were poorer and less educated. They were more religious though, and Judaism was a key to their attaining a foothold in U.S. society.

To the German Jews, Judaism was simply a faith that was not to interfere with assimilation into the core American culture and society. To the East Europeans, coming from the shtetl, or Jewish village, where religion governed all aspects of life, Judaism was an entire social world. (*Id.* 222)

The Germans viewed the new immigrants as illiterate, uncouth, and provincial greenhorns, who could only cause embarrassment to the American Jewish community and produce a backlash of anti-Semitism. By the 1890s, however, the divisions between the two groups were evaporating. (*Id.* 223)

So back to the question: how did the larger group of Jews rise in the U.S.? They did it by helping each other in certain ways.

JEWISH AMERICANS HELPING JEWISH AMERICANS

Jews found the United States a haven that provided for the first time a social atmosphere in which Jewish identity could be retained without fear of official repression and from which there was no need to contemplate flight. Jews in America also found their economic circumstances relatively unconstrained, in sharp contrast to the situation they had faced in Europe. (*Id.* 219)

Jewish Americans have had the most spectacular ascent of any ethnic group to come to this land. No single group compares to them when it comes to where the first generation started and the heights to which multiple generations have climbed. From about 1890 and the arrival of very poor eastern European Jews, to 1990 and the preponderance of Jewish Americans in the professions, their economic excellence has become a subject in ethnic studies. Shortly after entering the country, Jews by a greater percentage than other ethnic groups started small businesses—sometimes from a cart. They did well in the areas that they had historically thrived at as a people in Europe: they launched into the clothing, jewelry, and finance arenas from wholesale to retail.

KEYS TO HOW THEY ROSE

Some of this achievement has to do with the assistance of those who originally came over with business experience, families intact, and even assets they could bring with them. Some of the success has to do with the "achievement syndrome": high emphasis (some would say, over-emphasis) on achievement directed strongly at the children, but even on adults. This is best seen in their commitment to and resources poured into the education of their children.

Some of the achievement has to do with their lighter color, which was a little less of a threat than the darker race of Latinos/as and African Americans. Some of the success, I think much of it, has to do with the synagogue.

In other words, while the spiritual guidance in the Black community during the Civil Rights Movement rivaled the spiritual guidance in the Jewish communities in the 20th century, the spiritual guidance in the last decades paled in comparison. Overall, Jewish spiritual guidance has been longer, wiser, and more committed to the cause than was ours.

On the west coast they experimented with showcasing their plays using the newest technology at the time. In the process they established in Los Angeles a media core known as "Hollywood." As they rose financially they kept their families intact and invested generously in the education of their children. First they stressed education in the home and synagogue; then they added their financial resources to what they stressed; and finally they added facilities, when necessary, to their resources, setting up their own remedial or advancement programs, and then their own schools. All of this was shaped and buttressed by the insightful and community-building instruction of the rabbis in the local synagogues. They made sure that Jews in the U.S. patronized Jewish businesses as a matter of survival and godliness. They encouraged the structuring of no-interest lending societies to provide their entrepreneurs indispensable seed capital.

To see how high Jewish Americans have risen, one need only determine their percentage as attorneys, doctors, investment bankers, accountants, and managers of the most prosperous and prestigious companies. It will likely be something like 5 to 10% of the total, or much more. Then relate this to the fact that they are about 3% of the country's population. Whereas African Americans rate disproportionately high on the indices that are bad (i.e., unemployment, debt, and incarceration), Jewish Americans are disproportionately high on the indices that are good (i.e., stock ownership, income, and academic achievement).

Their economic growth parlays into economic and political power. Of late, at least one, and sometimes two, of the seven governors on the financially supervising Federal Reserve Board will be Jewish. They now have what is the most influential lobbying group as of this writing: the American Israeli Public Affairs Committee (AIPAC). Privately, AIPAC boasts of having successfully campaigned against the reelection of a number of members of Congress. That is power. Jewish Americans are disproportionately at the very locus of power in three important cities: in Boston, the investment headquarters of the U.S.; in Los Angeles, the entertainment capital of the country; and in New York, the banking and cultural core of America.

The family is very important to Jewish economic development. Parents and particularly fathers have been crucial. The matriarch and particularly the patriarch are important to their economic and political development, as an education is especially emphasized. But their help was more than personal or familial. They helped each other as a people.

Marger believes that the differences were resolved because of "humanitarian motives and partially by the concern that they might be lumped with these poor and religiously traditional Jews in the eyes of their Christian neighbors" (*Race & Ethnic Relations* 223). I believe that the rabbis, working from a four thousand year old religious tradition, had a lot to do with the change.

> *German Jews now accepted the responsibility for uplifting and assisting their East European cohorts (Wirth, 1956). By the end of large-scale immigration in the early 1920s, the subdivision of the American Jewish community into German and East*

European groups was no longer apparent (GLAZER AND MOYNIHAN, 1970; YAFFEE, 1968)" (QTD. IN MARGER, RACE & ETHNIC RELATIONS 223).

Association is more important. When at least five males convened to worship together a synagogue was established. The synagogue is the life of the Jewish people. The rabbi is important for spiritual development and sub-cultural awareness. The rabbi is also impactful in economic cooperation.

I think that another key is that Jewish Americans added hard work and knowledge of business to a thorough understanding of capitalism. Jews had to learn to excel at business early on in their survival. The capitalists' capitalists are bankers and financiers. Some of the greatest in Europe were Jews like the Rothschilds, who lent money not just to people but to nations. The greatest critiques of capitalism are works by a Jew: Karl Marx. Happenstance seems to have made similar the pronounciation of the English words "jewry" and "jewelry", but for all intents and purposes they could have come from the same root, for Jews have wise been adept at dealing in precious metals. This work in business—whether in precious metals or textiles—started early on as was earlier referenced in the quote to the Hebrew book of Jeremiah, chapter 29.

The most successful ethnic (religious) group in America provides a good example to strive for. A group stands to gain a lot by studying the rise of Jewish Americans in the U.S., especially since 1880. Their 120 year ascendancy to the highest levels of economic, political, and social power presents a lesson in the heights a group can attain. Jewish Americans show that it has happened. If it has happened, then it could happen for us.

VIETNAMESE AMERICANS: PERSONAL APPROACH

The dramatic modernization of the Asian economies ranks alongside the Renaissance and the Industrial Revolution as one of the most important developments in economic history. (LARRY SUMMERS)

Vietnamese Americans are the next ethnic group to discuss. They also have sought economic development upon receiving citizenship rights (even before receiving such). When I bring up Jewish Americans, Blacks who see development as a pipedream can counter, 'Well, the Jews are White.' But they cannot say that about Vietnamese Americans. The Vietnamese also deflect the argument that ethnic groups cannot rise now in White-controlled U.S.A., for Vietnamese have forged their business corps mainly since 1975. This is pretty recent.

Vietnamese Americans have used an approach that is based on the extended family, buttressed by the associations. They, like the Chinese and Japanese, are another study in the ascendancy of an ethnic group in American society. The power of their story, however, is that this mainly occurred since 1980 and started in or near African American communities. The springing upward of Jewish Americans originally occurred long enough ago that Blacks can say that it cannot happen again. Moreover, Jewish Americans look White. Vietnamese American uplifting represents that ethnic groups can rise today, and that non-Whites can do so.

EXAMPLE OF VIETNAMESE DEVELOPMENT

Vietnamese Americans remove from Black scoffers the counter argument that no group can rise from the ghetto. In point of fact, the Vietnamese moved into the poorest areas in whatever cities they gravitated too, as they escaped here from the persecution of the North Vietnamese in their country of origin. Sometimes they lived two families to an apartment. Many, if not most, started for a time on welfare. Many, if not most, did not speak English. The Vietnamese lived so close to Blacks that their children went to school together, each group has a sense of the other's story, and they at times shared the same tenement buildings.

Blacks have watched from a distance the economic rise of Vietnamese Americans. In fact, some of the businesses that the Vietnamese purchased were Black owned or at least operated. Ironically, Blacks are the major patrons of some of the hair supply, auto, or clothing stores that the Vietnamese own. Theirs has been a remarkable success story. How did they go from many on welfare to many owning businesses in one generation?

KEYS TO THEIR SUCCESS

The entrance of Vietnamese into the United States is unique to other Asian groups and probably could be only compared to Cubans. Most came as refugees subsequent to the end of the Vietnam War. In contrast to the Cubans, they came as a result of a political situation that the United States had everything to do with. Consequently, we were duty-bound to receive them. They had helped us during that war, so we owed them. Moreover, some had children who were fathered by U.S. servicemen, so this was partly their home as well.

How did Vietnamese Americans do this? It came as a result of an extended family and associational drive for prosperity. The Vietnamese emphasized their own economic development. Individually, they worked as many jobs as they could handle upon entry in the country. They kept their marriages and their families largely together (although this is changing, as they are approaching the incidence of divorce of the larger society). The younger family members respect the elders in the family, who have directed the investing the family has to do to prosper.

Vietnamese Americans minimized expenses and saved as much as they could. They cumulated their savings in family or associational pools. Their elders determined who would be the first to receive business seed money. They jointly established businesses, and their families assisted with the work. In so doing they enjoyed labor savings.

Then they put heavy pressure on their children to excel in school. Vietnamese parents are earnest about telling their children that the family's honor rests on their performance in school and in business. Perhaps it is too much stress, but I, for one, love the academic results they achieve. Vietnamese children score high in science and math, rivaling the results of Chinese and Japanese children. The oldest child has the job of tutoring the younger children, and of being the interpreter for the parents, if necessary. Clearly, everyone in the family has a role to play for the uplifting of the entire family (although Vietnamese women may lament that the role is traditional, maybe even sexist).

The academic success of many Asian students, and increasingly Vietnamese American youth, is the subject of analysis. They particularly rise to the head of the class in math and science, subjects the average American students struggle with. Their academic success garners for them high marks on standardized tests, acceptance at major universities, scholarships, and grants. This kind of achievement draws resources and investment from outside of their community into their children for the good of all of society.

> *Asian Americans are hard workers, are inclined toward business, and their children do well in school. With respect to work, "The rate of labor force participation for Asian Americans is higher than that of any other ethnic category, and the range of occupations held by Asian Americans is broad, extending from working-class jobs to professions such as medicine and engineering."* (MARGER, RACE & ETHNIC RELATIONS 2D. 355)

THEIR UNMISTAKABLE SUCCESS

The businesses they develop and the higher education they earn prepare them to move into the professions nearly in mass. This is how a people propels itself forward by Olympian strides. The results are too plain to miss.

Between 1966 and 1975, some 20,000 Vietnamese arrived in the United States...In the nine years between 1975 and 1984, more than 700,000 Southeast Asian refugees came to the United States, most of them Vietnamese. (*Id.* 348)

> *Most of the refugees coming in the second wave were unlike the earlier Vietnamese in that they were relatively unskilled, less educated, and spoke little English (Wong, 1986). For example, almost 80 percent of the Vietnamese coming to the United States between 1965 and 1969 were college graduates, as opposed to less than 16 percent of those who arrived between 1975 and 1980 (U.S. Commission on Civil Rights, 1988). Their adjustment to American society, as a result, was far more difficult, and today they remain the most economically depressed element of the Asian American population.* (MARGER, RACE & ETHNIC RELATIONS 2D. 348-9)

> *[A]lthough, nearly 60 percent of employed Asian Indians and over half of Chinese and Japanese are professionals or managers, only 27 percent of Vietnamese and 18 percent of Cambodians are in such occupations (U.S. Census Bureau, 2004f). The income and educational levels of the latter are also considerably lower than those for other Asian American groups.* (MARGER, RACE & ETHNIC RELATIONS 2D. 353-4)

In 1999 the average median family income of all American families was $50,046. The Vietnamese family income was $47,103, which is pretty good for one generation in this country. By contrast, the median Black family income was $31,690 in 2000. Vietnamese have surpassed African Americans in this regard already. "The family income of Asian Americans far exceeds that of most other minority ethnic categories, and, with the exception of the Southeast Asians, surpasses most Euro-American groups as well" (*Id.* 354).

The Vietnamese poverty rate is 16%, whereas the average U.S. family comes in at 12.4%. Given that many, if not most, Vietnamese who entered the country in the second wave received some type of governmental assistance, this is exemplary. In 2000, the percentage of Africans in poverty was 22.5. Again, in one generation Vietnamese Americans have climbed out of poverty to a greater degree than Blacks have.

As to small business involvement,

> *"A salient feature of the economic role played by Asian Americans today is the unusually large numbers who choose to own small businesses. Indeed, Asian Americans have the highest rate of business ownership of all U.S. minority groups. Thirty percent of all minority-owned firms and over half of all sales of such firs are Asian (U.S. Census Bureau, 2001j)."* (QTD. IN MARGER, RACE & ETHNIC RELATIONS 356)

Their formidable one generation advances augur well for them in the future. Who knows how far along they will be when they have been in this country as long as Jewish Americans. Their example can teach African Americans a lot and can remove a bevy of excuses. To recap, Vietnamese Americans have used an approach that is based on the extended family, buttressed by the associations. Associations are helpful. Buddhist, Taoist, and Christian groups provide a means of community contact and sub-cultural acculturation. However, the real development and linking in the Vietnamese community happens with the family and particularly the elder males.

ETHIOPIAN AMERICANS: ELDER APPROACH

Ethiopian Americans are the last group demanding consideration. They are still largely in the middle, if not early in, their first generation in the U S. Yet, their gains can already be appreciated. Ethiopians in the U.S. are faring as well, if not better, than first generation Jamaican Americans, a group known over the years for doing markedly better than African Americans in general—that is, who do better in their first generation.

Incidentally, this subject presents a language problem. Both Ethiopian Americans and African Americans are, in fact, African Americans. Obviously, Ethiopian Americans are mostly recent arrivals, whereas the bulk of "African Americans" came here well over a century ago. Though messy, I choose for convenience to refer to Ethiopian Americans as if they are not in the class of African Americans although they actually are. These labels are inadequate. I want Ethiopian Americans to know that I see them as part of one diasporic family, a family in which they hold a special place by virtue of coming from an area that sits astride the civilization originating Nile River.

THE IMPORTANCE OF THEIR RISE TO AFRICAN AMERICANS

Like first generation Jamaican Americans, Ethiopian Americans are hitting the American soil running. They form businesses as first generation Americans. What is unique and telling about their grasping of the American dream is that they are making their way in or near the African American community as Africans in America (or as African Americans). They remove the excuse that Blacks cannot rise in this land.

Like Vietnamese Americans, Ethiopian Americans nix a number of excuses that Blacks simply just have to overcome. Some African Americans (who have been in the U.S. 50 or more years) say, "You know Vietnamese Americans may not be White, but they are not Black either." Well the typical Ethiopian is as dark, or darker, than the typical African American.

Other African Americans feel that with the Gingrich Republican Revolution of 1994, the country has turned against Blacks in a way reminiscent of the 1950s. Even if this is so, how does one explain Ethiopian Americans opening stores, restaurants, and gas stations; taking over the local taxi-cab industry; and acquiring a healthy percentage of the parking lot business? This is legitimate, lucrative business development that the footings of a renaissance can rest on. Ethiopian Americans have done this in a quarter of a lifespan.

KEYS TO THEIR SUCCESS

How do they do it? As I have been able to determine, their methods are a mixture of what both Jewish Americans and Vietnamese Americans have done. With intact families, their elders guide family protocol. Family members get whatever jobs they can and work hard. They save as much as they can in order to raise start-up capital. The elders direct where the capital goes: to whom, and to what ends.

The church or mosque aids what family elders do. Ethiopian Orthodox Christians priests and other Christian pastors teach the necessity and godliness of transcending native tribal differences. They instruct on the ways Ethiopians in this country can work together, at least as separate families. They offer the churches and mosques as centers for society, education, and business development.

Ethiopian parents and pastors emphasize education like Vietnamese parents do. They may not as of yet invest the resources of Jewish parents, but they employ Asian- like pressure on their children to succeed. Ethiopian American children do well in school. Their success is much higher than the African Americans on the whole; Ethiopian children's success in school is comparable to Vietnamese American children.

As a result, Ethiopians have been rising as a people right before the eyes of African Americans. Viewing their economic accomplishments has not been easy for Africans who have been in the U.S. 50 years or longer. There has been some ill-will, perhaps even enmity, between Blacks and Vietnamese Americans, and now between Blacks and Ethiopian Americans. In Seattle, there have been incidents of violence between the groups, mainly from African Americans towards Ethiopians here. It has led to shootings on the streets and in the cabs.

Efforts are underway to stem this tide and to foster harmonious relations. Blacks and Ethiopians have good reasons to resolve their differences. African Americans who have been here longer than 50 years need to learn from Ethiopians about their ancient history, about family and culture. For, it is becoming increasingly clear that the earliest humans came from near Ethiopia in Africa, and the West Africans, from whom Blacks have come, came from East Africa. Moreover, Blacks still do not know a lot generally about families from the Motherland. Ethiopians can teach Blacks the eastern story, which may be the generic story.

Ethiopians in the U.S. can use the political assistance and cover African Americans can provide. As the government comes too harshly and broadly against East Africans under the guise of terrorism, Ethiopians here have needed to appeal to the NAACP and to Black churches for assistance. As Ethiopians experience discrimination, they feel the need to resort for advice to the people who knew best the civil rights laws and activism. One group can help the other. But what Blacks need most to know from Ethiopians is what they are doing in detail to gain a foothold locally in pockets all around this country.

The Ethiopian story is still very new. There is still a question about whether they will fall victims to the experience of second and third generation Jamaican Americans. Something happens to the children of Black immigrants, even Jamaicans, which makes it progressively more challenging for them to produce the academic and professional results of the earlier generation of children to come to the country. What does this mean? It means that there is something real and sinister going on in the U.S., a covert racism that grinds down even those who come here with the best of intentions, the hardest of workers, and who start off as small entrepreneurs.

Alternatively, every year more of this institutional racism is confronted; every year it fades; every year its pillars are rooted out. So, maybe the combination of elders in intact families and the guidance of strong religious institutions will steer Ethiopians in the U.S. around the experience of Jamaican Americans. Time will tell. In the meantime, I am making overtures to the Ethiopian American community in order to give what I can and to learn what I can. Where they come from and their success thus far here are all I need to sit at their feet to learn something.

Jewish Americans had a meteoritic rise in this country from the 1900 through 1990. If Jewish America can do it, then so can Seattle African America. Vietnamese Americans are rising fast now in the U.S., with Ethiopian Americans just a decade or two behind. If they can do it, then so can Seattle African America. All of these groups have developed and are developing from different plans like the one herein. This is how Blacks have to do it. It is time to develop a clear, comprehensive plan.

EMAIL TO BLACK LEADERS IN SEATTLE ABOUT COMPENSATION IN A NOVEL WAY ON A CONSTRUCTION PROJECT

As most people know, an owner is quite reluctant to go with anyone but the prime on change order work related to another prime contract. Owners want to give the work to the prime presently under contract and performing. **Therefore, we have to give a strong argument for *why* we should receive such work and then make another strong argument about *how* it could be done immediately**.

Our reason for **why** are the claims we have presented and continue to present. We have not made an argument about ***how*** it could be done. Here is that argument:

We could **put together 2 or 3 teams:** one with the prime as the largest black electrical contractor and the other with the prime as the largest mechanical contractor. On each team the structural subcontractor will be the White prime of the related contract (who thought for sure he was going to get the change order work). If the new Black prime is the electrical contractor, then a Black contractor will be the mechanical subcontractor.

The challenges will be threefold: **bonding**, **carryover** of the underlying contracts, and making the **White structural subcontractor** do right by the Black prime. We can handle each matter as follows. **First**, the Black prime can be responsible only for 10% of the performance bonding (or whatever he/she can afford); [the governmental entity] will have to secure the rest. They have the capacity to get it. I think that we should have the bonding go through [a Black who was formerly in the bonding business], to put him back in business.

Secondly, on the underlying contracts (for specialty equipment. specialty supplies, general subcontracts, temporary power, etc.) that the White prime now subcontractor had worked out, [the governmental entity] will have to help the new Black prime get extension contracts at the price that the general had gotten. [The governmental entity] will have to get the information from the general with guarantees that the representations are true and correct and then still run the numbers to see if they are profit worthy (because they may lie about them). [The governmental entity] and [Black community] members will need to monitor the contracts to ensure that the new Black prime is getting performance to the same quality, quantity, and timeliness that the White prime now subcontractor was getting. Having the White subcontractor on this portion of the work should help all of this.

Third and last, [the governmental entity] will have to help (and the [the Black community]) the Black prime get the maximum participation of the White subcontractor. To a great degree the Black prime will be benefiting from the White subcontractor (having in a sense stepped into the extension of the project, having stepped into many of the terms of his subcontracts and supplier contracts, working along side of him such that he can learn on the inside about how he staffs a project, and growing to a point that he might be competing with the new Black prime for subsequent work). So, it is likely that the White subcontractor will try to undermine the project. But this is what we always have had to deal with.

What is the benefit? There is nothing like controlling a project ourselves. Moreover, these are how we best take care of our own people and build the kind of track record that will grow our business, as well as give us bonding capacity capability.

#1: Black prime (electrical) / #2: Black prime (mechanical)

Black mechanical sub
+ White structural sub / Black electrical sub
+ White structural sub

Let's put our teams together immediately and draw up how this can be done. Let's get the agreement of the contractors who are willing to do this. Let's see if Tyner wants the bonding brokerage business. Then let's go out and ask for some real money; like $50 million dollars or more.

SLIPPIN'

The Black community is slippin',
staggering like a drunk in an alley,
bouncing from one wall to the next.

We are limpin',
refusing to stop
but unable to run forward with power in life's race.

We are scrimpin',
having to reach down in this race to pick up a dime on the ground,
miraculously making ends meet.

We are driftin',
drifting from our true course set by our leaders of old,
the Menes, the Hatshepsuts, the Tubmans, the Kings.

Yes, the Black community is slippin'.

And why are we slippin'?

We are slippin' because our great leaders are missin';
our current leaders are trippin'.

Missin', like Harriet Tubman and Frederick,
Ida Wells and a Garvey named Marcus,
Fannie Lou and Malcolm too.

Missin', especially King
who led us top of the mountain of Jim Crow,
downward moving into the valley
to snatch the black face off of featureless Mr. Poverty.

Missin', as King stayed on the trail
despite death firing rounds at him,
and firing at him,
and firing,
. . .
until Martin
and not death
was missin'.

Missin', like your momma being gone
when it is dark outside

and there are no cartoons on;

like being cornered in an alley
when all of your homies are missin'
indeed.

The great leaders are missin and thus
the Black community is slippin'.

Now our current leaders are trippin';

Trippin' by following the path of least resistance,
selling the children's birthright for a pot of white chowder.

These leaders are dissin',
playing power games on each other,
serving as jack-o-lanterns of division
instead of candles of umoja.

They too are missin':
missing out on living heroic lives
by settling for merely getting paid
—the 'okey doke'.

The everyday leaders are trippin
and hence the Black community is slippin'.

These leaders are —
  Primpin',
  caught up in style
  and mesmerized by their image in the mirror;

  They are tippin',
  talking what is right
  without taking care of their wives and kids.

They are pimpin',
taking the people's money
without leading us into the real promised land
— nothing for something.

  They are sippin',
  giving their palates to thunder's bird
  and their noses to white lines on a 'TV' tray
  by the bed.

The Black Community is slippin',
the great leaders are missin',
and the current leaders are trippin'.

But given history
Blacks know we are not in a fix.

Instead, . . .
we are fixin'
to get out of another mess.

We must do some siftin',
separating the wheat from the chaff:
throwing the old guard onto the heap of the dead ideas;
loving Black elders
but kickin' "niggas" to the curb.

We must do some shiftin',
turning our attention towards a new leadership,
who will pay the cost to be the boss,
who'll purge the dross,
then gain the lost.

To promote our buildin',
repairing every darker institution,
until our green money
is as great as our black power;
and our black power
is as beautiful as our rainbow love
for each other
and everybody else.

So we can prepare for our liftin',
to see the dawning sun
which the ancients said was the closest thing to the great God.

Soon there will be no more slippin',
our feet fully grippin',
and like an army we will be steppin'
into the resplendent sun.

—CARL L. LIVINGSTON, JR.

ENDNOTES

1. This is called "broken windows" policing. It became big in the wake of the SWAT and anti Black Panther policing of the 1970s. Broken windows policing is an approach that targets the owners and occupiers of dilapidated buildings and blighted points in communities. There police cited owners, arrested loiters, and vagrants. It expanded to being an approach that posted a police dragnet in certain areas with orders to make stops, arrests, and to enforce beat control. New York Mayor Rudolph Guiliani added his variation to this by creating an environment in which his officers targeted people in addition to blocks. Members of the African American and Puerto Rican American communities retorted that they were being racially profiled.

2. Wayne Perryman did something like this regarding the racist past of the Democrat Party in his book *Unfounded Loyalty*. It was published in 2003. The Republicans saw that it could be used especially in Ohio, one of a handful of swing states in which the Republicans felt things were too close. They purchased hundreds of copies of the book and helped Perryman with a few speaking engagements. One of which CSPAN aired to the world. The Republican Party was hoping that the civil rights community, and particularly Blacks, would not connect the dots of the White Southern Democrats' past and Republicans Southern Strategy present. They had to hope that Perryman would not make that case as well. He came close to doing so; he hinted at it in the question and answer time. To the fortune of the Republican Party, the Democrat Party of the distant past looked bad in ways that cast a shadow on the Democrat Party of the present; and the Republican Party of the present did not look bad despite their being in the present the new home of the Southern Whites whose thinking was still too much like the past.

It was a high wire act that required great political deft and skill. It equally showcased the political ineptness of the Democrats. One could argue that it also showed how deft Wayne Perryman is. His community needs him now, as one of the foremost writers on the subject, to expose the Southern Strategy with the same analysis and gall he used to reveal the racism of the Democrat Party.

3. I think this is the perception, but that it should not be—the perception is patently wrong. State races are so close in the swing states that our votes are desperately need-

ed. Moreover, the Rocky Mountain states, and even the South, are changing. Race is strong, but not nearly as strong of a wedge as it used to be. More and more Whites are giving less and less significance to a candidate's color. Moreover, there is a huge potential electorate—one half of the people—that could vote but are not. The more of these folks that are brought in, the more the Democrats will benefit.

4. Being in what is known as the federal district or city, the mainly Black residents of D.C. have no representative or senator in Congress with voting rights on the floor, so the Blacks there do not directly participate in democracy in America, nor in ultimately running their own city. No other citizens in the U.S. are treated in such an undemocratic way, their rights being very slightly above the rights the U.S. affords Puerto Ricans in Puerto Rico. For Puerto Ricans in Puerto Rico have a shadow representative in the U.S. Congress, are given rights to welfare, and have rights of entry in this country because Puerto Rico is part of the U.S. commonwealth.

5. Arthur Schlesinger, in his work the *Disunting of America*, wrote about the problems to this country posed by ardent multi-culturalists, especially the afrocentrists. Andrew Hacker's work *Two Nations: Separate, Hostile, and Unequal* has very sensitive, well written selections on the concern of Americans that the country will have actual and all-out race war. He quoted Alexis de Tocqueville's *Democracy in America* and his predictions that this would eventually happen.

However, the most widely distributed work and critically acclaimed may be Samuel P. Huntington's *Clash of Civilizations*. In this work, in the middle, he warns of Asian and even more Latino Americans causing a cleft and then moving to break in this country. He says that the group that poses the greatest danger on the ground in this country are Mexican Americans. He gives four reasons for this (slowest assimilation, proximity to Mexico, Atzlan identity movement, and knowledge that the U.S. forced the Southwest from Mexico arguably wrongfully). These reasons, he said, may lead to feelings that Mexican Americans should fight to take the region from Texas to California back.

Later in Huntington's book he flags his most pressing concern in these matters. It is the multi-culturalists, particularly the afrocentrists. He quotes Schlesinger. Huntington says Americans have a choice: do we want to be the United States or the United Nations. He calls this the real war in the U.S. Then he says that things are already being done preserve this country's connection to Europe and its eurocentric cultural core.

Following him, former presidential candidate and television commentator Patrick Buchanan wrote *The Death of the West*. In it he makes Huntington's points about the threat of the multi-culturalists, and especially Mexican Americans. Buchanan has a chapter entitled "La Reconquista" (the re-conquest) that focuses on them.

It is not just the writers of trade books for the public. Textbook writers have also discussed this, most notably in field of Ethnic Studies. In Martin Marger's text, he cites that scholars used to think that ethnic group relations would get better over time, especially as ethnic groups and the larger society prosper. He states that scholars no longer feel this way. After the 1980s and 1990s with break up of the Soviet Union, Yugoslavia, Czechoslovakia, and the ethnic civil wars of Rwanda scholars hold that the future of ethnic relations may be hostile or civil depending on the circumstances.

In their text, Aguirre and Turner state that it may turn on how long and deep has been the discrimination ethnic groups have suffered. The shorter and milder the discrimination, curiously, the more it becomes part of the bonding agents as the ethnic group assimilates across the board in the society. On the other hand, the longer and harsher the discrimination, the more it creates cleavages that causes ethnic groups to identify with people like them, and not with the country at large. Then Aguirre and Turner end with these remarkable and chilling statements:

> *But when discrimination is intense, long-term, and inhibits assimilation, then it creates cleavages along ethnic lines, and such cleavages are among the most volatile forces of human organization. And so, if discrimination over the next decades prevents African Americans, Latinos, and Asian-Americans from adopting the cultural core and from fully participating in the society, and at the same time heightens their ethnic identity, it will increase the level of ethnic tension in America, perhaps to the point of societal disintegration.* (AGUIRRE AND TURNER, *AMERICAN ETHNICITY: THE DYNAMICS AND CONSEQUENCES OF DISCRIMINATION*, 2D. 247)

6. Over the last thirty years, something has been amiss with Seattle's political and spiritual leaders. They are not bad; they just have not been big enough to provide the kind of grand direction to lead the people to where they need to go. For instance, the I-90 corridor was cut through a part of the Black community. The community did get promises from the governmental leaders about relocation assistance for the Blacks moved out, about work to be given Blacks on the project, and about Blacks who would be moved back into the community.

The relocation assistance was not what it was promised to be. Then, Black businesses did not get the percentage of work that was fair given what was told them. Still, the amount of money awarded Black contractors was more than they had seen before in this area. Yet its reach in the Black community tapered, as legitimate Black businesses had problems completing performance while front businesses siphoned work to illegitimate Black businesses. What should have been a renaissance in the Black community was merely an upturn that lasted a little while and then leveled. When it came to building the housing, a lesser percentage of the work went to African American contractors. Then came the selling of the units: Blacks were about 50% of the community at the time the promises were made; about 10% of the sells went to Blacks. How could this happen right under the noses of Black leaders?

Time for a second example. Between 1970 and 2000, the downtown doubled in space, if not tripled. This was construction work in the tens of billions of dollars. Even 2% of it would have been at least $400 million dollars (2% of just 20 billion). Black leaders did little to address this situation. Perhaps the fact that it happened progressively, was mainly privately done, and occurred during the conservative backlash had a lot to do with this. Still, leaders have to see the bigger picture.

Finally, public works like the Sound Transit Light Rail and Commuter Train project cannot be allowed to disfavor local Black communities. The phase of this project from the airport to downtown Seattle will total over 5 billion dollars worth of design and construction work by 2010. The Black community is 8% of Seattle. If one were to assume that Blacks are 2% of the local construction industry, then they could fairly advocate for about 2% of the total work. Two percent amounts to $100 million dollars. $100 million dollars would have gone far towards helping to finance the kind of Black renaissance of which I have been speaking.

Yet, the leaders in the community and those on the Sound Transit board fell short of achieving such gains for the community. The Black board members only talked a good game; the community leaders met, raised their voice for 6% of the money after about half the contracts were let, and even shut a jobsite down once for half a day. However, they lacked the clear and sustained effort to mobilize their Black and non-Black supporters effectively to achieve something like 2% of the total. Thus, the local Black contractors received something like .2% of the total. Something similar happened to the Black designers and workers on the project. It was an affront to us as citizens of the country, residents of the state, and taxpayers in the city. I hope this is the last time that our people allow the board of a major public works project to so disregard them.

OTHER WORKS BY THE AUTHOR

Affirmative Action on Trial; the Retraction of Affirmative Action and the Case for its Retention, article, Howard Law Journal, 1996

Poems for the People I

Poems for the People II